# BANKSY

THE MAN BEHIND THE WALL

# BANKSY

## THE MAN BEHIND THE WALL

Will Ellsworth-Jones

Aurum

First published in Great Britain
2012 by Aurum Press Ltd
74-77 White Lion Street
Islington
London N1 9PF
www.aurumpress.co.uk

This paperback edition first published 2013 by Aurum Press Ltd

**THIS BOOK IS 'UNOFFICIAL'. IT HAS NOT BEEN AUTHORISED BY BANKSY OR PEST CONTROL**



A catalogue record for this book is available from the British Library.

ISBN 978 1 78131 520 0

1 3 5 7 9 10 8 6 4 2
2013 2015 2017 2016 2014

Typeset in Kepler Std Light by SX Composing DTP, Rayleigh, Essex
Printed and bound by CPI Group (UK) Ltd, Croydon, CR0 4YY

For Lara and Daniel and in memory of Barbara

# Acknowledgments

First to my wife Barbara who died in February 2012. Despite extended stays in hospital and all kinds of pain when out of hospital she was determined that none of her trials and tribulations were going to stop this book being written. Sometimes in hospital she worried much more about whether I had done enough writing that day before coming to see her than she did about her own far more pressing problems. In times of despair, particularly early on when it seemed it was going to be impossible to get through the wall of silence that surrounds Banksy, and I doubted if I would ever finish the book, I told myself that I could not conceive of letting her down.

Next my thanks to Graham Coster, Publisher at Aurum Press, who had the original idea for this book, helped me develop it and was a very understanding shoulder to lean on during all the usual – and unusual – ups and downs.

There are a few people who were of considerable help to me but who would not thank me at all if I named them here because they would then be cast out from the Banksy magic circle. But they know who they are – many thanks and thanks too to all those who did help and are named in the book.

My thanks to three people who showed great patience in initiating me into the world of graffiti. First Nico Yates, a young graffiti artist who writes under the name of Spico who, over breakfast one morning in a café in Deptford, gave me my first long lesson in graffiti. Thanks too to David Samuel and John Nation who, with similar patience, expanded this lesson on the streets of London and Bristol.

My thanks as always to Don Berry who gave me key advice at awkward moments along the road and then made the first edit of the manuscript – as always suggesting many changes for the better. My thanks too to Bernie Angopa, Drusilla Beyfus, Mick Brown, Jessamy Calkin, Gary Cochran, Jon Connell, Carolynne Ellis-Jones, David Galloway, Gail Gregg, Cathy Giles, Jonathan Giles, Henry Greaves, Nick Greaves, Rory and Michael McHugh, Vicki Reid, Mern Palmer-Smith, Francesca Ryan, Claire Scobie, Robin Smith, Emma Soames and Angela Swan who all helped in various ways. The mistakes, however, are all mine.

# Contents

# Introduction

He is the outlaw who has been dragged reluctantly, but relentlessly, ever closer to the art establishment.

He is the artist who mocked museums and art galleries alike. Yet he chose to mount his first major exhibition in one of the crustiest museums imaginable – amidst the stuffed animals and the antique pianos of Bristol City Museum and Art Gallery – and made a huge success of it.

When, in 2010, *Time* magazine selected him for its list of 100 most influential people in the world, along with the likes of Barack Obama, Apple's Steve Jobs and Lady Gaga, he supplied a picture of himself with a paper bag (recyclable of course) over his head. For he is an artist unique in the twenty-first century: famous but unknown.

He claims he needs this anonymity to protect himself from the forces of law and order. This was true in the past, but at this stage in his career most cities would welcome a new Banksy on the wall. The argument would be how best to preserve it, not how to lock up its creator.

This book does not attempt to unmask him. Tales of scuttling around his home town of Bristol trying to convince childhood friends to reveal his identity would not make for very interesting reading. More important is the fact that fans, followers and even those who are just vaguely aware he exists, don't want to know who he is. The *New Statesman* critic who derides it all as 'ostentatious anonymity' is very much in the minority. We all enjoy the mystery of the man who has somehow managed to get himself described as 'Robin Hood' even though he is hardly robbing the rich to feed the poor.

What this book does do, however, is to follow his upward spiral from the outlaw – just one of many – spraying the walls of Bristol in the 1990s to the artist whose work commands hundreds of thousands of pounds in the auction houses of Britain and America. The outsider who has become an insider.

It has not been an easy voyage. Pest Control, the appropriately named organisation set up to authenticate the real Banksy artwork from the fake, is also involved in protecting him from outsiders. Pest Control uses everything from a tightly drawn up legal contract to a carefully timed phone call from the man himself where necessary to maintain its control.

Hiding behind a paper bag or, more commonly, email, Banksy wants to protect and preserve his own narrative and he does this very well. Pest Control has asked that this book be marked 'unofficial' to 'avoid any doubt with the public that the book might be sanctioned by the artist' and, yes, it is completely 'unofficial' – utterly unauthorised. It is perhaps ironic that a graffiti artist appears to be trying to authorise the way people both think and write about him. Which is sad, for his work speaks for itself. His unique talent puts him at the head of a whole new movement in the world of art: street art. A technically skilled artist who has – literally – taken art into places it has never been before, he marries this skill with an acute eye for the world around us. He is both artist and social commentator with the humour of a great cartoonist.

Inevitably what comes with all this is a certain amount of baggage. There is the paranoia, which if anything has grown over the years, and then of course there is the money. He says, 'I don't make as much money as people think,' and it is true, he is not – yet – in the Damien Hirst money-making bracket, but money he certainly makes. In his earlier days, when his prices suddenly started to rocket upwards, often it was not Banksy who was making the huge amounts that captured the headlines but his fans. Usually they were from his home town of Bristol, fans who had bought a painting for a couple of hundred quid not as an investment but simply because they liked it and were selling it a few years later for thousands. For a short time it was that elusive commodity called people's art. But when the art investors moved in the money started to flow to Banksy himself.

He accuses others of being capitalist but, despite giving away some pictures for charity, funding events for other graffiti artists, trying to sell prints at a reasonable price only to see them more than double in value on eBay, he too is a capitalist – albeit a reluctant one. With all the compromises and fudges that this entails, this is the side of life that he is most uneasy in dealing with.

With his success comes the inevitable envy and accusations of being a sell-out. Certainly there are many people in the street art world who criticise him, but almost universally, whether they be gallery owners or street artists who have found a market for their work, they admit, if sometimes a little grudgingly, 'Without Banksy I wouldn't be here.'

For he is the standard bearer for a whole new movement in art, whether its practitioners be 'pure' graffiti writers, stencil artists like himself or even artists who crochet their own graffiti. It is a movement which has sprung off the streets and into a much wider public consciousness. In an emailed interview to publicise his film *Exit Through the Gift Shop*, Banksy suggested: 'There's a whole new audience out there, and it's never been easier to sell it, particularly at the lower levels. You don't have to go to college, drag 'round a portfolio, mail off transparencies to snooty galleries or sleep with someone powerful. All you need now is a few ideas and a broadband connection. This is the first time the essentially bourgeois world of art has belonged to the people. We need to make it count.'

He is right, up to a point. There is undoubtedly a new army of Banksy fans thriving on the internet, who will queue for hours to see the very few exhibitions he has put on or queue all night to buy a new print when it is released. When you meet a Banksy fan you can mention *Trolleys* or *Morons* or *Flying Copper* and many of his other works and both of you will know instantly which of his many prints you are talking about. Club Banksy is a club which you don't need a degree in art history to join.

In the long run Banksy will certainly, as he suggests, 'make it count', although, like the members of many other movements, it is difficult to imagine that many of his fellow artists will be remembered. Nevertheless it is remarkable how far street art has travelled in the ten years since Banksy rose to the surface.

The strength of an art movement is all too often measured by the prices the movement's leading figures command in the auction houses. But there are ways other than the price of a Banksy to measure how street art has become an accepted, if slightly confusing, part of our lives.

At the end of 2010 I travelled to the Herbert Art Gallery & Museum in Coventry for the opening of a travelling exhibition of street art prints from the collection of the Victoria & Albert Museum. All the big names were represented in the exhibition, from Banksy to D*Face; Swoon to Shepard Fairey. But there was more than that; six 'emerging' artists from the street had been invited to paint on the white walls of the gallery. A DJ had been imported to give the opening night a little edge, and there was even a wall provided for artists to spray their stuff in some sort of competition with each other. The city council condemns graffiti as an 'illegal, anti-social activity' and spends thousands of pounds a year washing it off, but here was the council's chief executive welcoming – when he could be heard amidst the slightly raucous opening-night crowd – street art both figuratively and literally as it came in from the cold.

Quite soon afterwards I was in the middle of Hackney, east London hunting around the frozen streets for a community centre where a meeting was being held to 'Save the Rabbit'. There was no DJ, no free booze here. The night before, the centre had hosted a bingo session for the local residents. But tonight a rather different, more earnest audience was gathered together to try to save a huge – about twelve foot high – and very attractive rabbit. The rabbit had been painted by the Belgian street artist Roa on the side of a recording studio (with the owner's permission) on one of the main roads through the borough. The council had warned the studio's owners that the unfortunate rabbit was 'a blight on the local environment' and would have to go. What the council had failed to take into account was both the new popularity of street art and the new power of the internet. And what an animal to go into battle against! Not a rat, nor a snake, but a nice cuddly rabbit.

An online petition gained more than 2000 signatures in a week – 'The rabbit must live','Fur Pete's sake', 'Just because it's not a Banksy doesn't make it worthless', 'Don't scrub the bunny' were a few of the comments that came with the signatures. In general the belief was that the rabbit was probably the best thing that could happen to a fairly dismal road in the middle of Hackney that needed all the lightening up it could get. Eventually the local authority relented and the rabbit was saved, as they woke up to the fact that cleaning up graffiti or street art had become a much more confusing task than it used to be.

An artwork a little further down the same road in Hackney better illustrates the way graffiti jousts with the mainstream. It was a huge piece of typography, made out of smiley faces, which spelled out very simply THE STRANGEST WEEK. Apart from its size, it was not exactly an arresting slogan unless you knew the story behind it. For the piece was painted by Ben Eine, Banksy's one-time printer, a graffiti artist in his own right with about twenty arrests and seven convictions for graffiti vandalism to prove it. Shortly before this work went up Eine had received a telephone call from the Prime Minister's office asking if he would provide a painting to give to 'the most powerful man in the world'. ('I didn't think it was going to go to Ronald McDonald,' Eine said, 'so it had to be Obama.') It had indeed been a very strange week; David Cameron on his first visit to the White House as Prime Minister had given President Obama a painting by a convicted graffiti artist. It was this that Eine was commemorating on Hackney Road and indeed Obama proved useful, for Eine was painting alongside another graffiti artist, Pure Evil, on a site where they only 'sort of' had the permission of the owner. When the police duly turned up it was the link with Obama that helped convince them not to make any arrests.

Eine was now famous, his prices went up and at a show he held in San Francisco every piece was sold. And while the rise of street art is confusing to city councils, it is also sometimes confusing to the artists themselves. 'I'm going to travel as much as I can, paint as much as I can and sell as few paintings as possible. I'd rather not earn money,' said Eine shortly after his show had done exactly that.

Graffiti can still anger me intensely, in the same way as it does councils trying to clean up depressing neighbourhoods, especially when I see it on the outside of the flats where I live; I think, 'Who's done that and what's the point?' But what surprised me in talking to graffiti writers – not the Banksys of this world, but others who have made it a little lower down the ladder – is the redemptive power that graffiti sometimes carries. The fact that on occasions it can bring hope and even a life to kids – nearly always male – who were going nowhere until they found the excitement and the skill in painting graffiti on the street.

A minuscule number of these taggers, if any, will get anywhere near what Banksy has achieved. But without Banksy it is impossible to imagine that graffiti art, or as it is now more often called 'urban art', 'street art' or, more ridiculously, 'outsider art', would occupy the place it does today. In 2001 Banksy self-published his very slim, first book – and how many artists, graffiti or otherwise, have ever done that? In it he wrote: 'The quickest way to the top of your business is to turn it upside down.' What this book attempts to do is to travel with him as he does just that.

# One
# The Art of Infiltration

One Wednesday in mid-October 2003 a tall, bearded man, looking slightly scruffy in a dark overcoat, scarf and the sort of floppy hat that cricketers used to wear, walked into Tate Britain clutching quite a large paper carrier bag.

Banksy, for it was he, walked straight past the security guards, who were probably more worried about what visitors might be taking out than what they were bringing in, and made his way unchecked up to Room 7 on the second level. It was a well-chosen spot that he must have researched beforehand. For it is not a gallery you simply stumble into: there is no direct entry from a main corridor, you have to go through another gallery to reach it. It is usually quite quiet there, which allows the museum attendant to move in and out between galleries rather than having to sit covering just the one room.

Having chosen his gallery, next he had to choose his spot on the wall. He found enough room between a bucolic eighteenth-century landscape and the doorway leading to Room 8 and claimed it for his own. He placed his paper carrier bag on the floor, dug out his own picture from the bag and then simply stuck it up.

It was a pretty ballsy thing to do; the Tate would not have been too happy to find a man stealing not their pictures but their space. But perhaps his earlier years spray-painting the streets of Bristol helped steady his nerve, for he showed no signs of panic as he reached down into his bag for a second time and pulled out an impressive white stiff board on which was mounted the picture's caption. This he stuck neatly beside his picture. And then he was off.

Banksy was once asked by an American radio interviewer if he carried out this sort of incursion alone. He answered, 'I do, yeah, you don't want to bring other people into that.' And strictly speaking he was right – he was the only man sticking the painting to the wall. But others were involved in the planning. One of them remembers sitting with Banksy in a café going through the options: 'We said to each other, "It's like planning a bank robbery."' He had at least one accomplice and possibly more in the gallery, for we only know precisely how he achieved this coup because someone was filming him do it. Once the film had been mildly doctored so as to obscure his face, it went out on the web. Eventually a set of stills were to find their way into his best-selling book *Wall and Piece*.

As for the painting itself, Banksy said it was an unsigned oil painting he had found in a London street market. He claimed he found it 'genuinely good' but he was being kind; it was an uninspiring countryside scene with sunlight just managing to filter through the trees on to a meadow and what looked vaguely like a chapel. Across the foreground of the picture he stencilled the sort of blue and white police incident tapes that you usually see keeping gawpers away from an accident. The picture was titled *Crimewatch UK Has Ruined the Countryside for All of Us* and the caption he stuck up alongside it was one of the first of Banksy's many pronouncements:

It can be argued that defacing such an idyllic scene reflects the way our nation has been vandalised by its obsession with crime and paedophilia, where any visit to a secluded beauty spot now feels like it may result in being molested or finding discarded body parts.

(Originally the caption was rather more jokey, adding: 'Little is known about Banksy whose work is inspired by cannabis resin and daytime television', but interestingly, as Banksy became more mainstream, this was edited out of the caption when it eventually appeared in *Wall and Piece.*)

The idea of converting the old into the new is not an original one, although Banksy said that when he first thought of it, 'I was completely convinced it was a genius idea nobody had had before, and I thought, how do I stop people from stealing this idea? And I thought the best thing to do was to get it hanging up in the Tate with my name next to it.' In the 1960s, Asger Jorn, a Danish artist who was a key member of the Situationists, a small group with their base in Paris who argued that advanced capitalism had reduced us all to passive spectators in life, *détourned* paintings he bought in the Paris flea markets with his own swirls and splatters. In the catalogue to his exhibition in Paris he gave collectors and museums advice they were very unlikely to take: 'Be modern. If you have old paintings, do not despair. Retain your memories but detourn them so that they correspond with your era. Why reject the old if one can modernise it with a few strokes of the brush?'

In a more recent example, in 1980 Peter Kennard, an anti-war artist who was to become a friend of Banksy's, painted *Haywain with Cruise Missiles.* This is John Constable's famous painting detourned by Kennard, in a rather more startling manner than

Banksy achieved, by the addition of three Cruise missiles on the back of Constable's hay cart. The Tate bought this work from Kennard in 2007. But it did not matter that the idea of adding something to an old painting was not an original one, nor did it matter that Banksy's picture only lasted on the wall for three hours before the glue failed. (An art student who was there at the time said: 'When it fell to the floor a security guard went over to it in a bit of a panic. He then realised something was up and other security guards were called.') What mattered was that Banksy had stuck it up in the Tate and he had been *filmed doing it.*

Although remaining incognito, Banksy was happy to declare to newspapers reporting the story: 'People often ask whether graffiti is art. Well it must be, now it's hanging in the fucking Tate.' He suggested: 'To actually go through the process of having a painting selected must be quite boring. It's a lot more fun to go and put your own one up. It's all about cutting out the middle man, or the curator in the case of the Tate.' But it was actually about much, much more than that – it was a publicity stunt that had gone wonderfully right. And if it worked at the Tate, why not try it elsewhere?

Over the course of the next seventeen months he played the same sort of trick in seven more galleries in Paris, New York and London. It was fun; it was done with style and considerable cool; it hurt nobody; on the whole the museums took it in good heart; and it helped transform Banksy into an international name. The recognition that other artists spend years trying to achieve, he achieved in months.

He did not just stroll into these galleries and put up a painting on the first wall he could find. He did the reconnaissance first: 'It was funny. I was going to all these galleries and I wasn't looking at the art, I was looking at the blank spaces between the art,' he said. In 2004 he hit two targets. In April he installed in the Natural History Museum in London a rather complicated piece, a stuffed rat enclosed in a glass case along with a spray can, microphone, torch, backpack, sunglasses and a sign scrawled on the background in graffiti style announcing 'Our time will come.' Banksy's then manager, Steve Lazarides, claimed at the time, 'I saw a member of staff walk up to it, check it was attached properly, read the text and walk away.'

Recently the Natural History Museum were kind enough to try to discover what happened to the rat. A spokeswoman said, 'It wasn't long before museum staff noticed it and removed it and as far as we're aware it was returned to Banksy.' In fact it was Steve Lazarides who very swiftly asked for it back, in the hope that a photograph of the rat that had been in and out of the museum would generate even more publicity. But he was told he would have to wait, since the boxed rat was being kept in the museum's ice room to ensure that there was no contamination of any of the museum's permanent exhibits. When the rat was finally released and Lazarides was interviewed by the museum's security staff, he pointed out that there must be something wrong with security if a man could walk in with a rat enclosed in a substantial box and screw the box on to the wall of the museum without anyone raising an alarm.

Banksy also visited the Louvre in Paris. It is difficult to say just how successful he was here. Documented in his book there is a rather blurry picture of his own version of the *Mona Lisa*, transformed by a smiley face, hanging on a wall in the gallery. All does not look well in this photograph. We can see the back of a man, probably Banksy since his head has been deliberately blurred.

He looks in a hurry, pressing a caption on to the wall below his *Mona Lisa* with one hand while he continues to keep moving past. That's it. The video shows very little more than the photograph. As for how long it lasted, Banksy's book only says 'Duration Unknown.' But it was the Louvre, it was there for however short a time – it counts.

But he wasn't quite there yet; the Tate had won enough headlines but the Natural History Museum and the Louvre had not really taken him much further. It was next year that he really upped his game in both New York and London. Being a Sunday, 13 March 2005 was a busy day for galleries; nevertheless he managed to infiltrate four museums in New York without being stopped once. At the Brooklyn Museum he put up another doctored painting, this time of a bewigged and rather ridiculous-looking aristocrat, all ruffles, frills and sword. One hand is resting limply on the back of a chair, the other is holding a can of spray paint just as limply. All this is in bright colours, while the dark background behind him is covered in graffiti including a CND sign and a simple demand for 'No War'. At 61 cm × 46 cm it is the largest of Banksy's incursion paintings, and the video of him doing it is the clearest of them all.

The coat he used at the Tate had been replaced by an equally inconspicuous raincoat and the hat by a rather sturdier model, but the false beard looks as though it was still there and the carrier bag with his painting inside was almost laughably noticeable. Again he had chosen a gallery, the American Identities Gallery on the fifth floor, where there were not many visitors. We see him saunter into the gallery with a nerveless deliberation, put his bag down against one wall, extract the painting, turn and press it up against the opposite wall, pushing down on it with a manic intensity – determined that it was going to last longer than the three hours *Crimewatch UK* had survived at the Tate. Then he is off. The whole operation takes exactly thirty-three seconds. According to Banksy's book, the painting stayed there for eight days before being discovered. Reports at the time say it was three days. But even if it was only three days, it is still a slightly depressing comment on how much interest we take in some of the paintings on display as we trail around galleries. Explaining how he got away with it, Banksy said that the galleries 'do get pretty full but not if you put the pictures in the boring bits'.

In Brooklyn he had chosen a boring bit, but in Manhattan itself he risked the crowds and still got away with it. How? He explained that the accomplices who were filming him also provided distractions where necessary: 'They staged a gay tiff, shouting very loudly and obnoxiously.' But, more thoughtfully, he told another interviewer: 'I think it is a testament to the frame of mind most people are in when they are in a museum really. Most people let the world go past them and don't pay a lot of attention to most things. Not even apparently to people with big beards wielding around pieces of art and glueing them up.'

(All this talk of interviews makes it sound as though he was chatting to all and sundry, but of course he wasn't. He chose the people he would talk to as carefully as he chose the galleries: the *New York Times*, National Public Radio – the nearest thing America has to Radio Four – and Reuters. The interviews were conducted by phone or email and since no one got to meet him they had to take on trust the fact that they were talking to or reading an email from the real Banksy.)

He claimed that he had set a target of hanging his piece in the Metropolitan Museum of Art for at least forty-seven days. Why such a specific number? Because it was the time a work by Matisse, *Le Bateau*, hung upside down before it was spotted by a visitor who informed a guard of the mistake. (He had actually got his museums muddled – an easy thing to do. The mistake was made in the Museum of Modern Art, not the Met.) But Banksy's piece only lasted two hours and it is easy enough to see why. In the Great American Painting wing his modified portrait of a very proper society lady stared out at you; the gold frame fitted in well enough with the paintings around her, but she was wearing an antique gas mask. She was impossible not to spot. A spokeswoman for the gallery said that no damage had been done to the wall or to other artworks. She added, a little sniffily, 'I think it's fair to say that it would take more than a piece of Scotch tape to get a work of art into the Met.'

At the Museum of Natural History he hung an intriguing glass-encased beetle to which he had attached Airfix fighter plane wings with missiles slung beneath them. The caption declared it was a '*Withus Oragainstus*' beetle (you may have to read the caption for a second time to get the joke). On the third floor of the Museum of Modern Art (MOMA), home of Andy Warhol's *32 Campbell's Soup Cans*, he placed his own painting *Discount Soup Can* – depicting a tin of Tesco Value cream of tomato soup. He says in *Wall and Piece* that having placed the picture on the wall he took five minutes to see what happened next. 'A sea of people walked up, stared and left looking confused and slightly cheated. I felt like a true modern artist.'

Most of these successful incursions came with slightly irritating faux-naïf thoughts from Banksy. After his success in New York he emailed the *New York Times* to say he had thought about trying the Guggenheim as well but he was too intimidated: 'I would have had to appear between two Picassos and I'm not good enough to get away with that.' He said he preferred to be known as a 'quality vandal' rather than an artist and he went on: 'I've wandered around a lot of art galleries thinking "I could have done that", so it seemed only right that I should try. These galleries are just trophy cabinets for a handful of millionaires. The public never has any real say in what art they see.'

Having finished with New York, Banksy was back in London. In May he hit Gallery 49 of the British Museum, a busy gallery full of artefacts from Roman Britain. Below a statue of Atys (youthful lover of the mother goddess Cybele, in case you were wondering) and partially hidden by a first-century tombstone, he managed to stick up a convincingly rough piece of rock. Drawn across it, in the style of early caveman art, was a picture of 'early man' pushing a shopping trolley. The caption, which was almost identical in design to the British Museum's captions, read:

> The artist responsible is known to have created a substantial body of work across the South East of England under the moniker Banksymus Maximus but little else is known about him. Most art of this type has unfortunately not survived. The majority is destroyed by zealous municipal officials who fail to recognise the artistic merit and historical value of daubing on walls.

On his website Banksy announced a treasure hunt with a prize for the first person who could find the caveman's art and send him a photograph of themselves standing beside it; but the British Museum got there first, taking the caveman down before anyone could claim the prize. A spokeswoman for the British Museum said they were 'seeing the lighter side of it' and were 'still in the process of deciding what to do with it'. Since then it has become part of internet folklore, reinforced by a statement in Banksy's book, that the caveman was taken into the museum's permanent collection. However, a search of the permanent collection using key words such as 'Banksy Maximus', 'Early Man goes to Market', 'Post Catatonic' and, of course, 'Banksy', yielded no results. It seems a pity to spoil the fun but the museum responded to my request for information by saying, 'It wasn't acquired by the museum and isn't in the collection.' (In contrast, Riikka Kuittinen, then a curator in the print department at the Victoria & Albert Museum, says she was really hoping that the V&A would get one. She says she would have marked it 'accession into the collection', stuck a number on it and put it into store. But the artist never obliged and later the V&A had to buy its Banksy prints.)

These incursions were not only profitable in terms of publicity, they were – eventually – profitable financially. Banksy's *Crimewatch UK* was placed in the Tate's lost property office after it fell down. Quite what happened to it after that is unclear. The Tate says that at this point it has no information about where it ended up. But only days after the Tate incursion, another version of *Crimewatch UK*, complete with the video of it being hung, was being offered for sale by a gallery for £15,000. And six years later, yet another version turned up on the walls of the Black Rat Gallery in Shoreditch; this version was owned by a private collector who had presumably bought it from Banksy. The gallery had received an offer of £150,000 which the collector turned down. (There is a puzzle here. Banksy found the original painting in a street market and painted the police tapes over it; but he can't have found three *identical* paintings in the market. Somehow he must have transferred the image.

Similarly, a picture identical to that of the unfortunate society lady he used for the New York Metropolitan Museum turned up four years later in his exhibition in Bristol, but her gas mask had been replaced by a child's disguise: a big false nose, complete with a silly moustache and funny glasses. She looked better in the gas mask.)

The rise of Banksy's humble can of soup was just as swift as that of *Crimewatch UK*. Just three years after he had hung his first version in MOMA, a rather bigger version of the painting (measuring 48 in × 36 in, it would have been difficult to smuggle into MOMA) fetched £117,600 at Bonhams, after two rival bidders had driven it rapidly beyond the estimated price of £80,000. And this was at the height of the credit crunch. Certainly it was not the $15 million that wealthy friends of the Museum of Modern Art had paid for Warhol's *32 Campbell's Soup Cans* back in 1977. But this was fifteen years after Warhol had painted them and the price reflected the fact that Warhol's soup cans, glorifying such an everyday object, had come to be seen as changing the very nature of what was considered art. When Warhol had first painted his cans back in 1962, his new gallery in Los Angeles was trying to sell them at $100 each – and failing. (Eventually the gallery bought the whole set for $1000, an extraordinarily good investment but not much of a return for Warhol.)

Although these gallery visits were to earn Banksy good money in the years to come, this was almost certainly the last thing he had in mind at the time. It seems strange to say this about an artist who wishes to remain anonymous, but his incursions were about fame and recognition, about people who never went near a gallery or a museum seeing his pictures for the first time in newspapers or on television, and especially on the web, enjoying them and looking out for them in the future. Very swiftly Banksy became the first international artist of the internet. His anonymity meant he could not hold big press conferences or give television interviews, so he announced his coup in New York on the internet by giving a set of pictures to www.woostercollective.com, a New York site dedicated to street art of one kind or another.

He was not creating art on the internet, but he was building himself an immensely loyal following on the web, fans who were unlikely to visit a gallery but were more than happy to visit a website. He now shows his new works on his own site, www.banksy.co.uk. He can thus be spraying walls in Israel, Hollywood, Barcelona or London and everyone can see what he has done – it gives his art a lifespan that graffiti artists never had before. The wall might be painted over but the picture is still there. He can advertise his film, promote any new exhibition and through an associated site, www.picturesonwalls.com, sell his own signed prints and those of other artists. And apart from Banksy's own site a whole nest of other sites have sprung up to follow his work, argue about who he is, put up photos of 'a new Banksy' they think they have spotted, discuss whether this piece is *really* a Banksy, track his prices, slam him and champion him. In short, to give everyone a chance to feel they *share* some part of Banksy, even if they are not a millionaire with a Banksy on their sitting-room wall.

And beyond these dedicated fans, through both the mainstream press and the internet, Banksy had won for himself international recognition. Before he hit London, Paris and New York he was known – he had for instance provided the cover illustration for Blur's *Think Tank* album. But he was not *well* known; his first two small self-published books had been overlooked by all but his most committed fans. Now, by reinventing the rules, he had become a known name, and he had done it in such a clever way that he was not considered a publicity seeker, but more a battler for the little guy against the all-powerful galleries and art dealers. Instead of 'vandal', descriptions of him like 'The Scarlet Pimpernel' became common currency, culminating in the *Sunday Times* calling him 'Our unlikeliest national treasure.'

There is simply no other artist who could command the cover and the inside pages of the *Sunday Times* magazine, followed a few months later by an 'exclusive' interview heralded on the front page of the *Sun*. The fact that this *Sun* interview had simply been lifted word for word from the extras when his film, *Exit Through the Gift Shop*, was released on DVD did not matter – except perhaps to Banksy. What mattered was the fact that the *Sun* considered him interesting enough to their readers to devote two pages to him. He had come a long way in a short time from his early days in Bristol.

# Two
# Once Upon a Time

The Barton Hill district of Bristol in the 1980s was a scary part of town. Very white – probably no more than three black families had somehow ended up there – working class, run down and not happy with strangers of any colour. A series of high-rise council flats had been plonked there in the 1950s and it had a reputation for drugs and crime. The graffiti on the walls of Barton Hill shouted 'Fuck the Pope', but it was not a Protestant enclave, more an angry enclave. The National Front had got a foothold in the estate and, as one of its old-time residents says, 'No one was coming up here taking the piss.'

So when Banksy, who came from a much leafier part of town, decided to go there for the first time he was nervous. You never quite know with Banksy whether he is telling the truth, embroidering the truth or simply just inventing things. But he told his fellow graffiti artist and author Felix Braun: 'My Dad was badly beaten up there as a kid and had his trousers stolen, so he'd always put the fear of God into me about the place. By the time I'd worked up the courage to cycle over and check it out, I was so terrified I actually remember choosing my best pair of pants for the occasion just in case.'

Why would Banksy want to go there in the first place? The answer lies with John Nation, who Banksy described to Braun – correctly – as 'that shouty red-faced little social worker'. Nation was the man 'who made it all happen, [he's] had more impact on the shape of British culture over the past twenty years than anyone else to come from the city.' Today the link between Banksy, international artist and film-maker, and John Nation, now in construction and hating it, might seem improbable; sadly, when Banksy staged his exhibition at the Bristol Museum, Nation did not even get an invitation to the opening night – although by the time the exhibition closed he had taken himself there no less than eight times. But without Nation there would not have been the throbbing graffiti scene that developed in Bristol and there might well not have been a Banksy.

I met Nation on his home territory at Barton Hill. He arrived unshaven in his Ralph Lauren baseball hat, jeans, a light blue tracksuit top, a Bristol City three lions backpack and a cigarette lighter with a St George's flag positioned carefully on a girl's bare bum (although he has since managed to give up smoking). He says he has 'the gift of the gab' and he certainly has, it is almost impossible to stop him talking about graffiti in his round Bristol accent. He is generous with his time and generous with his gifts – for instance he pulled out of his backpack a set of twelve postcards from Banksy's Bristol exhibition and gave them to me; the web now prices them at an average $15. Now turning fifty with two grown-up sons, he looks back at his graffiti days as the best years of his life.

Nation's story is one of redemption. He lived on the fourteenth floor of a block of council flats from where you could look down and see the best thing going on the estate – the Barton Hill Youth

Club. From the age of eleven he was usually there four nights a week. There is a photograph from those days where someone has altered the sign on the club so it reads Barton Hill Yob Centre, instead of Youth Centre, and Nation admits: 'My mum didn't like me going there for it did have a reputation, very unruly, rough and tumble,' but the Club was better than home where his mother was 'a victim of domestic violence'.

At 15 he got involved in violence himself. It was very random. By sheer coincidence fans from Bristol City, the team he followed, and West Ham bumped into each other at Bristol station – they weren't even going to the same match. A fight followed, it spread outside the station, he picked up the nearest weapon he could find, a yellow flashing beacon that was protecting road works, and brought it down on the head of a West Ham fan. The fan ended up with a fractured skull and Nation ended up in detention centre, being given what William Whitelaw, Conservative Home Secretary at the time, called a 'short sharp shock.'

But John was fortunate. The club's youth worker realised that the middle-class workers commuting into the working-class ghetto every day were not gaining much respect. So John Nation was taken on first as a volunteer and then, at seventeen, as a part-time worker. The youth club might have carried on in much the same way, with a concentration on five-a-side football and occasional raucous punk rock concerts, but for two things. First Nation saw Malcolm Mclaren's 1983 'Buffalo Girls' video, a wonderful folding together of square dancing and hip hop, complete with scratching, breakdancing and graffiti writing. And then he went on a visit to Amsterdam. 'I've got to be truthful,' he says now, 'I went there for a smoking holiday and to visit the red light district. I was young, free and single. But the first thing that struck me about Amsterdam was the graffiti. Just seeing the sheer volume of it.' While there he came across the city's main graffiti collective and he was hooked. Barton Hill Youth Club, he decided, was going to become the graffiti centre of Bristol. No more tagging (writing) in the street, on the buses, on the bins, on the front doors. He would offer graffiti artists – 'aerosol artists' as he liked to call them – a home where they could paint all they liked but it would be completely legal.

He brought back from Amsterdam pictures of what he had seen. He got on the graffiti network and soon he was being posted pictures from around the world – this was in the days before everyone had a computer. He never tagged himself, but he photographed every piece he saw. So Bristol's vandals soon had a useful reference library, complete with sketch books of outlines and designs 'the lads' had done. To this Nation added a whole cupboard full of paint, marker pens and various mixing nozzles in the hope that this would keep graffiti writers from their usual practice of stealing the paint. Among the many people he approached for financial support was the Prince's Trust, but this was a step or two too far for the Trust. He did however have more luck with Dulux, who provided 'shedloads' of emulsion – the paint that often provides the background canvas for graffiti.

In many ways he succeeded. Barton Hill became the Mecca for graffiti writers, drawing them in first from Bristol, then from across England and finally from even further afield. A place buzzing with ideas, alliances, rivalries, a second family for teenagers in their rebellious years, it was a very, very unlikely creative hotspot, far removed from the sedate areas of the city's middle-class life. The walls of the club were soon painted, and they even climbed on the roof and painted that. One visitor from a different part of Bristol remembers going up to the club for the first time to play five-a-side football and being overwhelmed by the graffiti on the walls of the pitch that he was bouncing the ball off – he in turn became a graffiti writer himself.

Go to the youth club today and it is something of a disappointment. It is now the estate itself that is vibrant, with a multi-million pound makeover and people of all races living there. Even with John Nation as a guide, jabbering away enthusiastically about graffiti with a passion that remains completely undaunted, the club still looks unloved, only partially used, waiting for the day it gets redeveloped. But in the 1980s it was humming. Tom Bingle, or Inkie as he is known when he paints, says now, 'It blew my brains away as soon as I walked in. The graffiti on all the walls, people talking about it, people doing it and the train tracks right next to it – it was perfect.' It was, as John Nation rightly says, 'a bright beacon in a drab landscape', a beacon that would eventually attract Banksy.

Barton Hill was an inspiration, but as a method of stopping graffiti writers tagging the streets of Bristol illegally it was a complete failure. Nation says it was a 'place where people who were constantly being told that they're nobody in the world could say "I am somebody."' The trouble was they wanted to announce the fact all over Bristol. Inkie lived in Clifton, the affluent part of Bristol, and he says: 'We used to walk down the train tracks to Lawrence Hill [the nearest station to Barton Hill] and paint as we went. Everyone would tag from around there, the buses too, they'd be tagged out.' Or as the graffiti artist Turo tells Felix Braun, in *Children of the Can*: 'We were just basically destroying the city . . . Everyone would meet in Barton Hill, do pieces in the day then go out at night and do illegal pieces.' Even John Nation admits now that 'All the lads when they came here, they used to come up from the train station and cut through the estate and bomb all the bins and the doors. There was a lot of ill feeling from the local residents.'

It couldn't last and it didn't. British Transport Police started an elaborate surveillance operation – codenamed Operation Anderson – which went on for six months and reportedly cost close to £1 million. Eventually they got lucky: having arrested two lads they discovered that one of them had a diary in which he kept not only the phone numbers of other graffiti artists but also their tags – or names that they used to spray on the walls – right beside them. It was easy enough for the police to find the real names and addresses to go with the phone numbers and in March 1989 they rounded up seventy-two artists. The police arrived at six in the morning at Nation's mum's house and he was taken away in handcuffs to the youth club. 'I couldn't believe how many Old Bill there were. It was like they were looking for Ronnie Biggs or something.

'The officer in charge said, "We have established you are at the club to run this graffiti project," so straightaway I said, "No, I am here to run an aerosol art project and there's a vast difference." He replied, "I am not here to argue the whys and wherefores of graffiti art versus aerosol art. It's all fucking graffiti."' Inkie was seen by the police as the ringleader. John Nation describes him as 'a caner – he'd cane everything, when they raided his house they found he'd even tagged the walls of his bedroom.' Inkie says now, 'I think the first charge was for about £250,000 worth of damage, but I think there was £1 million pending against me. It was everything I had done on the train tracks, everything. And they had photographs to go with it.' But handwriting experts were brought in to challenge some of the evidence – their argument, for what it was worth, was that since the spray can had not touched the wall it was impossible to identify who had sprayed each tag. More important was the fact that there were almost too many photographs of tags to sort out exactly who was responsible for what. The taggers also benefited hugely from the fact that the prosecution was not allowed to lump everyone together to face one all-encompassing charge. In the end forty-six of the artists were fined, the amounts ranging from £20 to £2000. Inkie's fine was £100.

Nation himself was put up on the serious charge of conspiracy to incite individuals to commit criminal damage. There was certainly ample evidence to prove that John Nation encouraged legal graffiti – often dedications were written on pieces: 'to John and Lenny', Lenny being his Staffordshire Bull terrier – but no evidence to prove he was encouraging these same writers to commit criminal damage. In the end the prosecution never took the case to trial. He was formally found not guilty, although he agreed to be bound over to keep the peace for the next year.

The police claimed success with considerable justification, for although they had not been as triumphant in court as they had first hoped to be, at the very least they had made graffiti writers stop and think. But at the same time the case also gave the artists a lot of publicity – suddenly they were on national television. BBC2 ran a documentary on Barton Hill and Operation Anderson, Inkie and two other writers were invited to paint live on Granada TV's *This Morning*, John Nation appeared on *Richard and Judy*. For anyone deciding to retire from the scene rather than face imprisonment the next time they were caught, there were more than enough people ready to take their place.

John Nation stayed on at Barton Hill for two more years when, much to his regret, he fell out with the management of the club and was forced to leave. Perhaps *Richard and Judy* and all the other media appearances went to his head, for as he says, he was considered 'to be getting too big for my boots . . . I lost my focus . . . To be honest it was of my own making and I paid for it by losing my job.' His fall is a long, sad story, for in the unlikely setting of Barton Hill he provided the inspiration and the enthusiasm for many. The roll call of Bristol graffiti artists is a long one, starting with 3D – otherwise known as Robert Del Naja from the band Massive Attack – then Z-Boys, and going on through Inkie, FLX, Nick Walker, Jody, Cheo, SP27, Shab, Soker, Chaos, Turo, Xens, Sickboy, Mr Jago, Banksy, of course, and many, many more. They did not all paint at Barton Hill, but the great majority did and they were all heavily influenced by what was going on there. Some of course took it nowhere but others became model makers, TV editors, illustrators, animators, graphic designers, successful artists and mega-successful artists.

As Nation says, Barton Hill was an amazing mixture of graffiti writers. 'You had a lot of ragtag working-class kids from the big housing estates. Then you had an influx of middle class. But there was none of that class divide amongst them.' So where did Banksy fit in?

To answer that you have to decide who Banksy really is. And since at this point he is at the very start of his career, this is a good time to confront the issue. In 2010, when he was doing interviews by email to promote his new film *Exit Through the Gift Shop*, his publicist promised the *Sunday Times* magazine 'faithfully' that he was 'very working class'. She was thus having the best of both worlds, retaining his anonymity while moulding his image slightly, making him sound like the working-class vandal made good.

It is a tribute to Banksy that he has built around him a very loyal group of friends, people who might not have seen him for years but who still feel they are life members of Club Banksy and are nervous about letting slip the most innocuous of details. So throughout the research for this book I always told people who know him that I was not asking them to identify him.

In 2008 the *Mail on Sunday* produced a long investigative story by Claudia Joseph which did name him and detailed some of his family background. Three years later they named his wife. Banksy fans dismissed these stories as the *Mail* up to its usual tricks, but actually the paper's first story was a detailed, thorough investigation complete with photographs. There was one of him in his schoolboy days and another – taken in Jamaica, which Banksy had once visited – of an ordinary-looking bloke 'believed to be Banksy', with various bits of street art paraphernalia around him. Armed with his birth certificate, the *Mail* found neighbours who remembered him, a flatmate who tried his hardest not to remember him and parents who loyally denied any connection with the man the *Mail* thought was Banksy. The name does not appear here simply because I am honouring the commitment to people whom I asked for interviews that I would not identify him.

And besides that, as Adam Clark Estes wrote on Salon.com, 'Banksy's knack for anonymity intrigues us. Even if he stepped forward or another exposé were published, we probably wouldn't stop wondering because wondering is fun.' Certainly the reaction on the *Mail*'s website proved his point, for most people seemed to resent being told who Banksy was. Rather like Father Christmas, the legend was better than the real thing. One *Mail* reader wrote: 'Why have you done this? I don't understand. You have ruined something special.' When they named his wife the reaction was much the same: 'The vast majority of people don't want to know who Banksy is. We enjoy his anonymity just as he does. Leave them be and leave his wife's family alone! Spoilsports!'

Despite his PR's assurances, he is not 'very working class'. One of his friends says: 'This image of him as a lovable rogue, it's an image. He's public school educated and he's a very intelligent man.' Another says the idea that he is 'very working class' is 'a load of bollocks. I am not going to put anyone down for where they come from, but anyone who goes to Bristol Cathedral School is not "very working class".'

To survive in the rough and tumble of the macho graffiti world Banksy, like others, had to blur his background a little. 'Dare I say it, I think he made out he's a little bit less switched on than he is,' says another graffiti artist from those days. 'With the whole street culture thing you have to play it all down a bit, you can't go into it being all highbrow and intellectual. A lot of the places he painted are not the nicest places in the world and you can't go there all "Oh hi, hello" sort of thing. There's two sides to him and I think he kept the one side, the side that he went to one of the poshest schools in Bristol, very quiet. I think you will find quite a lot of his story is embellished. It sounds good but there's a lot of mystique about it all.'

Banksy was brought up in a leafy suburb on the edge of the city. It was not the most fashionable part of town – there was none of the buzz of Clifton – but still it was totally different from Barton Hill and it is easy to see how he would have been a bit nervous as he ventured into the high-rise council estate for the first time. In addition the school he went to was – at the time – no state school but the fee-paying Bristol Cathedral School (it became a free Academy school in 2008). Some years ago he told *Swindle* magazine: 'Graffiti was the thing we all loved at school – we all did it on the bus on the way home from school. Everyone was doing it.' It's a lovely picture of all these public school boys busy at being vandals, even if Banksy is mistaking everyone else for himself.

Quite how easy a childhood he had is unclear. In his first self-published book, *Banging Your Head Against a Brick Wall*, produced in 2001, Banksy himself tells one story from his childhood which is surely just too heartbreaking for him to have made up. 'When I was nine years old I was expelled from school,' he wrote, 'it was punishment for swinging one of my classmates round and round before dropping him onto a concrete floor.' The child was taken away by an ambulance that had to pull in to the playground to pick him up. He sustained a fractured skull and did not regain consciousness for a week.

'The next day I was made to stand in front of the whole school at assembly while the headmaster gave a speech about good and evil before I was sent home in disgrace. The unfortunate part of this story is that I never actually touched the kid ...' It was his best friend who had 'put him into casualty'. Banksy and another boy just watched – startled – as Banksy's friend swung the boy round and round until he was too dizzy to stand up. When the friend, who was a big lad, saw that things were serious he persuaded the other boy to lie: they both said that Banksy was the culprit.

'I tried many times to explain that I hadn't done it, but the boys stuck to their story. Eventually my mum turned to me and said bitterly that I should have the guts to admit when I was wrong and that it was even more disgusting when I refused to accept what I'd done. So I shut up after that.' He tells the story to illustrate that 'there's no such thing as justice' and 'there's no point in behaving yourself', but it might also suggest that something was not quite right at home.

He told one interviewer he did art at school but never made it any further. He never went to art college and he says 'I'm not from a family of artistic people.' But a fellow pupil recalls now: 'There were several good artists at school back then, but one really stood out and that was him.' However, the art department at school and Banksy did not appear to get on, for he says he got no more than an E in GCSE art. Asked if this was due to a lack of inspiration, he replied: 'That, plus I had also discovered cannabis.' (The school says it cannot discuss any individual pupil's achievements there.) From all that he says it appears as though he was miserable at school – it never made any sense to him – and it was only when he had an aerosol spray can in his hand that he discovered his voice. What happened to him between leaving school at sixteen and surfacing again as an up-and-coming artist remains unclear, although he claims to have spent much of the time apprenticed to a pork butcher. He says he was politicised during 'the poll tax, the Criminal Justice Act and the Hartcliffe Riots' (which developed after two men who had stolen a police motorbike were killed in a collision with an unmarked police car). 'I can also remember my old man taking me down to see the Lloyds Bank – what was left of it – after the 1980 St Pauls riots. It's mad to see how the whole thing of having to do what you're told can be turned on its head, and how few people it takes to grab it back.'

When Banksy did eventually make it up to Barton Hill he arrived at a good moment. He had started painting at the age of fourteen and he was only fifteen at the time of all the arrests, so he was not in any way involved and in many ways this was fortunate. Operation Anderson had not wiped graffiti off the streets but there was certainly a gap; it had made people pause and weigh up the risks and Barton Hill now had the reputation of being hot. Surveillance cameras were being introduced in force and there were fears that these cameras might have been installed in the area. Banksy and others were the second wave, the next generation, with new enthusiasm, new ideas, new ways of approaching things and no criminal record.

John Nation remembers him coming up towards the end of his time there. He finds it hard to believe that Banksy was as nervous as he claims to be, but for 'someone who wasn't from Barton Hill he probably was scared a bit . . . there were a lot of the lads who were there every day of the week, hanging out. He wasn't one of those, he wasn't one of the local lads. But there were a lot who came up at the weekends, you could have up to 100 people here . . . I can remember him coming up. He was a lot younger than some of the other lads that were painting and he would sort of tag along. There were always lads on the fringes who weren't so pronounced . . .'

Tucked away in the corner of the youth club's five-a-side football pitch there is a faded piece of graffiti that appears to be a Banksy. The wall has been sprayed silver and a poodle with what I took to be a goat's head has been stencilled across it (I read later that it was actually the head of a bulldog, not a goat). Bulldog, goat . . . it was not one of his best efforts and it was so faded I was not even sure to begin with if the body was a poodle, yet it was certainly his stencilled tag at the bottom. Over the next few years he began to make his presence felt all over Bristol and not just at the Barton Hill 'Hall of Fame' (the name given by graffiti writers to a large wall where anyone can paint legally).

He was experimenting with names – in these early days he sometimes signed himself Robin Banx, although this soon evolved into Banksy, which had less of the gangster 'robbing banks' ring to it but was much more memorable – and easier to write. He was experimenting too with styles. Was he going to be a graffiti writer, writing his name according to the strict set of graffiti rules? Was he going to be a freehand artist, using an aerosol nozzle against the wall in much the same way as a painter uses a brush against a canvas? Or was he going to be a stencil artist, cutting out the shapes he wanted on stiff card, placing the card against the wall and then using an aerosol can to spray over it so that when he took the card away only the shapes that had been cut out were left?

Graffiti artist. Stencil artist. Aerosol artist. To most people outside this closed world, the terms don't mean very much: graffiti is graffiti. But within this community they matter enormously. Thus a friend of Banksy's from way back says, 'He was never a graffiti artist who sold out, because he was never a graffiti artist to start with.' So what, or who, is a true graffiti artist?

# Three
# Graffiti Decoded

I was fortunate to find a friendly guide who would lead me through the world of graffiti, a world which he described very accurately as 'a lawless activity with a million and one laws'. David Samuel grew up on a council estate in Kilburn, London. His own estate was tolerable but there were three others around it, one of which was 'horrifying'. He got into graffiti at fourteen, at about the same age as Banksy, and he says simply, 'It sounds very corny, but graffiti saved my life.' And this is one of the weird things about graffiti: to the outsider it *is* vandalism; to quite a few of the graffiti artists I have met it is a way *out of* vandalism – or, in the words of one academic, a 'tactic of the dispossessed in achieving a sense of identity'.

Now thirty-one, the child of a volatile mix: mother Irish, father – who he never knew – Egyptian, he calls his story 'the usual standard sob story . . . one parent family . . . didn't have any money . . . I was stealing from a young age. As a teenager you want to do something that makes you look good, to stop yourself getting bullied or beaten up. I was running around with a gang from south Kilburn, doing a lot of bad things with them. When I stopped running with them things got really bad, they all turned on me because I knew certain things that could get them in trouble. There was a load of madness, once they tried to stab me on the high road and there was a knife fight in the bakery . . .'

Instead of gangs he turned to graffiti, going straight into it from school rather like an Etonian might go into stockbroking. 'I thought, this will show I've got balls. This will show I can do things myself and I don't have to hurt anyone. That's what mentally saved my life. And many of those people who I was doing those mad things with are either dead or in prison.' He has stopped painting illegally and, having been helped initially by a £4500 loan from the Prince's Trust to establish a gallery in Brighton, he now runs his own illustration agency, Rarekind. But if you know where to look on the web you can still find a short video of him painting trains.

Graffiti on trains has always seemed to me to be annoying, exasperating, dispiriting – in short, hugely anti-social. But watching David paint part of a carriage on this video I can see the attraction: the combination of fear, adrenalin and satisfaction at having outwitted the rest of the world. 'That's the top, top thing,' he says. 'It's amazing when you see your train in the morning. You get there early enough and you see it pull out. Oh, I can't explain, but it's the best, best feeling.'

So why do they write only their 'tag' – in effect their signature? ''Cos that's all we care about,' says David. 'We don't go out there for no monetary gain. We go out there for passion and for fame.' There seems, I suggest, a fair amount of macho swilling around here. 'Oh God, man, it's all about it – how big are your balls. It's fame, ego, that's what I did it for.' But excuse me, he's not famous and Banksy is. No, but graffiti writers are not doing it to impress the outside world, they are doing it to impress each other: 'We're not talking to anyone out there apart from ourselves.' Getting your piece up, whether it be on a train or on a wall where no one else can reach, the adrenalin of painting when any moment you might be caught, beating the security system, chatting about it afterwards to fellow members of the club, like footballers dissecting their victory. This is what it's all about.

He loves Banksy's work: 'He's very clever. I think he's a genius man.' But Banksy, he says, is not a graffiti artist. Graffiti artists 'only write their name and do characters and it's a whole ego trip and it's all about us and our peers. It's not about the public.'

In contrast, for Banksy and other street artists like him, it is *all* about the public. Maybe they care about their peers, but what they are really concerned about is a much wider audience. They are painting the same walls as a graffiti artist but they are producing images which are instantly understandable – a gallery on the street that is inclusive rather than exclusive. The image can be pure humour or social commentary or both, but every passer-by gets the joke.

In addition, while some graffiti artists sketch out their work before going out to paint, most just go out and bomb. But for a stencil artist, the art is much more in the conception of the piece and then exactly where you place it than in how skilfully you can use a spray can. Stencils can take hours at home or in the studio to prepare, and if you venture beyond black and white each layer of colour demands its own separate stencil. Bristol stencil artist Nick Walker says some of his own intricate stencils 'take days to cut.' It is painstaking work cutting out accurately the shape on a piece of stiffish card. Banksy himself suggests card about 1.5 mm thick, 'much fatter and it's too difficult and boring to cut through. Any thinner and it gets sloppy too quickly.' Some artists now use Photoshop to create their image and computer-driven lasers to cut out their shapes, but Banksy preaches the joys of a 'very sharp knife' and pre-cut gaffa tape to stick the stencil on the wall in a hurry.

The stencil artist manages to marry the techniques of the studio with the thrill of danger that comes with graffiti art. There are other advantages. The risk of being caught painting on the street is diminished, though not eliminated. For once the cut stencil has been stuck temporarily to the wall, it is much quicker to spray over it than to paint the intricate, involved flourishes of the graffiti artist, although watching a stencil artist doing layer upon layer of colour I realise it can take huge patience and attention to detail. Also, if you feel like it, you can repeat the image, or a very similar image, again and again – one done by Banksy himself, of placard-carrying rats, being a good example (in more recent years he appears to have stopped these repeats).

So if Banksy and others out there painting the streets are not graffiti artists, what are they? Steve Lazarides, Banksy's one-time gallerist and former manager, has tried to promote the name 'Outsiders' and his book called, of course, *Outsiders*, declares it is 'Art by people.' But the fact that some of these 'Outsiders' sell in his gallery for up to £40,000 makes them feel like outsiders who have very much come in from the cold. 'Outsiders' as a collective name probably has a shelf life only slightly longer than 'aerosol artists', the term John Nation persevered with for so long. 'Aerosol art' has never made it and never will – even though, long before the days of Tracey Emin and her bed or Damien Hirst and his sheep, we often classified painters by the material they used – as 'oil painters' or 'watercolourists' for example.

Street art is the name that fits best. It can cover Banksy and his stencils, it can cover stickers, posters, wooden boxes, cardboard, woodcuts, pavement paintings, mosaics, even knitting and crocheting. Yes, there are 'yarn stormers' who use knitting to decorate everything from lamp-posts to buses and there are crochet graffiti artists – particularly Olek, a Pole living in New York, who managed to crochet a nice warm tightly fitting suit covering the whole of Wall Street's charging bull, a bronze statue which stands eleven feet tall and sixteen feet long. Sadly her work only lasted a couple of hours before it was cut off. And if the 'pure' graffiti merchants hate the title street artists – usually dismissing anyone using stencils as a 'toy' or an 'art fag' – then they can still call themselves graffiti artists.

And pure graffiti can in itself be far more complicated than it might appear at first glance. To understand graffiti you need to decode it and without the code you are lost. Again, to put it in academic terms, 'graffiti artists are modern day calligraphers. It [graffiti] is characterised by the redefinition of the alphabet and its metamorphosis into one of indecipherable chaos. This is to deliberately exclude those who are not part of the sub-culture by making the names and messages indecipherable.'

Anyone who lives in a city will have seen squiggles on a wall, some of them – the most irritating ones – nothing more than a squiggle, the ones that make you feel that all graffiti should be banished. These are done by the lads who will 'sacrifice mural quality for tag quantity', putting their name up wherever they can find a space providing it will enhance their exposure.

But then there are the elaborate ones, where what is important is the way the piece flows, the rhythm, the balance, the lean of the intricate lettering, the space between each letter – which can be just as important as the letter itself – the colours of the outline, the colours inside the outline, the colours for the background. And this is just the beginning of the list. The end result you might find just as irritating as the simple squiggle, but they are not mindless; they are very carefully thought out, they are painstaking, they are expressive, they are, in one word, *art*. And what the outsider seldom realises is that buried deep down in this piece is a name. Essentially a nom de plume has been assumed, because there is obviously not much point running from the police if you leave your real signature on the wall. For example, these are some of the names, each given a small chapter to themselves, in *Crack & Shine*, a book on London graffiti artists: Teach, Elk, Diet, Grand, Fuel, Pic, Zomby, Drax, 10Foot, ATG, Dreph . . . The choice of name is often governed not just by the sound of the name but the way the letters will look on a wall. Sometimes this intricate signature can be linked in with a cartoon character or two, either taken from a comic or a book or just made up. It shows you have skills – and imagination – beyond the tag.

David takes me down to Leake Street, which goes under the railway tracks leading out from Waterloo station, once one of the darkest little roads imaginable, and even now, flaming with colour as it is, still a tunnel you would not choose to walk through in the dead of night. It is a road which Banksy rented from the owners to allow artists to paint unhindered by the police. As we walk in a sign announces 'The Tunnel, authorised graffiti area' and then warns 'You don't have to be a gangster to paint here, so please don't behave like one.' Here, using as a teaching aid the graffiti that almost overwhelms us on these walls, David tries to guide me through this arcane world. It is a world so prickly that the purists would probably question every word I write, but in one paragraph it goes something like this.

A *tag* is the name you have chosen, and although it's the

lowest on the ability scale it is still very important. Next comes a *throw up*; this is two letters of the name in two colours, one being the outline and the other being the fill-in. This is followed by a *dub*, the full name in two colours. Next comes a *piece* or *masterpiece*, where your elaborate name is painted on top of a background that is sometimes almost equally elaborate. Next *wildstyle*, a jigsaw puzzle of typography, a form of competitive calligraphy where each artist is 'attacking' another's style; it is very intricate, and often almost impossible to read. Finally comes a *production* – usually on a bigger scale – and often done by a 'crew' or gang of friends.

All of this, however intricate, is done freehand, sometimes sketched out in detail beforehand and sometimes painted without any pre-planning. There is never a stencil in sight. Occasionally a young graffiti writer might pull out a bit of masking tape to do a straight line and he would be dismissed as a 'toy'. (A toy is, as Professor Gregory Snyder puts it in his scholarly book on New York graffiti writers, 'a neophyte writer with no skills and little clue of the history of the culture'.)

The pressure for legal space to paint is so intense that most pieces in Leake Street usually only stay for a week or two, often less, before another artist comes and paints over them. But now it is mid-afternoon on a weekday so the place is almost empty of painters. At one end we come across a crew of three teenagers, all hoodies and hip hop, the kind of guys who might be a little frightening to meet on a dark night but who are all down here painting with complete dedication if not complete skill. They each have a separate chunk of wall which in the end they will join up. David sounds a bit like a school art master as we look at them. The letters don't fit together quite right; the outlines are too simple;

there should be a stronger border on the outline not a mid tone; they have left too much space in the middle of the whole painting so other kids will come and take it . . .

Then we examine their paint. He borrows a can on which the manufacturers have written 'Use cans for art not vandalism', as though this somehow absolves them of all further responsibility. He steps up to the wall, shakes the can a couple of times and writes his tag and WILL in what I consider striking blue, as though we have been writing as a team for years. It's all done in a few seconds and I get a small whiff of the thrill of it all. Next he takes a look at a big can of household paint sitting open on the pavement which, slapped on the wall with an ordinary brush, has given them their white background. They have made a comic mistake. The paint is gloss not emulsion, so already the paint they have sprayed on top of it has begun to run, giving the whole piece a nasty cracking effect. 'Next time use emulsion,' he tells one of the lads who, drawing close in the hope that I can't hear, explains to David with some embarrassment that the paint was 'racked'. In this world 'racked' means stolen and it used to be part of the tradition of graffiti art that all paint was 'racked', So in short they stole the wrong paint. They have a lot to learn.

On the other side of the street is a lone artist with about a dozen cans of paint at his feet. He is wearing goggles and full breathing apparatus to protect himself from the paint fumes, so he looks more like a welder than an artist. Pilot, as he calls himself, is originally from Poland and he speaks with such a slow, sincere English he makes the language sound almost sad. He has been here since ten in the morning, painting a piece which suits his name, planes exploding like darts out of everywhere. He is not using stencils, but it is not traditional graffiti, rather it is freehand graffiti without a letter in sight; he is using the spray can to paint what he wants without following any of the rules.

'There's still a load of work to do. I will finish in two or three hours.'

'Will it last?'

'No, it won't last. The second I finish it I take the picture and I go away and someone will destroy it.'

'That doesn't worry you?'

'No, I do it for the pleasure of painting.'

And then he tries to explain the call of graffiti in an almost messianic way. 'Kids will only aspire to what they can see. And that's why you need to do your best work, so that kids can look and aspire to master the craft. Because it is a craft. It's almost illogical to do graffiti. You can spend most of your life and money on it and what you have is a picture on the internet.

'What I love about graffiti is there is a sense of belonging. Everyone seems to be coming from the same background. It feels like we are an entity. When I meet these amazing street artists my hat goes off to their work. But with street artists there's no sense of "getting up", it's just one stencil, one sticker and two thousand pictures all over the internet. Graffiti artists would go in the dead of night and would do it for themselves and they would go to the most audacious spots for the love of painting. For the craft . . .'

I went back to Leake Street the next day and was happy to see that everything was still there just as they had painted it. When I went back again two weeks later there was almost nothing of the original work to see and I remembered David, sounding this time a bit like a letter writer to the *Daily Telegraph*, as he told me, 'We call them rats, they come out and they paint over everything and they've got no respect. That's kids in society nowadays. It's not just graffiti, it's how kids are growing up.' Pilot's elaborate work had been completely ruined by tags and throw ups. But I know he would say it was worth it. Of the lads' work the middle part had survived, with the crackled effect caused by the gloss still showing. The work they had done to the left and right had been completely obliterated. So too had our tag.

Banksy was once asked to define graffiti and he made his definition as wide as he possibly could. 'I love graffiti. I love the word. Some people get hung up over it, but I think they're fighting a losing battle. Graffiti equals amazing to me . . . I make normal paintings if I have ideas that are too complex or offensive to go out on the street, but if I ever stopped being a graffiti writer I would be gutted. It would feel like being a basket weaver rather than being a proper artist.'

But although he is known by the outside world for his 'graffiti', it was very early in his career that he decided there was more to life than tags and masterpieces. And many, although certainly not all, hardcore graffiti artists are not happy with him for it – to put it mildly. His work, they say, is too easy, too glib. In *Crack and Shine* the graffiti artist called 10Foot (later imprisoned for twenty-six months) says: 'Banksy is a sell-out, a cross over and gets taken out because we hate street art and he's got no integrity. Getting properly up or having a wicked style is less pseudo-intellectual but takes more time, determination and talent.'

Banksy did attempt to reach this tough London crowd. Three years after he came to London he set up the Burner Prize – as opposed to the Turner Prize – for graffiti writers. He put up £1000 and even had a bronze statue made, rented out the basement of a club in west London and threw a party for about 100 people, all graffiti writers. There was a shortlist which included the ATG crew,

Cos, Kist, the NT crew, Odea, Oker, Take, Tox and Zomby. The front-runner was Tox but in the end the prize was won by Zomby. Unlike the Turner Prize there was very little argument, for almost all the writers agreed that Zomby was the king of the London scene and anyway the press was not too interested in a row over who was the year's greatest graffiti writer. There were two things missing from the award ceremony: Banksy and Zomby; but, sweetly, Zomby's mother was there to collect his award. David Samuel was impressed. 'I thought this Banksy dude, a stencil artist, bit of a writer from Bristol comes to London and does that with the money he's earning, that's amazing.' But it did not do Banksy any lasting good in this tight community.

For this is a world which takes no prisoners, where feuds can run and run and where women hardly get a look in. Riikka Kuittinen, who curated a touring exhibition of street art for the V&A in 2010, explains: 'It happens at night. It's quite physical, dangerous. It's mostly a boys' thing. There's also just the fact that women don't want to walk by railway tracks at night.' The feud or 'war' between Banksy and Robbo which stretched out for a year or so from the end of 2009 is an excellent example of the gulf between the world of hardcore graffiti and the world of Banksy. In the search for an arresting opening paragraph, newspapers ludicrously compared this spat to the rivalry between Picasso and Matisse, the feuds between Turner and Constable or Whistler and Ruskin, comparisons which – I hope – would make both Banksy and Robbo laugh.

Serious graffiti, sliding down dark holes, sawing through the railings, fixing up ladders in the dark, is a young man's game and Robbo, now in his forties, has a family to support. But he is a London graffiti artist from way back and is held in considerable awe as one of the 'kings' of the strangely hierarchical community of graffiti writers. In *Crack and Shine* the artist P.I.C. describes painting the tube trains with Robbo and Prime in Aldgate East on Christmas Day 1988. He gives a very good picture of how there is more to graffiti than just graffiti, there is the comradeship, the challenge and the fear.

It was Robbo who racked the Rubber Duck 'Stop That Leak' spray paint that was going to be their 'weapon of choice'; Robbo who did a recce of the station; Robbo who locked up a ladder near the spot ready for when they needed it; and Robbo who packed a little boom box in his rucksack to provide the music while they painted. After a day celebrating Christmas with their families (P.I.C. had dutifully listened to the Queen's Speech with his parents and grandparents) they drove to Aldgate on Christmas night. One by one they climbed over a high wall from the street, down the ladder, now extended, that Robbo had retrieved and on to the train roof. From the roof they were swiftly down beside the tracks. The CCTV cameras were put out of action and then the train was all theirs. They chose a carriage each and went to work.

'We were in there for just over four hours having our own special Christmas party. Robbo had supplied the sounds and pulled a bottle of Moet out of his bag, Prime had some ready rolled spliffs on the go and I had brought the turkey sandwiches. Perfect.'

Three years before this Robbo had chosen a hard-to-get-at wall alongside Regent's Canal in north London where he had spray painted 'Robbo INC' in huge bold letters. His work brightened up a dark space underneath a bridge, it looked good and it announced that Robbo was here to stay. And stay 'Robbo INC' did, for the next twenty-five years. In graffiti terms this was a landmark – there are very few pieces that survive twenty-five days, let alone twenty-five years. Certainly some squiggles had defaced it over that period, but essentially it remained 'up' until Banksy decided to have a go at the Regent's Canal. He painted a total of four pieces, all entertaining and close enough to Camden Lock for the crowds to enjoy; but it was what he did to the Robbo piece that got him into trouble, not with the police but with Robbo.

Banksy's piece was, as usual, a clever bit of work. He obliterated more than half of Robbo's original, painting it all a solid grey, and on this background he stencilled a workman with a paintbrush and bucket; the workman was posed perfectly so he looked as though he was pasting up Robbo's name, as if the work was nothing more than a few sheets of wallpaper.

Norman Mailer said in his exotically overwritten essay on graffiti in New York, first published in 1974: 'No one wrote over another name . . . for that would have smashed the harmony.' But here was Banksy writing over Robbo, and unless you are deeply involved in this whole world it is difficult to imagine how strongly people felt about his intervention – any of Norman Mailer's harmony that had ever existed was destroyed. The web was dominated by users attacking Banksy. 'Complete and utter sacrilege by Banksy,' was how one user described it. 'Blasphemous in the extreme. How dare he paint over history? What on earth gives him the right?' Revok, one of the West Coast's most famous graffiti writers – the news soon travelled – wrote: 'One of the "Golden rules" in graffiti is to respect your elders; foremost by not going over them . . . Particularly in the extremely rare scenario where something has lasted nearly three decades (the graffiti equivalent to a UFO sighting). I would assume Banksy would be aware of this rule, and respect it considering his roots lie in traditional graffiti . . . Apparently not.'

In contrast the street artist Gaia defended Banksy for daring to confront the 'unbending, intensely hierarchical and historically obsessed operations of graffiti'. He admired Banksy because 'instead of succumbing to graffiti's belligerence Banksy confronted and subverted its methods.'

It was graffiti war, childish only to the outsider. What happened next is best told by Robbo. Although elusive, he is not quite as elusive as Banksy, and I finally caught up with him in a pub in north London. Shaven headed, six foot eight inches tall, overwhelmingly built, he looks as though he could drink the pub dry. Although at times he can be very funny, I sense that behind it all there is quite a hard history to him that I will never quite know. Thus we are talking about the football team we both support and it puzzles me that he does not go to the games any more. Eventually he admits he has been banned, although he does not go into the gory details.

He met Banksy in the late 1990s when he was invited to a birthday party at the Dragon Bar off Old Street by Eine, who used to bomb up everywhere under another name until he turned respectable enough to have one of his pictures hanging in the White House. 'Eine introduced me to a couple of guys who were with Banksy. I had been retired a couple of years and these guys were saying "It's really an honour to meet you, a pleasure. You're Robbo. You're a legend." And I'm saying "Yeah, I've heard of your name too." I hadn't but it's good to be polite and stuff and I've always been courteous. Then I got introduced to Banksy. He was nothing at the time. And I said "Hello, I've seen your name about" – although I hadn't – and he went "I ain't seen your name anywhere." I went "What?" And he said "I don't know who you are." And I thought what the fuck. So I went bang and give him a backhander. I said "You might not have heard of me, but you'll never fucking forget me, will you?" Of course he had heard of me, but he was trying to play it cool. He was being disrespectful. He was a cocksure young toy really.'

It may all sound a bit like *Gunfight at the OK Corral* transferred rather shakily to Shoreditch, but it does illustrate the feeling between the two camps. I asked Robbo if Banksy said anything in reply. 'He got up off the ground, picked up his glasses and went off.' I suggested that Robbo's account might be slightly exaggerated; this was a mistake and I wondered for a moment if I was going to get cuffed too. 'I'm not one of those who over-exaggerate. I play things down.' It appears that many years later, as this story finally got out, Banksy took exception to it and felt the need to retaliate. Banksy completely rejects this story. He declined to be interviewed for a programme Channel 4 later made about the feud, but he did issue a statement saying: 'Is this a joke? I have never been hit by Robbo in my life. I don't know who he slapped but I hope they deserved it.'

Again it emphasises the strange position Banksy finds himself in: on the one hand the artist who collectors compete for at Sotheby's or Bonhams; film director; gallery artist and general all-round international star; and on the other still wanting to retain his links to vandalism on the streets. He told an interviewer in Los Angeles, 'I'm not so interested in convincing people in the art world that what I do is "art". I'm more bothered about convincing people in the graffiti community that what I do is really vandalism.' It's a difficult job.

'How can I consider him a vandal when he don't bomb or tag anywhere?' asks Robbo. Among some graffiti writers the belief is that his main train piece, a chimp wearing an apron reading

'Laugh now but one day we'll be in charge', which appeared on a District Line tube train in 2002, was actually painted by another artist who Banksy gave his stencils to rather than risk arrest himself. This has to be untrue, a libel on a vandal who, if this story were to be believed, is not as lawless as he makes out to be. Inkie for one is convinced it is untrue: 'From my experience I would say he's got some balls on him.' But it does illustrate how some in the graffiti world regard him now.

But whatever caused Banksy to pick on Robbo's wall, he certainly started something. 'It's an old school graffiti war,' said Robbo, 'people don't get it. They think I am bullying Banksy to get fame out of it. But I'm not. It's like you go over one of my pieces and I'll go over all your pieces.'

The problem Robbo faced in trying to get in his retaliation was that part of the reason his piece had lasted so long was that there was no towpath running alongside it. Originally he had reached this deserted side of the canal by getting through a fence, into a car park and thence down some steps, in full daylight on a Saturday afternoon. But that was before the canal had become a magnet for property developers and all the empty land had been built on. Today the only access is from the towpath on the other side of the water.

So he chose five o'clock on Christmas morning as the best time to take his revenge. 'Christmas has always been graffiti. You'd always go and do whole cars or whole trains on Christmas Day because it was the best day to do it. Everyone's more worried about the Queen's Speech and turkey and giving presents and stuff and they think even graffiti writers are going to have time off. And it ain't like that.'

He put on his expensive wet suit, which he uses for diving, and having put his paints and his track suit in a bag he flung it across to the other side. 'I'm in this wet suit. I'm cold. I've got this air mattress blown up and I'm thinking, you must be mad. But I lay the mattress down in the water and dived on to it and skimmed over to the other side. That was all good. But the ledge on the other side was high. And I'm thinking, how do I get off this thing without falling in? That's where my problem was. As I got up so the mattress went away and I was in the water.' Out he got, put on the track suit to protect his expensive wet suit and soon he was painting away. 'I'm doing my thing and I'm thinking this is good again and all of a sudden a bike goes by on the other side. And I thought, half past five in the morning, he must be a fucking nutter.' It is hard to imagine what the cyclist felt.

The piece took about twenty-five minutes and the whole time Robbo was thinking 'Don't get caught, you'll be in a cell while the kids are opening their presents.'

When I saw Robbo's piece it looked just as clever as Banksy's, even if the lines were not as perfect as Robbo would have liked. He had preserved Banksy's stencilled decorator, but instead of putting up wallpaper the decorator was putting the finishing touches to a huge dub: KING ROBBO – outline in black, fill-in in silver. Beside it there was a sign off: 'Team Robbo'. But to Robbo it was not as good as it could have been. 'I'd come back after a long lay-off which happened from what life is like – you've got kids, you've got businesses, you've got priorities, graffiti was on the back burner. The paint and the cans and the nozzles are all different now and I was rusty as well. I got given a 600 ml high pressure can and I went over there thinking it was a normal can. I go *pshhhhhhhh* and fucking hell, like I'm trying to get a little thin line and it ain't happening. It's just so wide and style went out the window. I want to get out of there before I get nicked. It come out crisp though considering, but the can just blew me away. It was like a fire extinguisher going off.'

For once even Banksy seemed to have a doubt or two, or at least thought he needed to explain himself and point out that the piece had already suffered heavy damage from other writers before he came along. 'I didn't paint over a "Robbo" piece. I painted over a piece that said "mrphfgdfrhdgf,"' he told the *Wall Street Journal*. (He told *Time Out* he painted over a piece that said 'nrkjfgrekuh', but whatever the exact lettering there were a lot of scrawls on it.) 'I find it surreal when graffiti writers get possessive over certain locations. I thought that having a casual attitude towards property ownership was an essential part of being a vandal.' Robbo and other writers say that if you paint in a legal spot you expect to see it painted over almost as soon as you have taken a photograph of it, but if you do a work on the street, particularly if it is a big piece, where you have run the risk of getting arrested, then you don't expect anyone to go over it – other than a council workman.

Across London both Banksy and Robbo were strutting their stuff. Banksy added FUC to the front of KING, thus making FUCKING ROBBO, so Robbo had to 'borrow' a canoe from the nearby boating club, suitably named the Pirate Club, and paint out the FUC before the council decided they had to paint over the whole thing. Then he went round London with startling determination defacing any of the remaining Banksys he could find – 'He started it, I'm going to finish it.'

When Robbo was first interviewed after his spat with Banksy he said he was contemplating doing a show in a gallery. 'I've done everything, everything for nothing,' he said truthfully. For there is no financial reward for painting the side of a train or the bleak wall of a canal. 'I don't think anyone would knock me for making money out of it. But it's never been my goal to make money out of something I love.'

Sure enough, within the space of a year Team Robbo – that's Robbo and his mates – had had not one but two exhibitions in galleries in Shoreditch. On the opening night of his first exhibition, with television cameras there at the ready, the canvases seemed to attract less attention than the feud, despite the fact that neither of the principals were there: Banksy didn't show and Robbo preferred to spend the time in a nearby pub waiting to see how the show was received.

There was one canvas that hit you as you walked in. It was heavy with colour and right at the point to which your eye is drawn, Robbo had written in easy to read lettering: 'R.I.P. Street Art.' But the fact both that Robbo had agreed to show in a gallery and that there was hardly a piece of 'pure graffiti' to be seen only underlined the reality that street art of the Banksy kind, which has nothing to do with the rules of pure graffiti, was not about to Rest In Peace. His second exhibition, entitled Team Robbo: The Sell Out Tour, showed that he had at least picked up one useful tip from Banksy: irony. His art still seemed happier on the street than it did on a gallery wall; nevertheless one piece, *The King*, was priced at an astonishing £12,000.

As for the beef with Banksy, at the time of writing Robbo had been in a coma for months after a fall outside his home. Graffiti writers were wishing him 'Get Well Soon', not with a card but on a wall. In September 2011 I went to an art auction like no other at Cargo in Shoreditch to raise funds for Robbo's family. You had to queue for forty-five minutes to get in and signs warned us: 'Please respect the Robbo event. No Bombing.' Inside it was like a football stadium in the days when fans stood on the terraces. For the most part this was a tight little circle of outlaws and their friends who made Banksy seem like part of some far-off establishment. The room was overflowing with macho, beer and a sort of fan worship for Robbo and what he stood for. On occasions there would be chants of 'Robbo, Robbo' pushing the bids higher. It was as far away from a Sotheby's auction as it was possible to imagine. The auctioneer, despite breaking his hammer early on, somehow managed to keep control above all this – just – and the auction raised about £30,000 from 150 donated works (there was nothing from Banksy). In addition, in the way these things inevitably work, Robbo's accident and the television programme about the feud had suddenly transformed him from an artist having difficulty selling anything into a hot number, and another £28,000 was later raised by selling his own works.

Robbo's accident, plus the fact that there were hardly any more Banksy pieces left in London to write over, may well have put an end to the feud. But graffiti writers will never see Banksy as one of them. At this point in his career you may imagine he no longer cares very much about what they think, but he very obviously does. At the end of December 2011 he put up on his website a slideshow of the whole Robbo affair, starting with the original piece, next showing how it had been partially defaced by others and then illustrating the tit for tat between the pair of them. The final picture was a black and white replica done by Banksy of the original piece, with the addition of a candle in the shape of a spray can spreading light amidst the dark; it seems to be some sort of homage to Robbo, lying in hospital in a coma. To emphasise the point he added elsewhere on his site: 'I would never deliberately cuss Robbo – he's a graffiti legend.'

# Four
# Finding His Own Style

There are a range of explanations that Banksy has given of his reasons for switching to stencils. The most romantic story comes in his book *Wall and Piece*, where he tells of the time when, aged eighteen, he was in the middle of painting a train with a gang of mates when the British Transport Police showed up. Everyone ran, but Banksy got 'ripped to shreds' by thorny bushes as he tried to make his escape. 'The rest of my mates made it to the car and disappeared so I spent over an hour hidden under a dumper truck with engine oil leaking all over me. As I lay there listening to the cops on the tracks I realised I had to cut my painting time in half or give up altogether. I was staring straight up at the stencilled plate on the bottom of a fuel tank when I realised I could just copy that style and make each letter three feet high.'

It certainly makes a good story, but in 2002 he told the *Observer* he abandoned graffiti because 'I was 21 and crap.' Stencils, on the other hand, were 'quick, clean, crisp and efficient. And that's quite sexy.' A couple of years later he told *Wired* magazine, 'I wasn't good at freehand graffiti, I was too slow,' and a year after that he told Simon Hattenstone of the *Guardian*, in the only face-to-face interview with a newspaper he has ever given, 'Because I was quite crap with a spray can, I started cutting out stencils instead.'

But perhaps it is all rather simpler than that, for he was most convincing when talking to author and friend Tristan Manco: 'I started off painting graffiti in the classic New York style you use when you listen to too much hip hop as a kid, but I was never very good at it. As soon as I cut my first stencil I could feel the power there. The ruthlessness and the efficiency of it is perfect.

'I also like the political edge. All graffiti is low-level dissent, but stencils have an extra history. They've been used to start revolutions and to stop wars. Even a picture of a rabbit playing a piano looks hard as a stencil.' A fellow writer from Bristol days confirms that it was more than just sitting under a dumper truck that persuaded him to abandon his attempts at 'traditional' graffiti: 'Stencils are no coincidence. He knows his history. He looked at Paris in the sixties and how quickly they got their message up.'

Almost from the start Banksy showed an unusual single-mindedness, which he very much needed. For Bristol was a hardcore graffiti town, heavily influenced by the styles that for a few years had overwhelmed the New York subway trains. Various artists from America – particularly Rock Steady Crew, who straddled both the music and the graffiti scene – brought their graffiti skills with them when they were touring here; but more than anything else it was one book that was the key reference point.

Martha Cooper was a photographer who had moved from Rhode Island to New York City, where she worked on Rupert Murdoch's *New York Post.* Henry Chalfant had arrived in New York as a sculptor, but with rather less success. Both had become disillusioned with what they were doing and had started photographing graffiti, first as sort of rivals and then as collaborators, producing *the* key book on American graffiti: *Subway Art*. It still remains an extraordinary record of the days when the New York subway system became one huge graffiti canvas. Over and over again graffiti artists say that this was the book that inspired them. Inkie, for instance, says, 'It was instant. Lots of us were punks at the time and as soon as I saw *Subway Art* I thought it was the perfect synergy between graffiti and my anarchist tendencies.' Jason Kelly, a friend who went on from graffiti to become a designer at the *Daily Telegraph* magazine and then start his own design business, even copied his tag, 'kid-ink', from the book. 'It's a great book, it was like gold dust in those days,' he says. 'It was like a bible,' says another graffiti artist.

The police, when discussing the case against John Nation, showed him a copy of the book they had taken from his office at Barton Hill as evidence that he was inciting young people to go out and paint illegally. He pointed out to them that he had bought the book at Waterstones and if they were going to prosecute him they should be prosecuting Waterstones and the publishers as well.

It was a huge book not only in its impact but also in its size, although sales were slow to start with – partly because the graffiti fraternity were stealing the book, despite its size, from bookshops in much the same way they stole their paint from paint shops. In the twenty-fifth anniversary edition, which came out in 2009, Martha Cooper remembers going on a promotional tour across Europe, visiting eighteen cities in twenty-one days, and 'in every city kids came up to me to tell me what *Subway Art* meant to them. More than one said "You saved my life." My favourite was the English writer who playfully shook his finger at me and said "You have a lot to account for."' The whole graffiti removal industry – for it is now an industry – would certainly agree.

A Banksy freehand 'tag' exists now only in old photographs and there were never too many of them in the first place, although there was for a short time a joyful 'Banksy' in big lettering on the side of a nightclub boat in Bristol harbour – 'That was so toy,' says one graffiti writer. His tag was the first thing that he put into stencils. It started off with simple lower-case lettering but soon evolved into the very distinctive signature – with the upright back of the capital B missing, the k relying on the n for support, the s with the top shaved off slightly and the final y that looks almost like a hieroglyphic – that he has continued to use ever since.

Although he had switched to a stencil for his signature he persevered with 'freehand' graffiti for some time. Inkie remembers this freehand stage well. 'He's a very talented artist quite apart from the stencils. If you look at his sketch book he's got fantastic concepts, an amazing sense of perspective and depth and vision. Personally I prefer some of his early stuff, the canvases or the sketches, over the stencil stuff. However I do feel that he gives depth to his stencils in a way that others can't do. It's a bit more organic.' But however talented Banksy was as a freehand artist, it is still fair to say that if he had stuck to his freehand style he would probably still be doing it in Bristol today, and probably no one other than the tight circle of the city's graffiti artists and ex-artists would have ever heard of him.

Even when he was painting with a 'crew', if there was intricate lettering to be done someone, often Inkie, or sometimes another friend, Kato, would do it, while Banksy stuck to illustration. The people, and indeed the apes, he drew in these early days all have a slightly strange, primitive feel to them. My personal favourite –

perhaps because it is still there to see – is a piece which greets you when you enter the Pierced Up tattoo parlour in Bristol. It is a painting of giant wasps (with television sets strapped to them as additional weapons) dive-bombing a tempting bunch of flowers in a vase with their long red tongues curling towards the nectar. What somehow makes this aerosol painting work is the fact that the flowers and their vase are encased in a wooden frame screwed to the wall, so the angry wasps are buzzing towards a traditional still life. The manager, Maryanne Kempf, says, 'It was an all-nighter and the next day when he came back he still wasn't sure how to finish it off. He saw an empty frame in a skip, screwed it to the wall and it was done.' It is a typical Banksy touch which lifts the painting out of the ordinary. (Like many early Banksy paintings, this one ended up on eBay, but the tricky problem of how to remove it from the wall was never solved because the bidding stopped at £6889 – below the reserve price.)

Perhaps the best judge of this early work is Banksy himself. In his three small self-published books there is not one example of this freehand work from his Bristol days. In *Wall and Piece*, which followed later, there are 316 photographs – give or take a picture or two – but amidst so many photographs only six of these early pieces are included. There is never going to be an exhibition of Banksy's 'Early Work' because most of it was soon painted over. But it was nearly always photographed before it was obliterated and these photographs do not appear to be memories he treasures.

Banksy was not the first to switch to stencils. 3D, Robert Del Naja, tried it in 1986 for the face of Mona Lisa – the body he did freehand – and, he says, 'the graffiti boys hated it.' But 3D had been one of the earliest graffiti artists in Bristol and no one was seriously going to give him much trouble.

Jody was another early stencil artist in the city but, without quite the same pedigree as 3D, he found life rather more difficult. In an interview with Felix Braun for *Weapon of Choice* magazine he says he ran into a 'notoriously intimidating' member of the United Bombers crew (famous in their day for tagging virtually everything that moved) just after he had finished stencilling his version of Warhol's Marilyn Monroe on the wall at Barton Hill. 'He stood right in my face and said: "You can fuck off with your fucking stencilled faces, you cheating ****! Nothing you've done will ever test my pieces."' It did, he admits, put him off stencils for a bit. Banksy has never even hinted that he got the same sort of treatment. Perhaps it was because he was not the first, but more likely it was because of the sort of character he was. 'To us stencils were taboo,' says Inkie. 'I would have just been laughed at, it was all about face. Even if you used a bit of paper or some sellotape or masking tape to do the sharp edges it was frowned on . . . But Banksy had a punk attitude. He didn't care what people thought, he had a strong personality.'

So it was not as though Banksy was the only person in Bristol to have thought about stencils; but he was one of the very few who dared to make the big leap. It was much more than just a change of style; he risked banishment from the strong subculture that was part of the lure of graffiti. This is perhaps why he did not convert to stencils overnight. It was almost as if he was testing the water, for although some of his early pieces look like stencils they are actually painted freehand to give the stencil effect. Thus in one early work on an Esso garage in Bristol, painted with other members of the Dry Breadz Crew, most of the length of the piece is pure graffiti, but at one end the two children who we are used to seeing on the lollipop lady's sign warning of children crossing, have been gently transformed by Banksy into robbers so the girl is carrying a gun and the boy is carrying a briefcase leaking money gained in their successful raid. It looks like a pure stencil, but it is actually freehand with Banksy trying things out. On other occasions he would stencil the face while painting the body freehand.

Once he had found the right medium he was on his way. Another of his Bristol friends says, 'From the first he was very ambitious and centred,' and another writer from those days told Steve Wright, author of *Home Sweet Home*, 'When I first met him, which was probably in 1993, even then he was very driven. He wasn't much concerned about what anyone else was doing, even though he was, back then, up for getting together and collaborating on projects and pieces, something he seems less likely to do these days. But he already had that "goal" then – wanting to get his message across, have that dig at the system, make that point. It seemed obvious that he was going to become big or well known, he just had that air about him.'

He had some sort of agent from quite early on and while others just painted at Barton Hill, he managed to stage his first show, with a few other artists, in the laundromat in the block of council flats next to the youth centre. He said later with some pride: 'All the people who lived there checked it out. It was really funny seeing trendy kids in Carhartt next to big fat ladies with Iceland shopping bags.'

Who were his early influences? Apart from 3D there was no one in Bristol who he could turn to, but in Paris Blek le Rat – a very genial artist despite his name – had been stencilling life-size rats across the walls since 1981. Blek, who has an impeccably bourgeois background, tells a romantic story of how he was inspired to go into graffiti by a fortune teller who told him she saw him working with walls. He studied architecture before moving on to stencils, so she was certainly in the right zone. Perhaps more to the point, he remembers being on holiday in Italy after the war and spotting an old stencilled propaganda portrait of Mussolini. What impressed him was the power of the stencil – still there long after the dictator had been done away with. The first time he ever saw graffiti as art was on a trip to New York back in 1971. He told *Swindle* magazine: 'I wanted to do American pieces like I had seen in New York. [But] I told myself, "No, I mustn't do that."' Why? Because he was determined, in a very French way, that if he was going to do art on the streets of Paris it had, somehow, to be graffiti in a uniquely French style.

In the early days, when he was besieging Paris with his rats, Blek needed to be as anonymous as any other street artist attempting to avoid the police, but now he is as open as Banksy is closed. Somehow an image of the street artist has evolved, all hoodies, jeans, sneakers and aggression, but Blek fails to meet the criteria. When I met the well-dressed, middle-aged Blek at a book launch party in London, he told me how excited he was to be flying to Brisbane in a day or two *first class*. He had never flown first class in his life and not only was his ticket being paid for, but he was being provided with a legal wall to paint on once he got there.

Quite when Banksy first learned about Blek is unclear. Blek suggests it may have been through their mutual friend Tristan Manco, who showed his work to Banksy at 'the end of the nineties', but it may well have been earlier than that, for a slim book called *Paris Graffiti* was doing the rounds of the graffiti writers in Bristol at about the time Banksy was coming on to the scene. (None of the graffiti in the book is attributed, but there is what looks like an early Blek rat and possibly other pieces by him – certainly the book revealed what the blurb called 'a new chic on the streets of Paris'.) Whatever the date, there is no doubting the influence Blek had on Banksy. Once you have seen Blek's work it is impossible to see a Banksy piece, especially his early work, without thinking of Blek. Blek does not play with words in the way Banksy does and he is also much less political (a rare political piece of his with David holding a rifle, done in support of Israel, did not go down too well in the street art community). Nevertheless the line between the two of them is a very strong one, for like almost any artist Banksy has been influenced by those who have gone before him.

The two artists are almost always impeccably polite about each other. 'Every time I think I've painted something slightly original, I find out that Blek le Rat has done it, too,' says Banksy, 'only Blek did it twenty years earlier.' And Blek replies with just a little more edge: 'People say he copies me, but I don't think so. I'm the old man, he's the new kid, and if I'm an inspiration to an artist that good, I love it. People want to know me now . . . I have a major book deal with the biggest publishers in the world. I have waited thirty years for this. It's only today that my street art has become big news, and that's thanks to people saying Banksy is inspired by me.' All of which is true, and only once has he been slightly less polite about him: 'I can tell you now that I have a stock of good ideas for him. Really, I do! I have many good ideas but this time he will have to pay because we all know that he is fucking rich. (laughs) . . . He takes, but we all take from someplace.'

Right from the start of Banksy's switch to stencils the humour, which was almost non-existent in his early freehand pieces, started to appear in his work. At Bristol harbour a sweet, but startling-looking girl appeared on the wall hugging a large bomb instead of a Barbie doll. He repeated the image in years to come, but the stencil work got cleaner and she got younger and grew a neatly plaited pigtail in place of her rather wild ponytail. The changes made the image even more arresting. He had two CCTV cameras grow legs and do battle like fighting cocks – the first of several pieces on the subject of surveillance – long before Ai Weiwei's troubling CCTV camera, carved out of marble, drew critics' praise when he was exhibited in London in 2011.

Other pieces from that time include a tiger that escaped his bar-code cage by bending the bars and elderly bowlers, properly dressed for the occasion and concentrating just as hard as every bowls player does, but using bombs instead of bowls for their game. The melding of the familiar with the shockingly unfamiliar; the humour, the quality and craft of the work; the way that even now, when the original has long gone and they are no more than photographs, they simply stop you in amazement immediately you see them, marks out Banksy as brilliantly different from the beginning. Forget all the hype, all the argument about the name, the influences, the money, the fame, here was an original artist – and apart perhaps from Jean-Michel Basquiat and Keith Haring, who in the 1970s and 1980s both jumped from New York's streets and subways into the galleries, he was making himself known on the streets in a way no other artist had done before him.

Quite apart from his skill as an artist, Banksy had another skill: he could organise. Kato, a graffiti veteran equally at home with lettering or characters, recalled in an interview with Felix Braun the day when he was painting with the Dry Breadz Crew and Banksy 'just turned up. He said he was into graf and wanted to paint with us. He was already doing stencils by then. He had a knack for putting them in the right places, and they always had just the right content. He invited us to do workshops and stuff and he always seemed to be able to blag good spots.' When Kato and Banksy painted the side of a house in Bristol it was Banksy who knocked on the door and persuaded the house's owner to give them permission.

Inkie was another key contact and friend he made in those early days. Inkie moved up to London about the same time as Banksy, and carved out a very successful career for himself both as a graphic designer in the video games industry and as an artist in his own right. He now has a family to support and unless fuelled by alcohol he is no longer quite the wild outlaw he once was, but in the early Bristol days, one writer remembers, 'When Inkie turned up at Barton Hill it was like the Pope coming to visit, the red carpet came out . . . he had a presence about him – and, of course, a reputation as a really good writer.'

He might not have been pope, but he was still a very useful man to know and Banksy had no qualms about introducing himself. Inkie was painting – legally – the shutters of Rollermania, a Bristol skateboard shop, when Banksy came by. 'He came up and introduced himself. I hadn't really heard of him to be honest. He said he knew the guys from Glastonbury, he'd got an opportunity to paint there and he invited me to come along. We did the main dance stage along with Dicy, Feek and Eko.' Their first piece there was a cartoon of Michael Eavis, who runs Glastonbury, on his tractor being chased by a herd of cows. After Glastonbury they started painting together quite regularly.

'From the minute I met him he was always quite motivational. At that point I was a bit laid back about it. As far as I was concerned I had become one of the best in the world. I had done what I had set out to achieve. We'd had our fifteen minutes of fame and I never thought of it as a kind of career or anything, I just liked doing it. But he was taking things to another level. I lent him my credibility in the graffiti world, which he didn't have at the time, and he used his organisational skills. It was a meeting of two halves really.'

Nowhere were those skills better displayed than at the Walls on Fire graffiti festival which Banksy and Inkie put together in 1998, with the city's agreement, using a line of hoardings stretching for 400 metres around building work at Bristol harbour as their canvas. Posters announced an event that sounded excitingly edgy: 'WALLS ON FIRE! Britain's top graffiti writers representing their skills in a massive paint battle over two days.' All this to be accompanied by 'raw hip hop and funk'.

Banksy might have been the young upstart but the event would not have happened without him. Inkie gave him his network of contacts, but it was Banksy who did most of the work. Here was a completely unorganised activity – graffiti – being organised: someone had to negotiate with the city agency to allow it to happen legally, someone had to find sponsors willing to supply paint, someone had to get the DJs. Most difficult of all, someone had to decide which artists were going to be invited to paint, and of course the key question: how much space each artist was to be given and where that space was going to be, nice and obvious or tucked away at the end somewhere. And pretty much all of this was done by Banksy. A picture still exists of a line of young graffiti artists working away on the wall, each sticking happily to their own space. They look very meek and mild, far from the 'BATTLE' the poster had been promoting.

Banksy's own work for this festival was largely freehand – a group of the gloomiest-looking doctors you have ever seen gathered around an operating table. At either end the piece was 'framed' by television screens, each with a different Banksy stencil on it. The operating table itself was obscured by elaborate graffiti lettering that ran right across the piece, reading ASTEK (a fellow graffiti artist), and there was a dedication in one corner which read, 'For Astek in the Scrubs'. The whole thing was Banksy with a foot in both camps. But no one complained. Unfortunately it rained most of the weekend but John Nation, whom Banksy tapped for sponsorship, says 'It was the best event ever.'

While Walls on Fire meant a lot to the graffiti world, a piece that Banksy did several months later endeared him to a much wider community in Bristol. *The Mild Mild West* (it's his title painted across the top) is a huge piece on the side of an abandoned building. A teddy bear manages to look quite cuddly despite the fact that he is about to throw the Molotov cocktail he is wielding at three riot policemen who are advancing on him. Eight years after it was painted, *The Mild Mild West* won a BBC online poll to find an Alternative Landmark for Bristol, getting more than double anyone else's vote. And it is easy to see why. Some saw it as a reference to the St Paul's racial riots of 1980 – the front line was just a couple of minutes away – others thought it more to do with the police tactics in breaking up the free party scene that was then thriving in Bristol. Whatever the influences, the message is clear: nice cuddly citizens represented by the teddy bear – he looks too nice to ever throw the Molotov cocktail – against heavy-handed police.

If the madam running a brothel has a little black book where she keeps the details of her finest clients, then some graffiti writers often have their own rather larger black book where they keep the preparatory sketches they make before they do their work. Banksy has said he never used sketch books 'in the way you imagine a "real" artist does', rather he uses them 'to note down great ideas of somebody else's I've just had'. But he certainly did a preliminary sketch for *The Mild Mild West*, the major difference being that in this sketch the cuddly bear was holding a spliff as well as a Molotov cocktail. Whether Banksy would have got more or fewer votes if the spliff had stayed we will never know, but the image he actually painted is certainly sharper without it. The teddy bear is still there – just – and in the spring of 2011 must have been watching with some amusement as below him life imitated art, with rioters and police clashing violently in protests after a new Tesco store opened in the area.

*The Mild Mild West* was one of the last pieces Banksy did before leaving Bristol for London and it is a good example of how his style was developing. Although this piece could easily be a stencil, it is actually freehand but it shows him already light years away from the traditional graffiti that was being painted all around him. You don't need any inside knowledge of the graffiti world to know exactly what is going on. The painting is instantly accessible and, like many of his pieces, shows a clever sense of timing in capturing an incident, a protest or in this case just a vague feeling of what people are thinking.

What followed next – the history of the piece – illustrates Banksy's extraordinary trajectory through the art world. First there was the excitement of actually doing the piece. It was painted over three days, with a friend holding the ladder up to the first floor site and keeping a look-out at the same time. Then a sort of anticlimax: nothing from the police, nothing from the anti-graffiti squad, no angry denouncements in the council chamber. Next, over the years, a growing fondness for the piece which became a part of the ongoing attempt to turn a rather tatty area into the sort of bohemian art district that every city covets. Then, as the area began to improve, and nine years after the piece was painted, an application by a property developer to redevelop the site around it into flats with a café on the ground floor covered in glass high enough to enclose the Banksy. So you could be sipping your cappuccino right underneath a Banksy.

Four months after this plan was approved by the council, the piece was splattered in red paint by someone wielding a paintball gun. An outfit calling itself Appropriate Media announced on its website that they were the perpetrators. Calling the work an urban 'masterpiss' by 'urban masterpisser, Banksy', they declared: 'Come on, you only care about it cos it's a Banksy and he sells his lazy polemics to Hollywood movie stars for big bucks. Come on, you only care about it cos it makes you feel edgy and urban to tour round the inner city in your 4 x 4, taking in the tired coffee table subversion that graffiti has become. Graffiti artists are the copywriters for the capitalist created phenomenon of urban art. Graffiti artists are the performing spray-can monkeys for gentrification.'

In response, one resident of the area who was interviewed by BBC Bristol amplified the confusion: 'I'm shocked. I know that in some graffiti circles he [Banksy] is not actually seen in the best light. But to do something like that is extremely disrespectful. You wouldn't do that anywhere, it's against the rules.' So somehow Banksy had become almost part of the establishment and others were the vandals breaking the rules.

But he was not going to hang around to debate all this. Within a few months he was on his way to London. Not only Bristol but the world of 'pure' graffiti was being left behind in favour of a style which did not need to be decoded and was instantly understood and enjoyed, and where Banksy could make his own rules or lack of rules. In 2010 he told *Time Out*: 'Traditional graffiti artists have a bunch of rules they like to stick to, and good luck to them, but I didn't become a graffiti artist so I could have somebody else tell me what to do.'

As for *The Mild Mild West*, when I last saw it the splatters of paint had been cleaned off by enthusiastic volunteers. The property market had not recovered enough for the flats to be built there. So, rather than being protected by the proposed glass-enclosed terrace, it still sits on the wall protected by one CCTV camera – the very security cameras which Banksy says today are 'one of the worst things about modern Britain'.

# Five

# All Aboard for the Banksy Tour

Some people go on a Jack the Ripper tour; I went on a Banksy tour. The day the contract arrived for this book I decided the first thing I needed was a total immersion tour around the streets of London where Banksy often paints, which are – conveniently – the streets where I live. Banksy must be the only living artist – and there cannot be many dead ones either – for whom you can buy a tour book giving you all the spots to find his work. The only problem is that despite regular updating, the book is always going to be out of date. You arrive and the wall is bare, painted over by council anti-graffiti teams, scrawled over by rival graffiti artists, or simply acquired by speculators.

The book you need is *Banksy Locations & Tours*, self-published by 'photographer, writer and street walker' Martin Bull, with a very significant proportion of the profits – almost £30,000 at the last count – going to the Big Issue Foundation. There is now a bulkier updated edition which covers the whole of Britain, not just London. Ten years ago Banksy said he wanted to paint every wall in the Easton district of Bristol: 'Next year they'll be selling little maps of it with little red dots where my paintings are. That's all I want.' It took rather more than a year, but here in this new edition are the very red circles he dreamed of, dotted not only around Easton but also all over Bristol.

With the lighter first edition in one hand, and a page of the London *A to Z* in the other, I was on my way. The first thing I discovered is that you can walk around London with your eyes wide open, yet tight shut. Quite apart from all the rubbish inflicted on us by kids with a spray can and an up-yours desire to leave their mark, there is a lot of very good graffiti staring you in the face if only you bother to look – and it isn't all by Banksy.

I had something of a head start. Months earlier, walking along the Essex Road in Islington, I had been stopped dead by a Banksy on the side of a chemist's shop – three children pledging their allegiance to a Tesco flag that had been run up on an electricity cable which Banksy had very cleverly transformed into a flagpole. As I stood there looking a man passed me by and said: 'A load of over-rated rubbish,' but he just kept walking as though he had not said a word and gave me no chance to tell him how wrong I thought he was. I learned later that the canvas version was called *Very Little Helps* and in 2010 was sold at Sotheby's by former supermodel Jerry Hall for £82,850. Towards the end of 2011 I passed the chemist's shop again; someone had taken the time and trouble to remove the top layer of Perspex protection and obliterate Banksy's painting with silver spray paint. I stood there mournfully with two other passers-by. Even though I had been told time and again how impermanent street art is supposed to be, it still seemed an utterly pathetic, destructive thing to do.

On my tour the first graffiti I came across had nothing to do with Banksy. It was huge, painted on a wall the length of a cricket pitch in an abandoned depot formerly used by Initial Washroom

Solutions. The depot must have been waiting to be turned into a block of flats but in the meantime it had become a playground for graffiti artists. There was the usual city rubbish, flattened water bottles, bike locks (where's the bike?), McDonald's bags, beer cans and a couple of buddleia, the one plant that thrives where everything else has long since given up the ghost. There was ample wall space to play with but there were locked gates to keep out all but the very determined – or those who, I was to discover much later, had negotiated a way in with the property developers.

The wall running along the side of a disused loading platform had been painted in a series of huge, curving zebra stripes. Pasted up in the middle of all these stripes was a page from the *A to Z*, enlarged to a giant size, perfect in the detail and name of every street, except for the fact that it was the wrong shape for a page out of the *A to Z*. But by standing back a bit the whole thing came into focus; it was anything but haphazard. The page was shaped – perfectly – like a revolver and running through the middle was the Lower Clapton Road. On the platform below was scrawled in crude letters: 'Murder Mile'. Googling Lower Clapton Road I came across an article in the *Independent* from January 2002: 'Eight men shot dead in two years. Welcome to Britain's Murder Mile.'

On one side of this piece was the signature 'Pure Evil', written at a size that would eat up all but the very biggest canvas. Google delivered once more, telling me that Pure Evil was a graffiti artist with his own gallery. The gallery blurb said he left England for California after the poll tax riots and spent ten years there 'ingesting weapons grade psychedelics' before returning to London to pick up a spray can. Just this one piece had given me a very good lesson on how graffiti can jump from the wall to the web to the gallery. The next morning I sent him an email:

Hello,

I was looking for a Banksy yesterday and just happened to stumble across your Murder Mile. I think it's wonderful. Presumably some day soon the site will get turned into a block of flats but for the moment it is an original delight.

Having discovered this morning you have a gallery maybe you make some sort of prints of your work. If you make one of Murder Mile I would like to buy one.

From *Murder Mile* I started sniffing around with a new enthusiasm and within an hour or so I had spotted four good pieces of art within spraying distance of each other – and still I hadn't found the Banksy. There was a 'paste up' of a woman wearing an elaborately patterned jacket which revealed a crudely stitched-up wound across her neck. Over her head was a sack as if she was awaiting her execution, except the sack was as elaborately patterned as the jacket. It was intricate and arresting, even though people had started to tear bits off the poster in passing.

I admit that until I started this book I had no idea what a 'paste up' was. Happily a young graffiti artist took pity on me: a paste up is a piece of work, usually in poster form, that you prepare beforehand and then, usually using wheatpaste, you stick up on a wall – simple.

Next to this woman seemingly waiting for her execution there was a black and white Pierrot figure which could have been a Banksy for all I knew, but it wasn't in the guide book. A street or so away someone had darkened the modern brick on the side of an office to provide the shadow that outlined a man's face. Clever, and very unclear how they did it, for the wall was so vast – did no one stop them or at least ask what they were doing? The only trouble was that someone else had got to it; there were white splodges roller-painted on to the wall and the whole thing had become a complete eyesore.

But where was Banksy? It turned out I had not been following the map correctly – I had the right canal, but the wrong bridge. Once at the right bridge it was easy enough. There was a hoodie under the bridge – almost life size – eating from a carry-out bag of chips, and because he was devouring them on the wrong side of the canal, the side without a towpath, no one had been able to reach him. Banksy must have had a boat when he painted it. On the bridge there were plenty of tags reminding me just how destructive graffiti can be, yet here was Banksy's hoodie still in his original state, peacefully noshing away. No council workers, no British Waterways workers and no envious graffiti artists. A Banksy, I had found a Banksy – joy; it was a treasure hunt, one down, hundreds to go.

(A year later I went back along the canal to see how the hoodie was faring. Sadly he had not survived the war between Robbo and Banksy. The hoodie had been black-painted out of existence and over this a great big red Rolling Stones tongue lolled out. Above the tongue was written 'I SEE A BANKSY AND HAVE GOT TO PAINT IT BLACK', while underneath it was signed 'TEAM ROBBO ROLLIN WITH THE STONES'. So much for my theory that the canal protected him.)

Encouraged by finding one Banksy, my next stop was Jamie Oliver's restaurant Fifteen; three of Banksy's many rats had once been lurking around here, but there was not a sign of them now. Across the side of the restaurant's van parked nearby was a message scrawled in graffiti-style writing: *personalised events created with love.* Although it was far too pink and clean to be *real* – quite apart from what it said – nevertheless it was another example of graffiti crossing over into the mainstream.

From there I went to Moorfields Eye Hospital. The guide book said there used to be a rat holding a microphone outside a disused entrance to the hospital but in December 2007 'a great big bit of wood was nailed over it. Dare I assume that it will be available to buy at auction soon?'

Well, it was a reasonable enough question for Martin Bull to ask, but he was wrong – or rather wrong when I arrived there. Peering between the wood and the tiles I could just see rat's ears and the glint of a whisker. The rat was still there! On the street a man shuffled gingerly by, a huge patch over his eye, reminding me that this was one of the world's leading eye hospitals. But I was celebrating the fact that I had found a Banksy that the author of the guide book thought would have been lost years ago.

The next morning I wrote another email. This time to John Pelly, chief executive of Moorfields Eye Hospital, or rather to his PA in the hope that she would pass it on:

> Dear Mr Pelly,
>
> I am a writer researching a book about the graffiti artist, Banksy. In the course of my research I came across a reference to a Banksy 'microphone rat' at Moorfields. It is at the disused entrance to the hospital on City Road which looks as though it is still used as a fire escape. Shortly before you arrived at Moorfields the rat was neatly boarded up. But looking behind the wood I can still see the rat's ears – I don't know if it has been daubed but my guess is that it is in reasonable condition. (I can direct you to a guide book which shows the rat before it was boarded up if this would help.)
>
> I am writing to you about the future of the rat. If it stays

there what is likely to happen? You could pick any one from a variety of things:

The steps could be knocked down one day and the rat with them. There could be a general clean up – although it has survived one clean up – and the rat would be washed away or broken up if the tiles were replaced. Someone with the right tile cutter could steal it. You could open it up to the public again and in time a rival graffiti artist (it's a funny world) would probably deface it.

None of those options are any good especially since someone at Moorfields went to some trouble to preserve it. So I suggest that you have it cut out (carefully). You could then either have it mounted on a wall somewhere at Moorfields – a genuine Banksy in the hospital would be a cool touch. Or you could sell it.

I have read that Banksy doesn't authenticate his street art; he said in a recent interview that 'that's basically a signed confession on headed notepaper.' But I suppose he might do so for the NHS and anyway I don't think anyone is going to suggest that it's anything but a Banksy.

I am sorry to trouble you with all this but as a local resident and a grateful patient of Moorfields in the past I thought that one way or another Moorfields could get something out of your own genuine Banksy.

I sent it off and forgot about it.

From Moorfields I went via five disappeared rats and one disappeared smiley policeman to a friendly-looking rat with a CND sign around his neck, holding a placard that, according to the guide book, said 'London doesn't work'. Amazingly, given the fact that he was close to the Barbican, right on the edge of the City, he had survived. But the placard now read 'I ♥ LONDON' (with the heart designating 'love' painted in red) and then in red: 'ROBBO'. So the 'war' between Banksy and Robbo had escaped the boundaries of the canal and any Banksy, particularly any Banksy rat holding a placard, was fair game.

Thus on a wall behind the Royal Mail sorting office off Rosebery Avenue there was a rat by the bus stop, which was the first Banksy I had ever spotted. The rat was holding a placard which used to read 'ALWAYS FAIL' – and my guide book informed me that this was the rhyming slang nickname for the Royal Mail. But when I returned to see how the rat was faring, his placard again advertised TEAM ROBBO. However, when I next wanted the bus down to King's Cross the placard was slogan-less, even though the rat was still there. I thought at first this was Banksy's own clean-up team in action, but Robbo later told me he had chosen the wrong paint – 'It faded because the ink was shit.'

I made a detour from the guide book up to Camden Lock to see what else Banksy had done on the night he had painted over Robbo's signature. The cleverest painting simply read (in graffiti scrawl) 'I DON'T BELIEVE IN GLOBAL WARMING'. In itself this was not a particularly original thought, but it was written so close to the canal that you could almost see the water rising inch by inch, year by year and eventually drowning this disbelief. But Robbo had been there and whitewashed key parts of it so it now read 'I DON'T BELIEVE IN WAR', and then by the side of it he added 'IT'S TOO LATE FOR THAT SONNY. TEAM ROBBO.' The rest of the Banksys along the canal had suffered the same sort of treatment.

Back on the guided tour, the book told me that in Fabric, the grooviest of nightclubs around Smithfield, was a Banksy bomb hugger sprayed on the wall by the toilets. 'They even put a frame around it.' So I put in what I thought was going to be an easy request to Fabric's head of press to come in and take a look at it out of nightclub hours. What followed was a good introduction to the weird world of Banksy.

To: Danna Hawley
Subject: Banksy

Dear Danna
I am a writer researching a book on Banksy commissioned by Aurum Press. I have been tracking down various Banksys in London – most of them have disappeared for one reason or another. However I read that a 'Bomb Hugger' was sprayed straight on to Fabric's wall some years ago and still survives today. I would very much like to see this survivor. It would only take about five minutes of anyone's time and since I live relatively close it would be easy for me to fit in to whatever time would be convenient for Fabric.

Thanks

Back came the reply:

From: Danna Hawley
Subject: RE: Banksy

Hi Will,
I hope this finds you well . . .

Can you please send us more information about the book?

We'd like to know a bit more about the project.

Many thanks.

So I told her:

To: Danna Hawley
Subject: Banksy

Danna,
In short it is the story of how Banksy turned the art world upside down . . . .

The chapter that involves Fabric will be about how we react to his art. Taking 'Banksy Locations and Tour' by Martin Bull as my guide I have now visited almost every one of the Banksy sites north of the river. Very few Banksys survive untouched. The majority have been painted over. Some have been stolen. Some have been protected by plastic covers, others have been boxed in with plywood or perspex. Some have been defaced by other graffiti artists. This chapter is not a tour guide but it will examine what happens to his work and why.

Regards, Will

You would think that at this point it would be easy. I was not exactly asking for a private viewing of the Sistine Chapel. But back came her reply:

From: Danna Hawley
Subject: RE: Banksy

Hi Will,
Thanks for the info, much appreciated.

Has this book been sanctioned by Banksy's management?

Best, Danna

I had had enough:

Subject: RE: Banksy

Danna,

Thanks,

Certainly not. The idea of a writer being sanctioned to write a book is as foreign to me as a graffiti artist being sanctioned to paint a wall. However what I have done is write to Banksy's pr, and told her about the book in case she or Banksy think he has some mad stalker on his trail.

Regards, Will

Despite making further phone calls I never heard from Danna or Fabric again, although I did read on the Fabric website the thoughts of the club on Banksy: 'Sadly, he's one of those authentic, exceptional artists that unfairly got caught in a fast moving hype machine . . . we know all too well from the obscene amounts of money we get offered for the Banksy piece on the wall outside of our downstairs toilets.' Perhaps Danna thought I wanted to buy it, not just look at it.

Many months later a good friend suggested that I had been a little bit wet in not just going there. So, one damp Friday night, having already bought a ticket online and attempted to groove myself up a little (orange sneakers and a sad O'Neill surf shirt!), I managed to talk my way through the army of the club's doormen and security guards, who were perplexed by this off-the-age-scale single man. They didn't quite dare to be brutally ageist about it and simply turn me away but instead warned me of a 'very heavy drum 'n' bass night' in the forlorn hope that I might just disappear.

Once in I felt a bit like a potholer must feel when he's not sure which way is safe. Marky and Friends were playing in one room, Urban Nerds in another, and amidst all this massive noise and crowd the idea of hunting down Banksy seemed absurd. But all of a sudden I came across it by mistake, right next to the toilets: a Banksy bomb hugger all alone on a wall and protected by a nice antiquey frame. There was too little light to judge how good a piece it was, but it really didn't matter too much. It was a well-preserved Banksy in its original context; it spoke of the early, uncomplicated days in his life and the fact that there was none of the usual fuss; that few people even seemed to notice it somehow added to the appeal. It had been worth the effort and I left while my eardrums were still intact.

Onwards. The rat on a street called Exmouth Market, famous now for Moro's restaurant rather than any market, had gone together with the video shop it had been painted on. In the plaster, which had been whitewashed over, a few small holes were visible as though an eager archaeologist had picked at the surface in the hope of finding a hidden rat underneath. A few doors along the newsagent's box with a Banksy on it had long gone, along with the Banksy. Someone will have made a killing.

One street away, however, there was still a large Banksy to be seen – just. Mark Ellis, a builder, was asked by the landlord of a derelict shop to come in and do it up. As he was prising off a large piece of rusting metal next to the shop window, there on the wall beneath it was a Banksy. 'I called Laurie, my daughter about it. I said, "You are not going to believe this, but there's a Banksy here." When she saw it she thought she'd won the Lottery. She said "Oh god, you've got to preserve it." It was in a dreadful state when we found it, absolutely mullered. Someone had already rollered over it. We cleaned it right up. We framed it. Put a bit of Perspex over it. Don't look too bad, does it?'

Well, it doesn't look too bad, but it doesn't look too good either. It's an odd one this; in the early photographs it was simply a cash machine stencilled on a bricked-up window with 'Di faced tenners' (a £10 note with a portrait of Lady Di replacing the Queen's head) spewing out on to the pavement. At some point most of the tenners had been done away with, to be replaced by an evil-looking robotic arm that was stretching out from the machine and lifting a terrified schoolgirl up off her feet into the machine. But this in turn had been attacked and largely ruined by someone who had roller-painted two white lines down it. Finally it had been given a Perspex protective shield by Mark Ellis.

His daughter had just finished university and they decided to go into business together. They would sell bagels to all the office workers nearby looking for a quick lunch. And what would they call it? Banksy Bagel Bar, and the bagels would have 'a Banksy edge' to them. I don't know about a 'Banksy edge', but I was thankful to the guide book for leading me to their smoked salmon and cream cheese bagel with seeds on top. The survival of this piece illustrates once again just how far Banksy's appeal stretches, for no one has ever cared to name their shop Seurat's Sandwiches, Kahlo's Coffee Bar, Picasso's Pizza or Hopper's Hamburgers. Just Banksy Bagels.

'When we first opened there were twenty people or more coming by daily to take snaps of it,' says Mark Ellis. 'We still have loads of people coming to see it. Loads of Japanese.' As we talk a young woman stops in her tracks, pulls out her mobile phone and snaps what is, at this point, quite a sadly defaced Banksy. 'You get three or four of them a day, the phone merchants . . . We get a few eccentrics coming in about it as well. Sort of well-to-do people who have lost their way in life a little bit. Seems to be a little bit of a statement for them.' But not enough of these eccentrics, photo-taking Japanese and fans were buying their excellent bagels, and a year after I saw him the business was for sale. A few months on it had become Diana's Dry Cleaners. The Banksy on the wall next to it looked even more forlorn.

From gentrified Exmouth Market I trailed up to very ungentrified New North Road, where Banksy's girl with a balloon had disappeared along with her balloon. Disappointing, because the photographs show a very poignant image: a little girl has let go of her red heart-shaped balloon which is floating away, its string still trailing – has she just lost her balloon or is she deliberately letting it go? It had not merely been whitewashed over; it had been replaced by a set of five toasters – yes, toasters. Four relatively small ones and one very elegant one about six foot high and ten foot across, set on an orange and white background. Obviously immense care and skill had gone into these toasters. But a toaster as art? Again the internet came to the rescue. According to the Nelly Duff gallery in Shoreditch the Toaster Movement was 'born on a cold New Year's Eve in 1998, over a kitchen table in Wolverhampton. The Toaster project started life as an idea of how to make a mundane object famous, subverting the image by its placement and its graphic rendering. The Toaster project grew and has inevitably over the years created more questions than answers along the way.' These toasters on the wall were all questions and no answers. But certainly they were a lot more life enhancing than the depressing squiggles in the nearby streets.

From toasters I moved to helicopters: Banksy's huge Happy Chopper, off Old Street, an ugly-looking, heavily armed attack helicopter with a pretty pink bow on top which somehow made it look even more menacing. 'HAVE A NICE DAY' was stencilled alongside it, although you knew that the chopper was promising anything but. It had outlived the previous occupant that sat below it, Franco's Fish and Chip, and now sat on top of Wa Do Chinese fast food. But the Happy Chopper was in trouble, for it had been surrounded, and although huge it was still very hard to find: above Wa Do there was a rampart high enough to partly obscure the bottom of the painting, while the top had been wholly concealed by a large electronic billboard. But by crossing the road and standing to one side I saw that the Happy Chopper was still there, although covered in large Perspex sheets hanging down in strips in front of it. Again it illustrates our slightly tortured view of Banksy. Is it here today and gone tomorrow – no worries? Or is it here today, so it's got to be preserved – it's worth too much to be gone tomorrow? In its present position it might as well not exist at all.

Sometimes it seems that Banksy can't win. He usually paints in fairly derelict areas of a city, but far from bringing down the neighbourhood even further a Banksy or two is often a sure sign that the neighbourhood is on the way up – where Banksy goes the gentry will follow. In Brooklyn, New York, a property developer used a Banksy skipping girl to help sell their $900,000 apartments at 'Urban Green – New York City's most exciting destination'. (It did not do them much good, the banking crisis proved more powerful than even Banksy and put paid to the development for some years.) But in Hoxton I discovered that Banksy's 'DESIGNATED PICNIC AREA', neatly stencilled on the entrance steps of an unoccupied building, has been washed off and the steps now lead to a newly opened estate agent catering to just the sort of people who might now buy a Banksy.

An even more complicated case of the Banksy effect is illustrated by a pub called the Foundry, near the Happy Chopper. In a previous life it was a Barclays Bank but when the banks started closing branches it had been turned into a pub/art gallery. It would be hard to imagine anything less like a bank than this. Inside it was undoubtedly the grungiest pub I have ever been in and, somehow, all the better for it; outside the wide pavement was a favourite spot for dispatch riders who could sit with a drink and watch the traffic go by instead of fighting it. Inside I discovered that there were two Banksys still in existence, but in a rather relaxed setting. The downstairs of the pub had graffiti on every spare space, even on the ceilings – the ladies' loo was just as overwhelmed as the gents'. 'It's an artistic dialogue going on here,' said one of the barmen. 'We don't judge, we leave it to the artists to make their own decisions.' Banksy's Grin Reaper, equipped with traditional scythe, black cloak and hood, but with a smiley face underneath instead of the usual skeletal one, was here, and a much smaller version of the Happy Chopper too, although it was more difficult to spot under rival graffiti. They were both still very much alive and visible amidst a lot of dross, so it was encouraging to see that in this 'artistic dialogue' in the pits of Old Street good art had triumphed over bad.

Again, the outside of the pub showed just how the relationship between graffiti artists and property owners has changed. There was a big piece of striking graffiti by Krah wrapped around part of the front, and a notice alongside announced: 'This painting is commissioned for The Foundry. Do Not Remove.' At the back a huge chunk of wall was boarded up by hoardings three storeys high to protect two big Banksys, one a rat and the other a television being hurled out of a window. This hoarding, which in turn had become an inviting canvas for other graffiti artists, rose from a car park which had all the hints of a property development coming soon in up-and-coming Shoreditch. Again it was the internet that told me what was going on.

On the *Guardian* website, under the headline 'Not all art is meant to last for ever', the journalist Nosheen Iqbal had written:

> A pub bearing his work is earmarked for demolition but Banksy has rightly rejected suggestions that his art should be saved. Having built a career on re-appropriating public spaces, it's a relief to see that Banksy has intervened in the bizarre fuss surrounding the Foundry. To recap, the east London venue which is most part pub to some part art space, bears a Banksy original on its walls. Last week, Hackney Council approved plans to pull the building down to make way for a luxury hotel and spa. Predictably, the decision was met with some protest: the local authority's response was to promise that at the very least, Banksy's mural would be salvaged and protected. It's a curious consolation and proof, if it were still needed, that street art has imploded on itself.
>
> To his credit, Banksy has appealed to the developers, asking that his work – a 6ft high painting of a rat, currently protected by hoardings – not be saved if the Foundry is to go. 'It's a bit like demolishing the Tate and preserving the ice-cream van out the front,' he told the Hackney Gazette.

The Foundry's keenest customers organised a squat to try to prevent the pub from coming down, but they were evicted without much trouble. When I last looked, the pub was boarded up waiting demolition before being turned into an eighteen-storey 'Art'otel'

– the name alone makes you want to vomit – with a publicly accessible arts centre and a design which, the developers promise, will 'fit perfectly against this fashionable backdrop'.

So, with Banksys disappearing all over the place, what hope was there for the Moorfields rat, neither dead nor alive, entombed behind his wooden screen? It was at about this time that I was slightly surprised and very delighted to receive an email back from the Eye Hospital's chief executive:

Dear Mr Ellsworth-Jones

Many thanks for your email, which arrived just before a three week absence overseas on my part and which I have only now had a chance to look at. I was made aware of the Banksy graffiti (graffitus?) soon after joining Moorfields two years ago. At that time we had had an 'offer' to buy it from one of our doctors and I asked for it to be valued. This achieved nothing, mainly because, as you say, Banksy appears not to want to see his art traded and there seemed to be no obvious means of getting an independent valuation of it. Thereafter it has, I'm afraid, remained very low on the list of things I need to think about!

Your email does, though, prompt me to need to think again about this, and I wondered whether you might be able to advise me on the valuation question and/or how to get it cut out. Neither is an area of expertise for me or any of my colleagues, so any advice you can offer would be most appreciated.

Kind regards

John Pelly

Chief Executive

Since I was hardly the expert he supposed me to be, I would have to do some research before replying. In the meantime it was back on the trail, although at this point I was spotting more toasters than Banksys and it was usually a case of spotting Banksy remnants rather than Banksy originals. Graffiti removal squads are obviously more interested in walls than pavements; thus a copper, snorting coke, had been washed away although there were still painted traces of the wonderfully long line of coke he had been snorting as I walked down the alley. A rat with an overturned barrel of poison had gone but the green slime that was spilling out of the barrel was still painted on the pavement. Two rats in dinner jackets going to a red carpet occasion had gone too, but parts of the 'red carpet' remained on the pavement. There was however no trace of a parachute rat – scrubbed off by the council years ago. In its place was a jumble of miserable scrawl. The building remained derelict and there was no evidence at all that by cleaning up the parachutist the council had cleaned up the site or the area.

There were many more occasions when I found the site of a Banksy but the painting had gone. At the old Truman Brewery site, off Brick Lane, I even came across an old Triumph GT6, painted pink, which had somehow been hauled up on top of a container, probably by Banksy, and then later encased in a Perspex box, almost certainly not by Banksy. He had painted the Grim Reaper – no smiley face here – looking scarily out of the driver's window, but some modern-day Houdini had come along and nicked the window from underneath the Perspex. The Triumph just looked a mess to be photographed by puzzled tourists. The whole thing looked bedraggled and it was the only time on the treasure hunt that I felt really let down.

Before the end of the tour there were still a couple of pieces of unfinished business I had to deal with. First I found Pure Evil, the man who had painted *Murder Mile*, a very jolly forty-something artist despite his name. Certainly, talking to him, street art seemed a little less edgy than I imagined. For one thing his real name, Charley Edwards, sounded rather less threatening than his pseudonym. For another it turned out that he had not climbed his way over the barricades to paint his *Murder Mile*; he had entered the site with a key to the big gates having first negotiated with the owners, Londonewcastle, developers of 'boutique flats'. While waiting for the market to improve they had turned this space into something of an open-air gallery – they required a sketch before they allowed him in – and Pure Evil would be followed by Mode 2, a graffiti artist represented by the dealer who used to represent Banksy. Furthermore it turned out that it was not just Pure Evil who was painting, but he had an 'intern' helping him; I thought 'interns' were the property of big corporations pleading tight budgets. But here were Pure Evil and his intern, who had come over from Paris for a month, painting a wall in Islington in a blizzard. (The intern went back to Paris and was soon being called by galleries wanting to use the graffiti skills he had learned.)

I bought my print from Pure Evil and I got some advice from him too, so I felt that I could now reply to Moorfields. It felt slightly scary to be treated as some sort of fine art adviser. Nevertheless I had a go:

> Dear Mr Pelly,
> Thank you for your email. I now see the problems you face. I would suggest that perhaps the best thing to do would be to write to Banksy's PR Jo Brooks explaining the problem and asking if she can help. [I gave her address.] Banksy has offered

works up for charity in the past so maybe one way or another he would be prepared to help the NHS. Even if he, or rather Pest Control who act for him, would authenticate the piece then at least you would be half way there.

I did discuss the problem with Pure Evil, a graffiti artist who also runs a gallery by the same name. He said it was perfectly possible for a restorer to sit down for a couple of days and using polymer and a releasing agent and other tools of the trade take the graffiti off the tile and put it on to a canvas. It sounded interesting until I asked what kind of money would be involved and he suggested about £30,000 for the right specialist. I can't imagine that Moorfields would want to gamble that amount.

The only other suggestion I can make is to contact one of the main auction houses. In case you want to follow this up these are the names I have found on the web . . .

I am afraid I have no knowledge of how best to cut it out from your wall, although if it came to it I am sure one of these contemporary art directors would know a man who knew a man who had an angle grinder or whatever is required.

Regards . . .

And there the tour had ended. I had one rather gloomy-looking revolver hanging on the wall; to be honest I think it looks better in its original context than it does on the inside of our house, although perhaps that is because it is hanging amidst rather more traditional scenes: quite a few sailing yachts, some gentle landscapes, family photographs. It is not very fair on Evil's artwork.

Of the fifty-two Banksys I was hunting for, forty had gone entirely, although at least two had been taken away by speculators hoping to make a huge profit, so these pieces had not quite been lost altogether even though they were no longer on the street. Another four (two inside, two outside the Foundry pub) looked like they would disappear too. Eight had survived (seven now that the hoodie has gone) in some form or another. Banksy would undoubtedly argue that this transience is part of the very nature of street art. It had indeed been a treasure hunt, where the disappearance of so many Banksys made it even more satisfying to find one still alive. You made a little effort for Banksy and he repaid you.

And there was an enjoyable footnote to this tale. For in October 2010 it was reported that the Moorfields rat was to go on sale at a charity auction. The rat had been successfully cut out of the wall and was to be sold for the benefit of Moorfields at a charity auction at the Saatchi Gallery, with Lord Archer wielding the auctioneer's hammer. The *Guardian* reported Mr Pelly as saying: 'As far as I can gather, it simply appeared on the wall outside our main entrance one morning. A member of staff subsequently offered us £5,000 for it, but we suspected it was probably worth a good deal more.' It was. It went for £30,000.

# Six
# Anonymously Happy

Anonymity can be a powerful weapon. Does the name Perry McCarthy ring a bell? And if you have no luck with him, what about an easier name: Ben Collins? It is hard to imagine that they are ever going to be much more than answers in a pub quiz or a round of Trivial Pursuit, but they were once famous in a very anonymous sort of way. Perry McCarthy was the original Stig when the BBC's *Top Gear* began. Ben Collins, his replacement, took Stig and the question of his true identity to another level.

For those who never watch the show, Stig set lap times for performance cars that *Top Gear* was testing as well as preparing celebrities for their drive on the show. His very anonymity – he never spoke, protected by his white full-face helmet and his white racing suit – turned him into a sort of human robot who couldn't answer back, a convenient butt for *Top Gear*'s jokes: 'His earwax tastes like Turkish delight . . . after making love he bites the head off his partner . . . the outline of his left nipple is exactly the same shape as the Nurburgring.' And it was his anonymity which transformed just another very fast driver into something much more intriguing.

The BBC knew just how valuable this anonymity was. When McCarthy confirmed that he was 'Black' Stig – so called because he was dressed and helmeted all in black – he discovered that his contract was not being renewed. It was all done in the best *Top Gear* fashion: he was last seen careening down the runway of the aircraft carrier HMS *Invincible* in a Jaguar XJS, 'missing his braking point' and disappearing over the side – a solitary racing glove found floating off the carrier was his farewell to the world. When it became clear that his successor, Ben Collins, was writing a book about his experiences as *Top Gear*'s Mystery Man he was not disappeared but taken to court to enforce the confidentiality clause in his contract. It was Collins however who won the right to go ahead with the book, for which he was said to have received an advance of £250,000. In the long run being Ben Collins might be more satisfying, but it is almost certainly rather less profitable than being Stig.

Banksy has the same allure of the single name which transforms the ordinary into something special: who would remember Ben Collins if he wasn't Stig, Paul Hewson if he wasn't Bono, Gordon Sumner if he wasn't Sting, Saul Hudson if he wasn't Slash or Cherilyn Sarkisian if she wasn't Cher? But in addition the way he guards his anonymity, although he is certainly not a recluse, gives him the added glamour of seclusion – the whiff of Syd Barrett or J.D. Salinger. Together it is a powerful mix.

Collins says that, as the years went by, preserving his anonymity 'became harder and harder because there would be these natural slips – there are all these little pitfalls you have to avoid and really I just had to keep myself to myself.' Perhaps he should have taken lessons from Banksy – if only he knew who Banksy was. For Collins' anonymity lasted – just about – for six years; Banksy's secret is still relatively well preserved after a dozen or so years. In May 2008, for instance, at the festival of stencilled graffiti that Banksy organised in a tunnel under Waterloo station, a French artist was overheard having a conversation with a fellow artist, telling him: 'I hope Banksy's going to show up today, it would be really cool to meet up with him.' Then they moved on. The Frenchman never knew that he had just had a conversation, however short, with Banksy.

So why the anonymity? Banksy's answer is usually twofold. One strand is the oft-repeated explanation with respect to the illegal nature of graffiti: he 'has issues with the cops'; authenticating a piece he has done on the street would be like 'a signed confession'. He has said in the past, 'I consider it to be a victimless crime what I do generally, but the criminal side is important. Any piece of graffiti is saying you are not going to be told what to do and you'll go out under your own steam and you'll make the city look the way you want it to look.' Certainly graffiti is more than a game – if you paint often enough, as often as Banksy has done, there is a real chance that you will get locked up. That's the risk that gives it the essential adrenalin rush that most graffiti artists talk about, and that's what they miss when they are painting on walls that have been provided as legal spaces. There is a story among graffiti writers in America – impossible to tell whether it is true or not – that the police in Los Angeles used to try their hand as agents provocateurs. They would put up their graffiti attempts on a wall then lie in wait for others to be tempted to put their tags up too. When graffiti writers duly arrived and contributed their own tags and vamps, the police would come out of their hidey-hole and arrest them. The police, or more often the British Transport Police, are not desperate enough to become involved in this novel form of entrapment but they are certainly after persistent offenders.

Take Sam Moore, twenty-four, of Newport in the Isle of Wight, known rather more romantically as 10Foot when he is writing his name across London. He is the complete opposite of Banksy – for him the 'getting up' is everything – and he is widely admired in the graffiti community for what he has done. He hates Banksy and his stencils and shows it by writing across his work. But in June 2010, before another graffiti 'war' could get going, 10Foot was arrested. He was let out on bail while the police used 'handwriting analysis' to link him with further tags, yet even in the months while they were carrying out this analysis he carried on painting with grim but foolhardy determination, only adding to his troubles. Eventually he pleaded guilty to twenty-five charges of criminal damage carried out over three years and was jailed for just over two years, receiving in addition a five-year ASBO which prevents him from carrying an extraordinary range of implements starting with any form of 'unset paint' and expanding through 'shoe dye, grinding stone and glass etching equipment'. So if you are caught bombing the town, the consequences are now much more severe than in the days of Operation Anderson twenty years ago.

Banksy himself has largely managed to stay out of trouble. He has always remained vague about his record, but Shepard Fairey, who has somehow succeeded in remaining at the pinnacle of street art in America while at the same time carrying on a very successful design business, says that Banksy has 'never been busted to the point of potentially not being able to do street art.' Translated, this means that he has never been fined or imprisoned on the scale of 10Foot where a subsequent offence would mean a huge fine or an even longer sentence. Piecing together what Banksy has either written or told interviewers, it appears that he was arrested once, many years ago, in New York, for painting a picture about corruption on a billboard. 'As a result I spent 40 hours in a cell with the cops taking the piss and telling me lies, followed by a spell of community service and hefty fine.'

In the late 1990s he spent a couple of years on and off in New York, usually staying at the Carlton Arms Hotel on East 25th Street, just north of the East Village, which had once been a port in a storm for welfare families, drug dealers and hookers of various descriptions before it cleaned up its act. As the hotel grew smarter, different artists were invited to decorate its fifty-four rooms – in return they got to stay in the hotel for free during the time they were painting. The room that Banksy painted has since been painted over by other artists but his bright, cartoony work along part of the corridor still exists. The hotel's general manager, John Ogren, says, 'We knew him when he was just beginning and he is one of the kindest, funniest, genuine, and genuinely talented artists I know.'

Not everyone felt that way. Banksy told one interviewer: 'You'd imagine that certain folk would kinda be on your side. But I was grassed up by some transsexual hooker looking to score brownie points with the NYPD.' In another version of the same story he said, 'You tend to think that certain people are on your side, but obviously they ain't . . . I got badly busted on that one. I had about seven cops raid me on a rooftop.'

But it is very difficult to imagine Banksy getting arrested now and being let out on bail while handwriting analysts decide which are genuine Banksys and which are fakes. Even prosecutors appear to put him in a different class from other graffiti artists. In June 2011 Daniel Halpin, a 26-year-old from Camden, north London, was finally brought to court on seven charges of criminal damage. Halpin was a prolific artist known as TOX, the scourge of

Transport for London, who sprayed his tag wherever he could find a space, and the prosecution, in trying to explain TOX's ubiquity, told the jury: 'He is no Banksy. He doesn't have the artistic skills, so he has to get his tag up as much as possible.' Quite apart from this misunderstanding of graffiti – the tagger's desire for maximum exposure, never mind if this means exchanging quality for quantity – it also seemed to put Banksy on an almost untouchable level, even though his art is just as illegal as Tox's. In the summer of 2011 Tox was jailed for twenty-seven months, the judge telling him: 'There has to be a deterrent aspect. These offences have gone on, in your own admission, since the year 2000 . . .' That period is only a little shorter than Banksy's career.

It has now reached the point where Banksy might still want to see himself as a bit of a vandal, but actually he is becoming something of a tourist attraction. When he painted a wall in north London in support of Tox, it was very rapidly covered in Perspex by the wall's owner. When he painted new work in Bristol and Croydon, both councils held back the graffiti clean-up squads and gave their citizens a chance to vote: should 'the Banksy' stay or go? After one early Banksy was whitewashed over by mistake, a councillor in Bristol proposed a register of outdoor artworks across the city to help protect them.

In Bristol the Banksy effect has turned graffiti into something of a growth industry, with one council officer suggesting the city now has three main tourist attractions: an old boat, a bridge (Brunel's SS *Great Britain* and his Clifton suspension bridge), and graffiti. The council now sponsors various legal graffiti events, the latest, in the summer of 2011, being an £80,000 extravaganza called See No Evil which turned the buildings in a drab street in the city centre into what the council hopes will become the biggest permanent street art gallery in Europe. The irony was that the man heading this project was Inkie, who twenty-two years earlier, during Operation Anderson, had been the key police target in the fight against graffiti, and the buildings painted included the juvenile and magistrate courts where Inkie and others who were arrested back then had made their first appearance in court.

As part of a difficult balancing act the council has produced a nine-page policy document on how to deal with graffiti, promising that in some instances there will be consultation on whether graffiti should be removed while warning that 'consultation is not a referendum'. In the first example of this consultation, back in 2006, 93 per cent of the people who voted wanted the work that Banksy had sprayed on the side of the Young People's Sexual Health Clinic – a naked man hanging from a window ledge to avoid a cuckolded husband – to be saved. So it is still there, now more under threat from fellow vandals with a paintball gun than from the council.

In Hastings Banksy painted a picture of a girl building sand-castles, making it look as though she had painstakingly pricked the word TESCO on the side of each castle. It might not have been one of his outstanding works but it was certainly a Banksy. The council's anti-graffiti team was about to wash it clean when first the local paper and then the council stepped in. Jay Kramer, the deputy leader of the council, said, 'I know that we have a zero tolerance policy on graffiti, and that is absolutely right. However, we have to be flexible so on this occasion I have agreed that Banksy can be an exception to our rule and can stay.' It is ironic that ever since having made this exception, the council has been trying to protect its Banksy first with Perspex and, when that was smashed, with some sort of protective spray. Other graffiti writers, who no doubt have suffered in the past from the council's zero tolerance rule, see no reason why Banksy should be treated any differently.

So, since Banksy is now being both tolerated and protected by councils, it would be more of an embarrassment than anything else if he was actually arrested. It is the second strand of Banksy's argument for anonymity which today is the more convincing one. At the time when his film *Exit Through the Gift Shop* was being launched in America, he told a Los Angeles journalist – anonymously: 'Charlie Chaplin used to say "once I talk, I'm like any other comic." I figured I'd follow his lead.' Several years earlier he had expounded at greater length on the theme: 'I have no interest in ever coming out. I figure there are enough self-opinionated assholes trying to get their ugly little faces in front of you as it is. You ask a lot of kids today what they want to be when they grow up and they say "I want to be famous." You ask them for what reason and they don't know or care. I think Andy Warhol got it wrong: in the future so many people are going to become famous that one day everybody will end up being anonymous for fifteen minutes.'

But there is more to it than this rant, interesting though it is. At the time of the launch of *Exit*, he also said: 'I don't know why people are so keen to put the details of their private life in public; they forget that invisibility is a superpower.' His good friend Shepard Fairey, whose statements sometimes make him sound a little critical, says, 'Banksy cares very much about selling art and what people think of him and he understands thoroughly that people's fantasy is a far better marketing tool than reality.' In 2010 Banksy told the *Sunday Times*: 'Sometimes it might seem like an elaborate public relations stunt, but the anonymity is completely vital to my work, without it I couldn't paint.' While this was certainly true in his early days in Bristol, it is not entirely true today when a considerable portion of his work comes straight out of his studio on to canvas, bypassing the street entirely. Anonymity, once a necessity, has become something of a marketing tool, for having stumbled into fame he has become remarkably adept in knowing how to use it.

It is a marketing tool he came across more by chance than design. At the end of the 1990s he was painting the side of a lorry at Glastonbury – Inkie was doing the lettering – and it became something of an open-air performance show, with no attempt to disguise who he was. But by 2000, when he gave a short interview to the BBC to publicise the opening of his exhibition in the Severnshed restaurant in Bristol, he had retreated into anonymity, although he was not using any of the voice distortion devices he uses now. (His voice sounds so ordinary on this tape, with just a gentle hint of the West Country in it, that you wonder why he bothers with voice distortion unless it is to increase the drama.) What he discovered was that anonymity created its own interest. An anonymous bad artist will remain just that and no one will have any interest in who he might be; but combining Banksy's talent with anonymity produced a remarkable effect.

Acoris Andipa, who has put on a succession of hugely successful Banksy exhibitions in his gallery in Knightsbridge – much to the chagrin of the Banksy camp, who certainly do not want to be associated with a Knightsbridge gallery – says: 'I think he operates on a very simple basis. He creates his work. He has no interest in being a celebrity. The fact that he has no interest has made him into a celebrity.' Would it make a difference if he wasn't anonymous? 'I just don't believe there would be much impact on his appeal and therefore his market prices.' But my own feeling is that his anonymity creates a buzz, an interest, a talking point. It widens his appeal and certainly increases the value of his prints, and possibly of his original canvases too. If you are in the street art world you know who Swoon, Faile, Fairey, Vhils, Inkie, ESPO, Blu, Mode2, Invader, Paul Insect and many, many others are; but to outsiders often the only name on the menu is Banksy. Would Banksy have been so successful if we all knew who he was? Probably not. I believe his talent is such that he would have achieved his success eventually, but it would have taken him much longer to get noticed by the wider world.

He is often likened to Andy Warhol, encouraged by his choice of subjects: where Warhol painted Marilyn Monroe, Banksy painted Kate Moss; where Warhol painted Campbell's soup, Banksy painted Tesco's soup. But in many ways they are complete opposites. Warhol bought his first house from the proceeds of his commercial work, mainly shoe ads but also ads for just about any other kind of 'ladies' accessories'. Banksy does not now accept commercial commissions. Warhol was desperate for gallery space; Banksy usually avoids it. Warhol loved celebrity and celebrities; Banksy can't stand them. Warhol, famously, would attend every fashionable event he could find: 'He would go to the opening of a drawer,' a friend once said of him. Banksy won't even attend his own opening, let alone anyone else's.

And yet they have both profited from the whiff of mystery that wafts around them. In his early days at least, Warhol preferred the telephone to a face-to-face encounter; Banksy now has the added armour of email, which he prefers to either the telephone or a face-to-face interview. The vaguer Warhol's responses to interviews became, the more they increased his appeal; the photographer Duane Michals told the authors of *Pop*, one of the key books on

Warhol, how surprised he was to see him 'cloaked in this air of mystery that people applied to him as if he was some sort of Zen philosopher and everything he said was a koan.' Banksy is not so vague, but he only answers the emailed questions he wants to and leaves the rest blank. Happily he is not treated as any sort of philosopher, but nevertheless his occasional pronouncements, however mundane, gain him at least as much importance – and notice – as any other British artist of his generation.

He has effectively stumbled into a place where he can pronounce on everything from the Israeli wall – 'the most politically unjust structure in the world today' – to the art world – 'it's a rest home for the overprivileged, the pretentious and the weak' – and be regarded as something of an anonymous authority. But retaining this anonymity has been a very calculated and determined act. He hires a public relations agency both to garner him publicity and to protect him from it and, when necessary, he hires lawyers to protect him even further.

Colleagues were usually amazed when I told them that Banksy had a PR agent – somehow it does not quite fit the image of the anonymous vandal. But he is now so famous that a sort of public voice is essential, even if it is only to deny that a 'Banksy work' is by Banksy. As soon as I started on this book I wrote a letter to this PR agent, Jo Brooks, at her office in Brighton, enclosing my last book so she could see how I wrote, advising her that I was writing this book and saying that I would very much like to talk to Banksy at some stage. As the deadline approached I made a more formal request for an interview, repeated it and repeated it once more. Eventually, with the deadline even closer, I had a note back asking for a copy of the manuscript. Since this is not an authorised biography, I declined this request. I was then told, 'We are keen to fact check.' I replied that this would change the nature of the book: 'The first thing to go in would be his name (which is not in at the moment) and I would then ask you to fact check if it was correct or not, etc, etc.' Instead I repeated my request for an interview to cover the wide range of subjects raised in the book, but heard nothing back. (Towards the end of these negotiations I was asked for questions to be emailed, but since the usual pattern has been for some questions to be answered and other key ones simply ignored I declined.) Although he has given a considerable number of emailed interviews when he has wanted to publicise an exhibition or a film, Banksy otherwise says nothing. Paul Wood, tracking him down for Radio Four's *PM* programme at the time Banksy was painting Israel's West Bank wall, said, 'I've had negotiations with wanted terrorists which have gone more smoothly than our attempts to speak to Banksy.'

A trip to Bristol showed me just how determined he was to protect himself. One of the reasons I went there was to discuss with Simon Cook, deputy leader of the city council and its executive for culture, the extraordinary success of the exhibition that Banksy had staged in 2009 at the Bristol City Museum. Part of the reason for the success of the exhibition was the element of surprise: it had been planned in complete secrecy and then, as the city's *Evening Post* said, 'appeared out of nowhere'. So I asked Simon Cook, when did he first know that the exhibition was going to launch? 'Sorry, I can't answer that.' It seemed an innocent enough question so I tried again, this time hoping that if I was a bit more ingratiating it might help: 'I was told you only knew about it a couple of days before it opened and that you were very supportive?'

'Well, as soon as I saw the exhibition I was very supportive. But

I can't really answer. It's a question to do with the planning of it and I can't. Sorry, it's just in breach of contract.' The contract that Banksy's lawyers had persuaded the city to sign before he staged the exhibition had tied everyone up in such knots of secrecy that even an innocent question about the planning, asked almost a year after the show's closure, somehow became a breach of contract. Mr Cook is an intelligent and enjoyable politician, so at least he could see the funny side of it: here was the city's most notorious 'vandal' using the full majesty of the law to protect his anonymity.

There are other instances too where the Banksy organisation appears to have moved swiftly to protect him. The copyright of the supposed photograph of Banksy shot while he was at work in Jamaica, used in the *Mail on Sunday* during its investigation of his identity, was bought shortly after publication by a PR company. The price was said to be £10,000, although this figure has never been substantiated. Selling the rights to use a photograph is how photographers make their money – and it remains their copyright to sell again and again. Selling the copyright, in other words the ownership of the photograph, is unusual. The photographer has always refused to talk about the arrangement he made.

A website that did use the photograph received a letter from media lawyers who were representing the PR company and have represented Banksy in the past, demanding that it be taken off the site within twenty-four hours or they would 'escalate' their action. The whole thing reads like a bad detective story: any link to Banksy could always be denied, but the PR company that bought the photograph has also represented Blur, a band with whom Banksy has had close links ever since he came to London. There is no evidence that the PR company had been instructed by Banksy to buy the photograph but it is impossible to see why the company would want to buy the picture other than to protect Banksy.

If he needs to call in a favour to prevent a chance of him being recognised he will do so, however small that chance is. In 2003 the *Observer* launched the first issue of its *Music Monthly* with a cover of Blur shot in front of a wall which had been specially painted by Banksy. One picture which the newspaper later used in reporting the whole shoot showed Banksy cutting the stencil he was going to use on the wall. The editor of the music magazine, Caspar Llewellyn Smith, says it was shot so you saw the back of his head, 'you couldn't tell who he really was at all. But he rang me saying, "Can you have a word and get rid of that picture off the system?" He made a real point of saying, "You have got to get rid of that picture, no one knows what I am like, I am asking you as a mate and as a favour and will you do that please." And I think I probably said to someone, "Do you mind just sort of losing that quietly," which I suppose I shouldn't have done.' The picture disappeared and the photographer, who has remained friends with Banksy, declined to talk about it.

Banksy is helped by the fact that people appear to enjoy a celebrity mystery just as much as they enjoy learning the 'secrets' of a celebrity – it lends a little variety to things. These are loyal fans who are determined not to know who he is. The *Mail on Sunday* reader who expressed anger at the way the paper had exposed Banksy's identity – 'You have ruined something special' – finds an echo in the galleries where Banksy's art is sometimes on sale. Robin Barton, whose Bankrobber Gallery specialises in trying to sell street works by Banksy, says: 'People really don't want to know who Banksy is. Even collectors don't want me to tell them who he is. It's weird but that's what keeps it fresh for me. In the same way

I don't want people to know who he is. Everyone can find out, it should be pretty easy, but it's more fun and much more profitable not knowing.'

And these are just collectors or fans who have no connection at all with Banksy other than their enjoyment of what he does and, importantly, who he is or who they imagine him to be. When you get anywhere near anyone who has had any contact with Banksy, the loyalty is even more intense. When I told a writer friend much more experienced in the alternative lifestyle to be found in the West Country that I was writing this book she emailed me back: 'Between you and me, would you secretly like to unmask him? I am sure you must be intrigued about who he really is.'

And I confessed: 'No, I don't have a desire to unmask him; but I do have a desire to join Club Banksy – the "I know who he is and I have met him, but I am not going to tell you" club.' It is the joy of being an insider matched against the outsider who is treated as something of a leper. No matter how many times I said I was not going to expose his identity, I was not after interviewing his mum and dad, I did not want to know what he ate for breakfast, it was not enough. If I approached anyone for an interview the first question I was nearly always asked was: 'Has Banksy authorised this request?' The irony of this question was simply never even considered.

Even someone like Acoris Andipa feels it. He talks about the Banksy camp: 'They are who they are and they do business in the way that they do it and nobody can crack into that – or definitely somebody like myself can't crack into that because I represent something that they want to be seen as not being involved in.' So does that bother him? 'On the professional front, no. On the personal front, kind of. Because I put my heart and my soul and my money into it. It would have been nice to get some sort of recognition, like "Look, we can't do business with you, but thanks mate, you've helped along in your own way." But I don't think it's ever going to happen.'

When I travelled to Bristol planning to see Simon Cook, I had also made an appointment to meet a graffiti artist who used to paint with Banksy in days gone by. He had agreed to this interview on the strict understanding that we would not talk about Banksy's identity. But soon after I arrived in Bristol I received a text: 'Hi there Will. Pest Control have been in contact today and would rather I didn't meet with you, so therefore, as this is the case I won't be. If you can clear it with them and I hear from them – great. But until then I am sorry I cannot meet up.' I learned later that he had received a call not only from Pest Control but also from Banksy himself. (The artist was so torn between his loyalty to his old friend via Pest Control and guilt about my wasted hours in Bristol that he kindly called again later that day and we did meet for a drink, but only on the understanding that we talked about anything other than Banksy – a surreal but enjoyable evening.)

It can of course work the other way. Old mates who have fallen out with Banksy might grumble about him, but they never want to grass him up. But people who have come across him later in life are not necessarily so loyal. I had one proposal, offering 'pretty much what every journalist/writer would like to know about Banksy and *Exit*' and then asking how much money I would pay him for all these promised goodies. The answer was no money, and I never heard from him again.

Bristol is a danger for Banksy; too many people there know him from the past. If he is waiting for a train back to London he tends to sit hiding behind a newspaper in the hope that no one spots him. Another danger is when someone comes up to him unexpectedly. Caspar Llewellyn Smith was at the Roundhouse in November 2006 listening to Daman Albarn's new band, The Good, The Bad & The Queen, when Banksy emerged from nowhere and came over to start chatting with him. Llewellyn Smith says, 'Here is a guy who doesn't want people to know who he is, and I had a slight sense that it probably gets quite lonely sometimes. If he is in a room which is a big social setting and it's a room where there are lots of people who seem to know each other it must be quite nice for him to have someone to talk to.' That was fine, but there was a problem: coming back from the gents to rejoin Llewellyn Smith was another journalist, Ben Thompson. What was the protocol, what introductions was Llewellyn Smith going to make? 'He said simply, "Oh, this is my friend Ben," and Banksy replied, "Hi, I'm John." Then he just sort of disappeared into the crowd. He had obviously had practice.'

So what kind of man lurks behind this well-constructed moat?

A man, one suspects, who enjoys what he is doing but who has trouble dealing with the fame, however anonymous it is, and the money that has come with it. After his triumphant show in Los Angeles in 2006 he said, 'The attention weirded me out so much, I refused to sell anything new for two years.' Yet he went to Los Angeles to do a big, big show to which he or his minders invited the likes of Angelina Jolie and Brad Pitt, the star of the show itself being a live elephant which enraged animal lovers and amazed visitors. These were hardly the actions of a man who didn't want anyone to know he was in town.

A certain anger – jokey, but anger nevertheless – runs through both his early books and interviews. For instance, in *Banging Your*

*Head Against a Brick Wall*, self-published in 2001 before he had gone more mainstream, he writes: 'You could say that graffiti is ugly, selfish and that it's just the action of people who want some pathetic kind of fame. But if that's true it's only because graffiti writers are just like everyone else in this fucking country.' Is he condemning himself along with 'everyone else'? In one of his first interviews he refers to the poll tax riots and says 'I like to think there's a side of me that wants to smash the system, f**k s**t up and drag the city to its knees as it screams my name.'

But those were the early days. Now he is thirty-eight years old and married to someone he sometimes calls his 'wall widow', the time is long gone when, as he told one colleague, he had no bank account and used to keep his cash 'under the bed' or give it to a friend to put in the bank.

He had always been involved in music – for a time in the early 1990s he had linked up with the self-described 'losers, boozers, cruisers, chancers and dancers' of Nottingham's DiY free party collective. And it was through music that he gained the use of his first studio in London. Soon after he arrived in London he linked up with Mark Jones, founder of the independent Wall of Sound records – and then with Damon Albarn and Jamie Hewlett, co-creator with Albarn of the cartoon 'band' Gorillaz. Jones allowed him to use a Wall of Sound studio on Acklam Road, west London, conveniently placed next to the tube tracks, and the arrangement was that instead of paying rent he would do the record label's flyers. One of his most memorable images, a partially masked demonstrator who despite radiating pure aggression is about to hurl not a Molotov cocktail but a bunch of flowers, first evolved in these early days in London.

The fashion designer Fee Doran, married to Mark Jones at the time, used the same studio. She remembers Banksy as 'a really nice guy, a man who was certainly up for a laugh'. They would have a drink, have a smoke and then he would 'go out and do some spraying'. She sometimes forgot how anonymous he wanted to be, a couple of times shouting 'hello Banksy', much to his dismay, when she saw him out on the street.

His anonymity is helped by the fact, as one American who worked with him in Los Angeles puts it, that he's 'another skinny English bloke. The sort of guy who you see in thousands of pubs in England, just a regular guy.' 'Ordinary' and, particularly, 'unassuming' are key words that crop up when anyone is describing Banksy. As another American who worked with him closely on his show in Los Angeles says, 'I always say he looks like a plumber, you know the man who goes "Knock knock, I'm here to fix the drain." He's just an average kind of a bloke really.' The sort of bloke who, as a colleague who worked with him in London puts it, 'is the most nondescript person you could imagine. He smoked roll-ups and he was always pretty scruffy. He certainly didn't strike me as ex public school, but you never know . . .'

The double lives he leads – Sotheby's vandal, famously anonymous, rich rebel – would be enough to make anyone a touch paranoid, and Banksy is no exception. Again he jokes about it – his film company is called Paranoid Pictures – but you feel it is not entirely in jest. In his second self-published book, *Existencilism*, he wrote: 'Nobody ever listened to me and I used to think that was their fault. Eventually I got to realise maybe it was the fact that I was boring and paranoid that was the problem.' A friend from Bristol days who still sees him occasionally says, 'He's paranoid and maybe he needs to be a bit, but he doesn't need to be as paranoid as he is.'

Certainly the circle around him appears to have got tighter and tighter, with old friends finding they no longer get through to him. In part this appears to be caused by the fact that he sometimes feels they are trying to profit from him, selling today for eye-watering sums pieces of art he gave them years ago – everyone wants a profitable bit of him.

But one man's paranoia is another man's straightforward desire to control what goes on around him. One collector who knows him says, 'It's nothing more than being a bit of a control freak who likes to be the centre of events.' Thus he was said to be angered when some of his prints were included in a 2010 exhibition of street art at the Museum of Contemporary Art, San Diego. He was just one of twenty artists rather than the key artist, but more important he had no control of the event or how the gallery obtained their prints. While other artists were given time and, more importantly, space to strut their spray can, pictures on the web show his print looking so forlorn in the gallery that his anger was understandable.

Everyone who has come across him says he wants to be involved. 'He's one of the hardest working people I've ever met,' said Steve Lazarides, 'he's a perfectionist.' If any artist brings a painting in to his gallery, Pictures on Walls, the staff will have to run it by him if they are thinking of taking it. He does not run the gallery – he has films to make, walls to paint, exhibitions to plan – but he certainly chooses the artists.

Another source who works with him (it is extraordinary really that Banksy has got everyone into such a state they feel disloyal if they even whisper a compliment about him) says: 'He is really involved in everything. I was always under the impression that the ideas were coming from him. He was a laugh, a lot of fun to work with and never anything but polite and friendly.'

Perhaps one of the best descriptions of the sort of man Banksy is comes from Caspar Llewellyn Smith, who spent most of one day with him back in 2003 and, unlike others, dares to tell the tale. Having lined up Blur for the first cover of the *Observer*'s *Music Monthly*, it seemed like a good idea to ask Banksy to do the illustration for the shoot, since he had already created the artwork for their album *Think Tank* (this artwork sold later for £288,000). The plan was to take Banksy up to the Leeds Festival where Blur were playing and squeeze in the shoot there.

'We met at the PR's house in west London early in the morning. It was at the time when there wasn't such myth around him. You sort of knew who he was because that was the idea to do it, but it wasn't as if you felt intimidated by the idea that he was a mysterious figure or particularly in awe of it. He just seemed a straightforward bloke. Very like someone like Damon Albarn. Very very clever, but a bit of a geezer.'

They piled into a minibus. Banksy's plan was to stencil a television set being chucked out of a window in typical rock and roll bad boy style and he brought with him a couple of pre-cut stencils and a load of spray paint. Nevertheless they had to stop on their way through Leeds when Banksy realised he was missing a piece of kit and went into 'somewhere like B&Q' to find it. Eventually they arrived at 'some strange back bit of the festival' and went looking for a wall for Banksy to paint on.

'We spent twenty minutes going around and we would say "What about this?" And he would be saying "It's not big enough, it's not this, it's not that," and getting slightly panicked because there wasn't a suitable surface for him to work against. We knew that the band would only be available to us for half an hour and we had to get this thing done in that period, so in a light panic we then piled back into this minibus and drove off into the countryside thinking, "We are just going to have to bloody find somewhere."

'We saw a farm, drove up the farm road, piled out, the farmer and his wife came out looking a bit bemused and we said, to paraphrase slightly, "Hello, we are north London media ponces. Can we have a look round your farm because we are trying to do a photo shoot with this band Blur who are about to headline the Leeds Festival." They said, "Oh yeah, our daughter has just come back from uni and she's at the festival and she's a big fan. She loves them, so have a look round." We looked around, Banksy found the side of a barn with all these tiny little ducklings in it and he said it would work fine. The band turned up and said hello and they were sort of larking around with him a bit. It was done fairly quickly. The farmer's daughter turned up with her boyfriend. They were quite pleased because they got to meet the band. We left, I am not sure if we gave the farmer any money but he had this Banksy TV stencilled on to the side of his duck shed. He also had something on a gate which was Banksy testing one of his cans, shaking it up and spraying it on a stencil to see if it would work all right. [As we shall see, both these two pieces were later to find their way on to the art market, with very different results.] Then we went off to the festival and came back to London late.'

Did he stress that everything had to be secret? 'There was no sense of ducking and diving at all. No feeling of "Oh, I can't be seen here." When we were with the farmer there was no great secrecy around it. He just did it and buggered off. I don't think we paid him for anything. There was no contract about you have got to keep your mouth shut. He was well known enough at the time that we definitely felt it was quite a cool thing to have got him. And we weren't going to betray him.'

How quickly did he work? 'Oh, really quick. I remember him cutting some shapes when we got there before the band turned up. He had come with some stuff and I think he was just adjusting it or fixing it for size. And then it was very, very quick. Five minutes, if that. The thing that took time was the photographer, because photographers always take time.'

Talking to Llewellyn Smith, the words he uses to describe Banksy include 'approachable', 'funny', 'friendly', 'a nice guy', 'very sharp'; but the one phrase he used most frequently is 'a bit of a geezer'. So does that mean if he came from London he would fit the stereotyped image of the norf London taxi driver? 'No, not a taxi driver, not rough round the edges in that way, but the sort of slightly classless sort of person you find in the record industry a lot, although quite a bit smarter than that.

'In the music industry, or the photography and fashion world, you meet a lot of terrible idiots and he certainly wasn't that. He knew his music. He was quite self contained and he just got on with it. There was no hamming around, there was no bossing other people about. There were no great airs and graces. It wasn't "Look at me, I'm the great artist and this is how you need to behave".'

# Seven
# The Artist and Organiser

At the beginning of May 2008, forty stencil artists from around the world were put on alert. They were not told exactly what was going to happen but they were told to be in London for the week. Those coming from abroad had their air tickets paid for.

When they had all arrived in the city, they were summoned to a hotel where they were let into the secret. Banksy had rented Leake Street, the street under Waterloo's railway tracks which he described correctly as 'a dark, forgotten filth pit', and they had all been invited to paint there. Pure Evil was one of the artists invited to the hotel. 'It was pretty exciting. I saw artists that I knew from Poland, artists from Italy, everywhere, everyone had been brought in. I came back to the gallery, grabbed all my stencils and went straight down there and spent the next three days there. The first night I was there it was just great because Faile was doing some pieces, 3D from Massive Attack was doing a piece, Banksy was painting. There wasn't really anyone else around there on the first night. I think everyone was in London and having a look around before they got down to work the next day. What was quite cool on that night was there wasn't any of the weirdness about secret identities, everyone was getting on with it and just doing their thing. It was like a little group of people that he knew. So the identity wasn't really an issue.'

There were plywood barriers and security guards to make sure that they had time to paint before the public were allowed to enter. Various props were brought in, including an ice cream van which has adorned more than one of Banksy's big exhibitions, and an assortment of wrecked cars were delivered by trailer. Someone even produced an unfortunate tree, growing CCTV cameras rather than leaves. The event was christened the Cans Festival and advertised as a 'stencil art street battle' – much like Walls on Fire – attempting to link it to graffiti battles of the past; but it was hardly a scene of conflict. The walls were all painted clean ready for the artists and they had all been allocated their spaces. Even their meals were laid on for them. The police could not touch them. In fact the biggest problem was probably the fumes from the spray paint they were all using in the enclosed space of the tunnel. Inkie said later, 'Paint fumes had always messed with my head. The worst time recently was Cans Festival Two down in that tunnel – I vomited!'

Entrance was free and the art was not for sale. The programme theoretically cost £3, though at some point it was being given out free. Thirty thousand people queued to get in during the three days over the May bank holiday. Once the show had opened, artists who came along with their own stencil could put that up too; there was even a blank piece of wall reserved for them. All the important figures in the street art scene were there, and each of them received a 'thank you' piece of art from Banksy – a laser print of a cowgirl riding a bucking spray can, each with a small dedication from Banksy which might make the prints difficult to sell if their recipients ever wanted to. Three weeks later Tate Modern opened its own exhibition of work by urban street artists. It was a major, major step for the Tate but it didn't quite have the down and dirty edge of Leake Street.

At the end of the summer Banksy staged a second show at Leake Street, curated like the first by his friend Tristan Manco, author of several books on graffiti. But this time it was the turn of the 'old school' graffiti writers. It might have had the slight whiff of a consolation prize, for as one old school writer says, 'They saw we were pissed off about not being included in the first show – we wanted a go.' Nevertheless it was a pretty cool consolation prize.

Again about forty artists were invited. There was no hotel briefing, but Leake Street had been completely cleaned up for them and a new array of wrecked cars deposited, ready to be painted over. For the first time in these graffiti writers' lives they were protected by security guards rather than being hunted down by them. David Samuel, who was one of the participants, says: 'We spent the weekend there with breakfast, lunch and dinner being served out of the arches. Like full gourmet meals. You'd go in in the morning and breakfast was there, all the chefs were there with all their catering thing. Lunch was called, everyone puts their paint down and goes in the arches for lunch. I thought, what a dude, man.' Banksy was neither painting nor watching over this show as he had the first time, so it did not have quite the same frisson. Nevertheless it was a second impressive show, and Banksy somehow retained use of the tunnel, so writers have been painting there legally ever since. The two Leake Street shows gave graffiti writers of all persuasions their biggest ever showcase in London, and together with the Tate exhibition helped raise street art to an entirely different level of recognition.

Waldemar Januszczak, the *Sunday Times* art critic, once wrote that Banksy's 'chief achievement, and I believe it to be a mammoth one, was finding a way to operate so successfully outside the art world.' It seems in a way a rather back-handed compliment – better perhaps at getting noticed than at his actual art – but is it true anyway? Acoris Andipa sees much more in his art than the way he has managed to get it displayed. 'I don't understand what's new about the way he operated. Basquiat and Keith Haring were painting just as actively in the subway in New York while at the same time they were showing at the Castelli Gallery. Banksy did the usual thing that most artists do, going from one small gallery to another, hosting your own exhibition, finding the right space, buying into a champion who happens to have influence over that space whether it's a restaurant or an empty venue, inviting all your mates and their mates along and hoping that somewhere along the line someone has some cash in their pocket.' But it is not as simple as that. Leake Street is one of five exhibitions that marked Banksy out as an artist with a very different and very successful way of marketing himself.

Oddly, having arrived in London, his first show opened in February 2000 back in Bristol, at the Severnshed restaurant beside the docks. At this point he was following the traditional path, doing just what other young artists do, finding the right *free* space. The restaurant was adorned with Banksys; there was even cheeky monkey, using a bomb as a surfboard, high up in the roof space.

This was Banksy's first real move from the streets to an exhibition space. He had to overcome his dislike of galleries – although this wasn't quite a gallery – and canvases. Even though he had told one interviewer, 'Canvases are for losers really,' he explained to the BBC: 'I am trying to make canvases work better than graffiti can work because obviously you can take time on it. Graffiti doesn't always come out the way you like it because you're rushing, you're panicking, whatever. The question is to try to get the adrenalin rush that you get when you are doing graffiti into a canvas, that's the problem that I am having.' He seemed to have solved the problem, for it was a very strong exhibition, and if it was a stepping stone for Banksy it was a Lottery win for anyone lucky enough to be there.

Everything was priced at under £1,000 and one of the paintings he sold was his *Self Portrait*, a painting full of mixed metaphors in which Banksy, whose head has been replaced with a chimp's head, is depicted firing both spray cans like a cowboy. Seven years later it fetched £198,000 after a short bidding war at Bonhams. Another piece in the exhibition, *Riot Green*, one of the most famous Banksy images – the masked flower thrower – was bought by a student who splashed out £300 from his student loan even though he had originally mistaken the Banksy signature as Banoy. He hung it over his bed – uninsured – until he couldn't resist the lure of the art market any longer, when he sold it at Sotheby's for £78,000.

What followed next in London, Los Angeles and Bristol was far from the traditional way of selling things. His first exhibition in London, if exhibition is the right word, took place in Rivington Street in 2001. In *Banging Your Head Against a Brick Wall* he explains the show better than anyone else could: 'We came out of a pub one night arguing about how easy it would be to hold an exhibition in London without asking anyone's permission. As we walked through a tunnel in Shoreditch someone said: "You're wasting your time, why would you want to paint pictures in a dump like this?"

'A week later we came back to the same tunnel with two

buckets of paint and a letter. The letter was a forged invoice from a Mickey Mouse arts organisation wishing us luck with the "Tunnel Vision mural project". We hung up some decorators' signs nicked off a building site and painted the walls white wearing overalls. We got the artwork up in twenty-five minutes and held an opening party later that week with beers and some hip hop pumping out of the back of a Transit van.' About 500 people turned up to an opening which had cost almost nothing to set up – 'We nicked all the materials except for about four pounds worth of black paint,' Banksy told a fellow graffiti writer who interviewed him soon afterwards.

There were twelve stencilled images painted on this clean white background, edged in black, and below them a message that read 'Speak softly. But carry a big can of paint.' The whole thing was so informal that it was virtually painting to order: you could actually see a stencil on the wall, put down a deposit and a week later go round and pick up your painting in a version stencilled on to canvas. It sounds incredible now, but this was in the days before the name Banksy meant anything to anybody beyond his own world. No one was making big money and no one was asking for provenance. Soon after the exhibition finished, the wall which he had used to display his wares was knocked through to provide one of the entrances to Cargo, one of the new restaurant-bars springing up across Shoreditch. They did have the decency to give him an exhibition, and a couple of well-protected Banksys can still be seen on the wall of Cargo's yard.

In the same year there was another Banksy exhibition that is hardly ever mentioned now. In March Banksy and a small gang of helpers hired a van and slogged up to Glasgow for an exhibition called Peace is Tough, which was to be held at the Arches, another café-bar/restaurant. To be fair to Banksy, he was not headlining the exhibition; Jamie Reid, the man who in putting a safety pin through the Queen's lips defined the visual style of the Sex Pistols, was supposed to be the crowd drawer. But punk was a little too old and Banksy a little too new, and the crowds never came. 'No more than five people turned up,' is how one person who was there remembers it. It can't have been as bad as that, but measured by the exhibitions that followed it was the only real failure Banksy has ever had.

Next came a very small and slightly chaotic show in a right-on Los Angeles gallery and bookshop called 33 1/3. It was advertised as an 'exhibition of graffiti, lies and deviousness' and although it is hardly remembered now it almost sold out. Banksy in those early days could afford to be rather more casual about his identity than he is now. One collector who bought a canvas there remembers him hanging around the show 'eavesdropping on people's comments without identifying himself. The idea seems to be that if he can earn his daily bread by selling paintings rather than by clerking or delivering pizzas, why the hell not.'

At the end of 2002 he launched the first of what has become something of a Banksy institution – if there can be such a thing: Santa's Ghetto. This first one was upstairs in a small room at the Dragon Bar in Leonard Street, Shoreditch, which at that time was one of the favoured hangouts for graffiti writers. A collector who visited it said, 'There were canvases all over the place. It was pretty chaotic and a one-off became almost an edition.' The poster for the ghetto advertised 'gift wrapped trinkets of vandalism for the whole family' and anyone lucky enough to be shopping for Christmas presents could buy some very valuable trinkets. An artist who was there said, 'A friend of mine and his girlfriend bought one for about £300 and ended up selling it for about £70,000.' It was here too that his canvas of Queen Victoria enjoying oral sex from one of her female subjects was given its first showing; it was to be sold at Sotheby's in 2008 for £277,000.

But although Santa's Ghetto continues, selling the work of Banksy and other artists (for Christmas 2011 it was replaced by an exhibition of prints at Banksy's gallery), the days of the small exhibition were over. With one exception Banksy was now going for size and surprise. Turf War, his breakthrough exhibition in July 2003, was staged in a former warehouse in Hackney, a true 'pop-up' show in the days before 'pop-up' had come to mean semi-permanent. It lasted for only three days but it established Banksy as the leader of the new movement in British art, the street artists who were prepared to come in from the cold – artists who painted walls *and* sold canvases.

When Andy Warhol first exhibited at the Stable Gallery in New York in 1962, a rival gallery manager noticed that 'There were lots of young people there and I didn't know where they came from; they weren't from the art world.' The art critic William Wilson called it 'the first circus opening, the first gallery-event . . . the first party opening'. Banksy was not only using some of Warhol's images, he was using some of his party tricks too. You could call the show a bit of a circus but that was what it was supposed to be. There were no performing dogs, no circus lions, no elephants (those were to come next). But there was an attention-grabbing cow sprayed with rather macabre images of Warhol, pigs sprayed in blue and white police colours, sheep painted in concentration camp stripes, the Queen portrayed as a chimp, Churchill with a green Mohican – very much an exhibition that shouted 'Look at me.' A fan who was there on the first night says, 'It really took off. The private view was so dangerous. It was really crowded. Everyone was smoking. People were graffitiing the walls, writing things like "you fucking sell-out" on the stencils that he had done on the walls, and amazingly Banksy didn't seem to mind at all. There was a random mix of celebrities. There were queues outside and girls from *Vogue* in high heels and high fashion demanding that they didn't have to queue in front of some really skanky warehouse in Dalston – this was in the days before Dalston got cool.'

Just before the exhibition opened, Banksy told Simon Hattenstone in the *Guardian* how excited he was. 'A part of me wishes I could go because I've put together a really nice setup.' He decided it was too risky to be inside on opening night but some years later he revealed he was on the pavement outside. 'I saw a load of local yoots, some famous people in a Mercedes, two pimps shouting, four broadcast units from TV stations, and two Koreans selling food from the back of their car to the people waiting in line to get in. I guess it was what you'd call cosmopolitan.' The day after the exhibition opened Banksy went inside. Unfortunately his timing was not very good, for the police had got there just before him and were asking one of the exhibition staff if Banksy was there or not. 'I'm sorry I can't help, I don't know who Banksy is,' the staff member lied to them. 'But just as I was saying this I saw Banksy stroll into the exhibition. He must have seen the police at that moment, because he moved along quite quickly as though he was looking at the paintings and then he very calmly walked straight out again.'

For all Banksy's genuine dislike of brands, the exhibition itself did receive some small financial backing from Puma, a company that had been involved in the exhibition in Los Angeles and which obviously thought being associated with Banksy would do its street cred good. Visitors were given three postcards and a single black latex glove with the Puma logo on it, as a slightly unusual way of reminding them that Puma was providing some sponsorship. In addition you could buy a sort of official Banksy T-shirt with the Puma logo on the sleeve.

As for the painted animals, Banksy offered two explanations for them. One went: 'If you come from outside London they give you a lot of shite about being a country bumpkin. So I thought, right, I'll give 'em country bumpkin – I'll just get all these animals together and paint them.' The second was rather more serious: 'Our culture is obsessed with brands and branding. I'm taking the idea of branding back to its original roots, which is cattle branding. I call it Brandalism.' In truth the animals needed no explanation. They did the trick; they were a very good publicity stunt. When one of Banksy's camp called animal welfare campaigners and gave them a tip-off – anonymously of course – that the animals were being mistreated, there was another round of publicity. An animal rights protestor chained herself with a bike lock to the railings which penned in Andy Warhol's cow. Steve Lazarides' response was simple enough: 'The animals are well cared for and I'm just going to leave the protester to it. Visitors will just think she is part of the exhibition.' The show had to close a day early but it didn't matter: Banksy was not yet a household name but he had gone way beyond the boundaries of the street.

After the first Santa's Ghetto in Shoreditch, Banksy continued to create a pop-up Ghetto almost every Christmas, starting in Carnaby Street in 2003 and then sticking closely to the Soho area except for a rather distant diversion he took one year to Bethlehem. They were always slightly haphazard, fun and very different from most art galleries. One year, for instance, there was a wall downstairs called the Chancer's Wall: if you were a chancer, you could take your canvas or whatever you wanted, put it up on the wall and hope a buyer would chance upon it. Pure Evil put up a Panda print there; Banksy's girlfriend bought it and eventually it was released by Banksy's gallery as an edition of 700. The next year Pure Evil was back at the Ghetto manning a 'remixed' fairground stall where you could throw hoops over the Virgin Mary and other religious icons. As we talk a few years later in his own gallery, he says simply: 'I wouldn't be sitting here if it wasn't for Banksy.'

In those days the Ghettos were still relatively casual. In 2006, for example, a blackboard announced: 'Events for December' and the events chalked in casually below included 'Mon 18th New Banksy print. Edition 1000. Unsigned. £100. One per person.' In contrast, the next day there was going to be a performance by 'Dynamo The UK's finest street magician'.

But these Ghettos housed other artists and other japes. Santa alone was not going to do it for Banksy, he had to go it alone. And 2005 was the year that helped turn him into a superstar. His punk incursions into galleries in London, New York and Paris were followed by a trip to Israel to paint the concrete wall on the West Bank, part of the barrier built to try to stop suicide bombers. Banksy was not the first to paint on the wall but he was certainly the best. Everything good about Banksy was on display in these paintings. They made his point about the awfulness of the wall, but they made it in a subtle way, far better than any slogan could. They were very specific to the site; they were poignant and there was no need to walk into a gallery to see them.

Whether it was the pony-tailed girl hanging on to eight balloons as she gets lifted to the top of the wall, the two stencilled children with bucket and spade dreaming of their own bright and colourful Caribbean beach (the effect achieved by a coloured poster pasted on to the wall), or the boy with a simple escape route: a crude ladder painted all the way to the top, all the images talked of escape from this depressing, dispiriting environment. None of this lasted very long but it did not matter, they were photographed and soon up on the web for all the world to see.

So, by the time of Banksy's next show, Crude Oils, two months after his trip to Israel, his name was much better known and he did not need all the razzmatazz of Turf War. This time his exhibition might have had the feel of a slightly more traditional gallery show, but there was one important difference: 164 rats – real rats – running around the gallery. For twelve days he took over a shop located between a hairdresser and a smart restaurant on Westbourne Grove, west London. A man wearing a fez and handing out free postcards of Kate Moss remixed by Banksy in the style of Warhol's Marilyn Monroe (yours now for £4.99 plus postage on Amazon) was at the door holding back the first-night crowds. Banksy later claimed proudly: 'On the opening night, the neighbours showed up with some cops and six different health-and-safety inspectors, but they never managed to shut us down.'

To begin with, at least if you did not have the right pass, you were allowed in for only three minutes, which did not give too much time to dodge the rats and see the paintings. There was a lot of very clever reworking of masters old and new: Hopper, Monet, Van Gogh, Warhol all had the Banksy treatment, and even *Modified Oil Painting No 6*, the painting he had slipped into the Tate two years earlier, made another appearance. While no longer in the Tate, it was at least hanging close to a museum attendant, or rather the skeleton of a museum attendant, slumped against a wall with the rats finding a home amongst all his crevices. Despite the rats, or maybe because of them, the exhibition did not create quite the stir of his first big show, although the Kate Moss canvas and print first shown here was eventually to prove one of Banksy's biggest money-spinners.

But there was another money-spinner still to come the same year, this time from an unexpected source. In November Century launched *Wall and Piece*, essentially a glossily repackaged version of his three self-published books with some additions – and a few deletions, usually for taste reasons. Thus in his self-published *Cut It Out* he describes precisely the ingredients and the fire extinguisher involved in spraying 'BORING' in huge ten-foot letters on the National Theatre and ends by saying: 'the perfect accompaniment to a night out drinking heavily with friends.' Whereas in *Wall and Piece* all this comes down to a much safer caption: 'Fire extinguisher with pink paint. Southbank, London 2004.' Similarly his detourned painting of the Virgin Mary holding baby Jesus with a suicide bomb attached to him had the caption beside it: 'Suicide bombers need a hug' in the original; perhaps understandably, this has disappeared in *Wall and Piece*. Again, his caption for Queen Victoria having oral sex reads much more rudely in the original than it does in *Wall and Piece*.

It is a book with instant appeal, enjoyable even for people who hate graffiti; it catalogues a great deal of his early work but nevertheless remains as far away from a catalogue raisonné as it is possible to imagine. At the front of the book he attempts to preserve his outsider status with a rather lame compromise: 'Against his better judgement Banksy has asserted his right under the Copyright, Designs and Patents Act, 1988 to be identified as the author of this work.' It is fortunate he could overcome his scruples, for the book has become something of a publishing phenomenon.

It is difficult now to find many mainstream reviews of the book, although the *Guardian* called it 'a grossly self-indulgent look at his work'. But it did not matter, for Banksy speaks and paints to a world beyond reviewers. Century's clout meant that *Wall and Piece* was placed at the front of bookshops, and from there browsers could pick it up, have a good laugh, buy it and tell their friends to buy it. Figures from Booktrack in the spring of 2012 show the hardback had sold over 135,000 copies, meaning a turnover of over £2 million for the publishers, and the paperback had reached 300,000 copies with a turnover of £3.5 million. But these figures probably represent no more than 70 per cent of sales, for while they include results from the bookstores and Amazon, they do not include places like HMV, Virgin and Urban Outfitters where Banksy was to be found, nor do they include foreign sales. Whatever percentage of all this Banksy was on, it was certainly worth him asserting his copyright.

If *Wall and Piece* spoke to fans way beyond the traditional art world, so too did his next two shows. The first, in September 2006, entitled Barely Legal to give it a little edge, was held in Los Angeles slightly less than a year after Westbourne Grove. The show seemed to be both a triumph and something of a disaster for Banksy. A triumph because the opening night was all valet parking and limos and Hollywood royalty, and so he made a lot of money – a reputed £3 million, although this figure has never been confirmed – while also making a name for himself in America, which was vital when his film came out just over three years later. A disaster because every story thereafter tended to have a clause in it that went something like this: 'Banksy, whose work is collected by Angelina

Jolie and Brad Pitt among others . . .' For many artists the fact that Jolie and Pitt eventually spent over £1 million on their work or that Christina Aguilera spent £25,000 would seem like good news. Indeed Brad Pitt himself seemed envious; he told *The Times*, 'He does all this and he stays anonymous. I think that's great. These days everyone is trying to be famous. But he has anonymity.' But for Banksy it appears that the fame, the movie stars and the money caused him considerable confusion for some time afterwards.

The show was classic Banksy. A few months earlier Joel Unangst, who owns a 12,000 square foot former warehouse in downtown Los Angeles named The Poodle Parlor, got a call from a location service telling him, 'Hey, this guy wants to come by and look at your place for a potential art show.' He had never heard of Banksy but told them to send him on over. The warehouse, built in 1937, originally stored salt, then fruit and vegetables, but from 1996 it had operated as a location for music videos, commercials, still shoots; people bored with the idea of a hotel ballroom even staged their weddings there. But never an art show. The warehouse is in a slightly dodgy part of town, dodgy enough anyway for one Sotheby's executive visiting for Banksy's opening night to say she 'really worried about getting out of my car'.

Unangst describes what happened next: 'The first walk through it was Banksy and Thierry Guetta [of whom more later]. They showed up in Guetta's Bronco SUV – the thing was a piece of shit. Thierry was there with his camera filming and Banksy is wearing black shorts with some paint smudges on them, sneakers and a T-shirt with more paint on it. He seemed a nice enough guy.

'They did a quick walk through and then a group came back three weeks later and said they wanted to use my space.' When they arrived at the end of August to set up the exhibition, Unangst was impressed by Team Banksy. 'They brought with them a core group of about twelve from England and hired others from LA. These guys got down and got to it. They weren't a bunch of fuck-offs, they were serious.' So who was running the operation? 'There were some other people who were more in charge of running the crew and stuff. They were trying to free him up a little bit so he could concentrate on the work. Thinking in film terms it's like the director having an assistant director and production manager and that kind of thing, so that Banksy was a little bit insulated from the day-to-day stuff. He was there all the time.' Banksy, he said, 'has a fantastic mind even though he's quiet and little bit unassuming.

'They liked to relax and have fun, but it was a brutal schedule and it was pizza, beer and ska music that kept them going. They'd come in at ten or eleven in the morning then work until midnight, go out until three or four putting stuff up all over Los Angeles and then come back and do it all over again the next day.'

The scale of the whole operation, creating all the artwork, shipping it over, hiring the warehouse – $25,000 for about three weeks – flying over the whole team, seemed beyond Banksy. The story in Los Angeles was that it had all been funded by Damien Hirst, but although it made a good rumour it was completely untrue. It is a measure of how far they had come in such a short time that with the proceeds of their two main British exhibitions, Turf Wars and Crude Oils, Banksy and Steve Lazarides took a big gamble and financed the Los Angeles exhibition themselves. At one moment it looked as though their gamble might fail: a semi-trailer full of Banksy's work had reached the West Coast but had then been held by US customs. When it was eventually released, what should have been a leisurely final ten days was forced into a frenetic three.

# SPRAY IT OUT LOUD

**Barton Hill Youth Club's unique experiments with graffiti art have brought it an international reputation. And the less welcome attention of the local police, who maintained that the Club's activities were the cause of criminal damage elsewhere in Bristol. Dom Phillips reports. Pics by Carrie Hitchcock.**

'YOUTH LEADER IS CLEARED OVER VANDALISM' screamed the recent Evening Post headline - final chapter in a court case saga that's been running for over a year now. Barton Hill youth club leader John Nation, the man behind the successful graffiti art project at the club that's attracted national as well as local media attention, was cleared of inciting young graffiti artists to commit criminal damage. The prosecution invited the judge to return a 'not guilty' verdict, offering no evidence on the original charge - that by providing a legal site for artists to work on, John Nation had in fact been inciting them to graffiti illegally.

This was the final court case from Operation Anderson, last year's West Country police crackdown on graffiti. 72 artists were arrested in total; names and addresses taken from the club, John Nation's collection of photos (running

All of these artists have benefitted from the Barton Hill project — which has brought together youngsters from all over the city, channelled the energies and talents, and brightened up a blighted clubhouse, now a beacon of colour in a grey high-rise landscape.

Barton Hill Boys Club was established in the 1920's, later moving to its present site and becoming Barton Hill Youth Club. For many years it stayed predominantly white and male; hostile to outsiders, the club maintained a strong identity and territorialism. Then in the

graffiti groups in this country and abroad. There's been visits to and from Europe; New York's Vul
pay their respe
walls they've be
up are adding a
Pauls and Newt

Publicity has
(Jody) was featu
and the club ev
1989 World Str
judged by Sub
Chelloni, among
need is space a

*Venue* magazine reporting on Barton Hill Youth Club which John Nation had turned into the home of graffiti in Bristol. *Courtesy of Neil Clark*

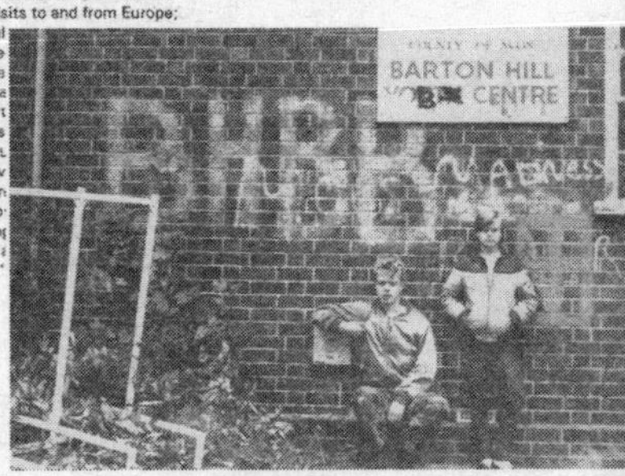


A wall of the Youth Club before and after (below) graffiti writers had got to work. *Courtesy of Neil Clark; Courtesy of Cheo*

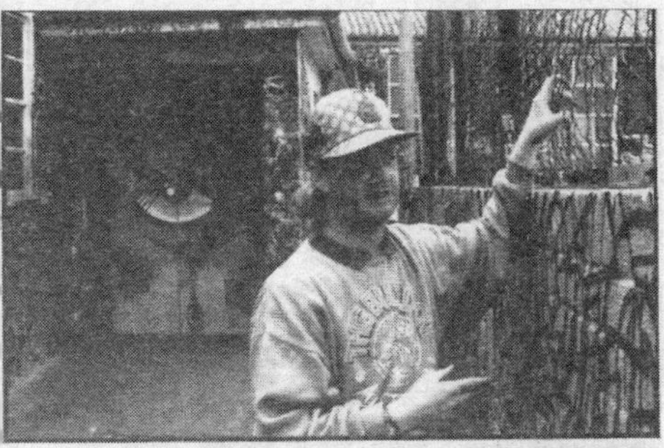

**John Nation. "People don't want to give credit to something that is primarily a working class movement".**

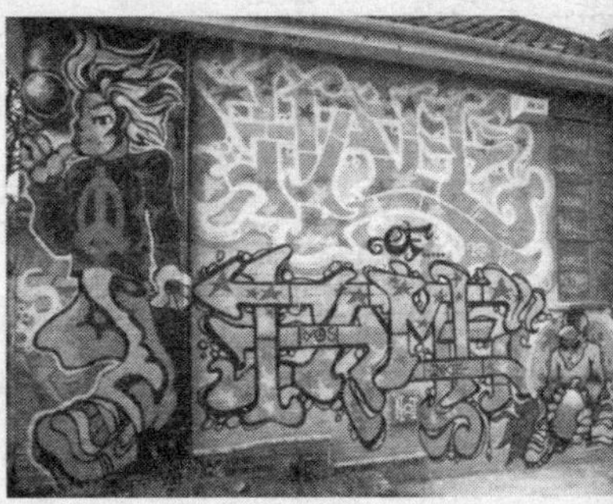

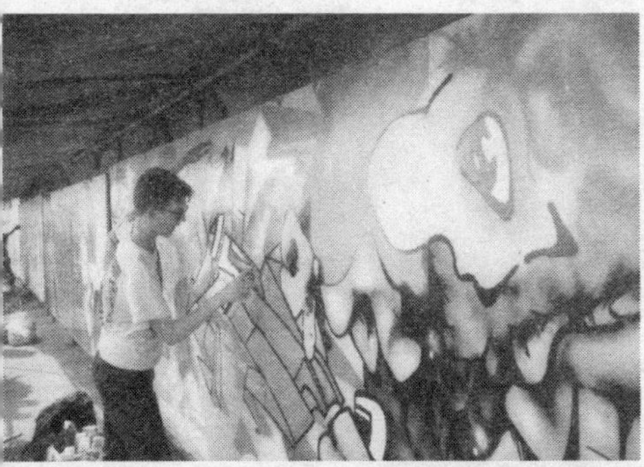

Bristol graffiti artist, Inkie, painting at the World Graffiti art competition in 1989 – he and his fellow painter Cheo came second. *Courtesy of Cheo*

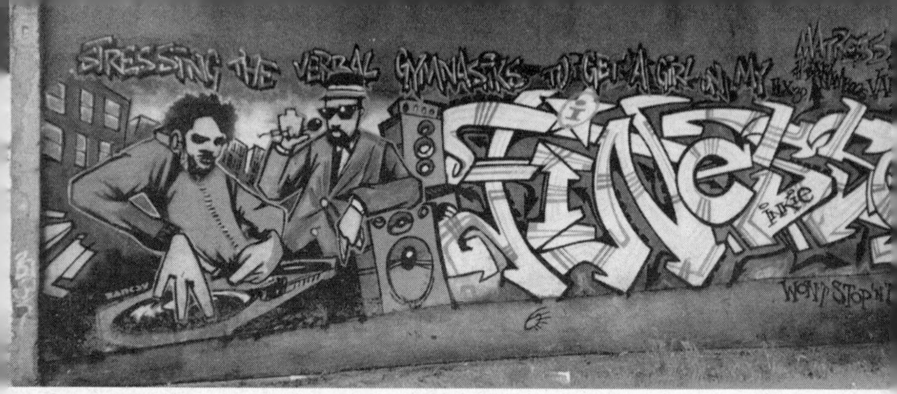

Banksy, with the DJ on the left and Inkie with classic graffiti lettering on the right, collaborated on this piece in St Paul's, Bristol in 1999.

Two panels from Walls on Fire, a graffiti exhibition organised by Banksy and Inkie in 1998 using 400 metres of hoardings around building work at Bristol harbour. The right-hand piece is by Inkie.

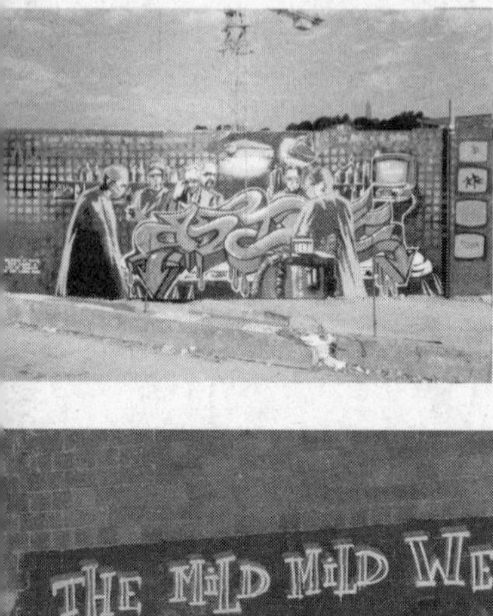

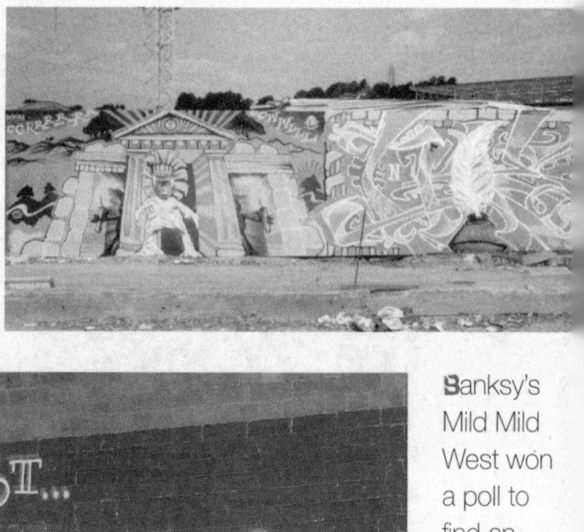

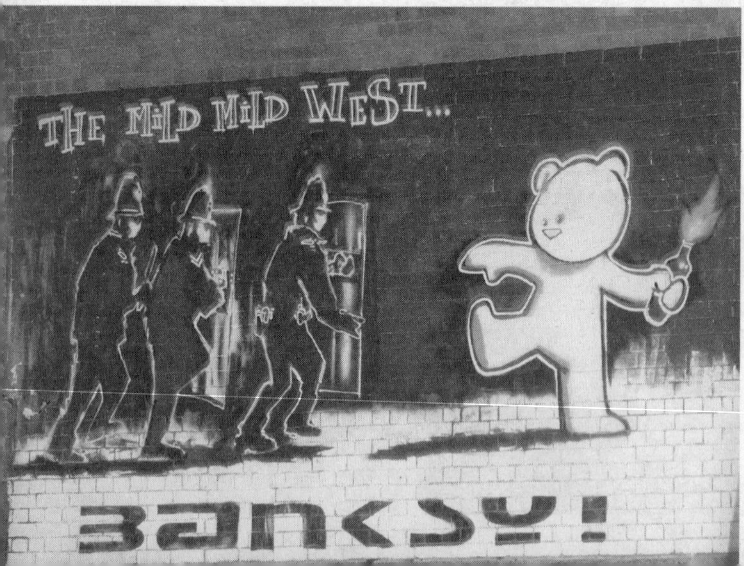


Banksy's Mild Mild West won a poll to find an alternative landmark for Bristol. It has been splattered in paint but not destroyed.

*John Mills/ Rex Features*

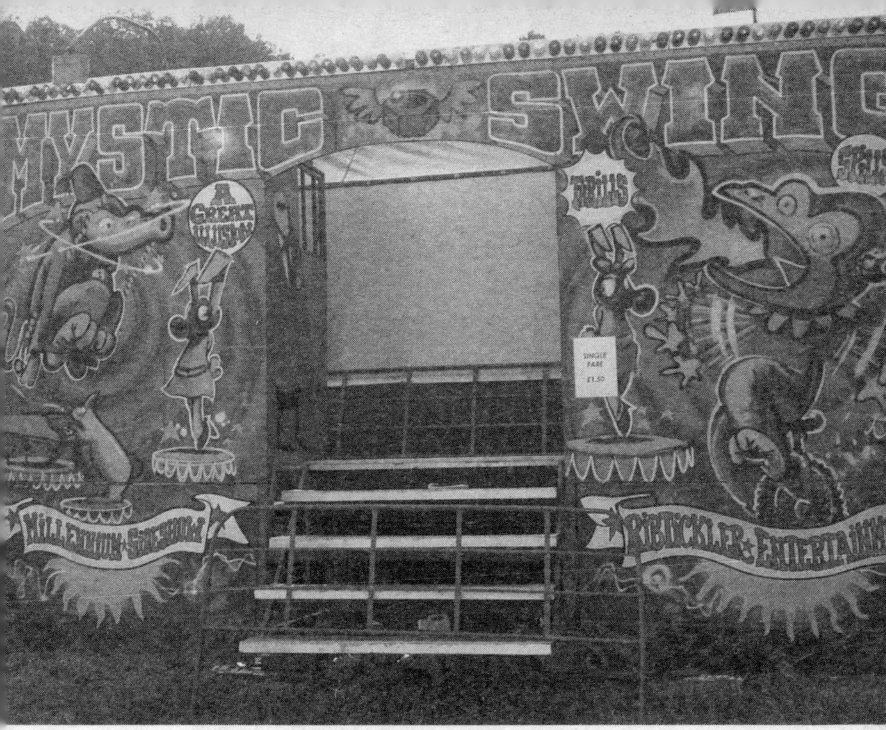


The front of the travelling fairground ride, Mystic Swing, painted by Dave 'W.E.T.' Panit and Banksy in 2000. Panit painted his section by day and Banksy used a headtorch to paint at night. *Courtesy of Mark Walton (tmunki)*

A punk having trouble with the instructions on a wall near the IKEA store in Croydon. The wall was cut out by two Banksy fans who have turned down an offer of £240,000 for it. *© JCB-Images/Alamy*

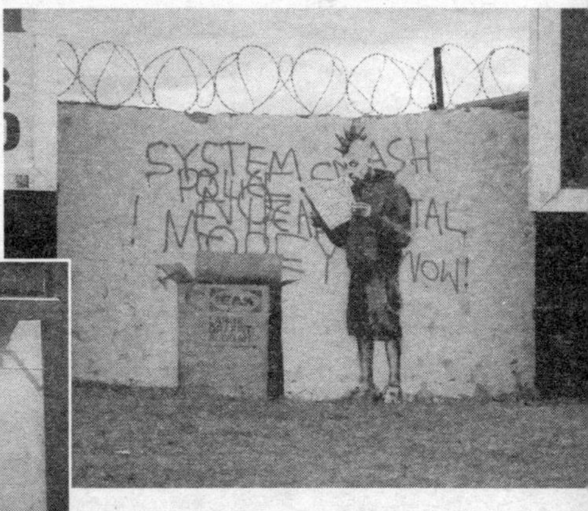


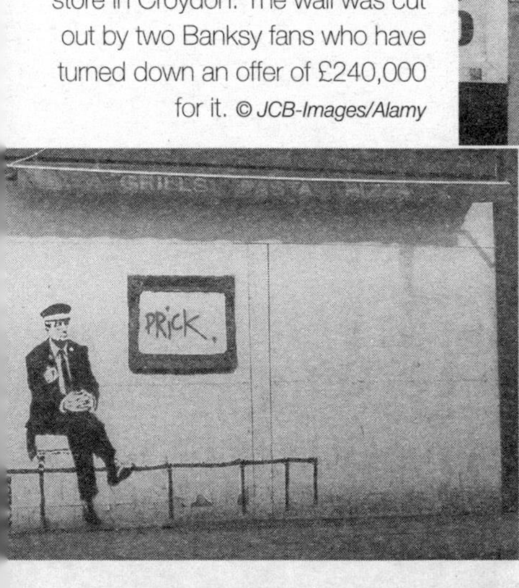


PRICK painted on a boarded up shop in Liverpool. Bought for £500 and sold for around £200,000 in New York although never authenticated by Banksy. *William Fallows*

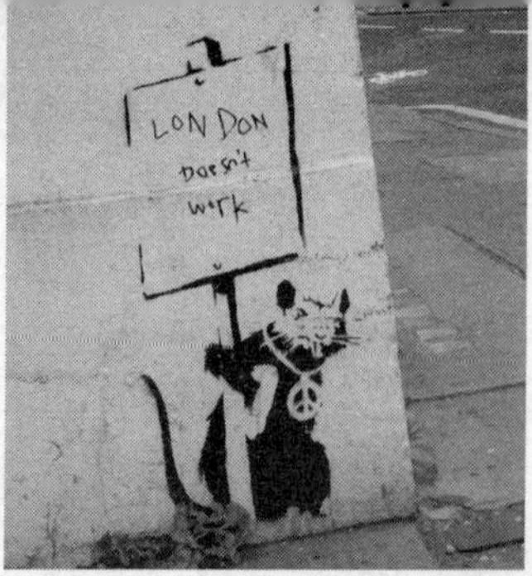



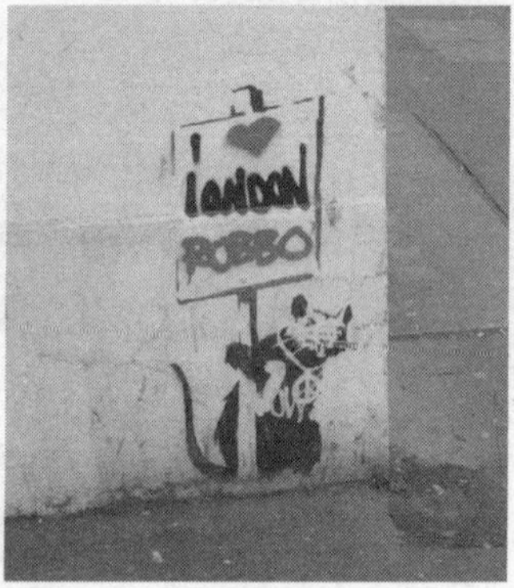



A Banksy placard-holding rat near the Barbican arts centre in London. The placard was later transformed by Team Robbo to read 'I love London'. *Nicholas Baily/Rex Features; Author's Collection*

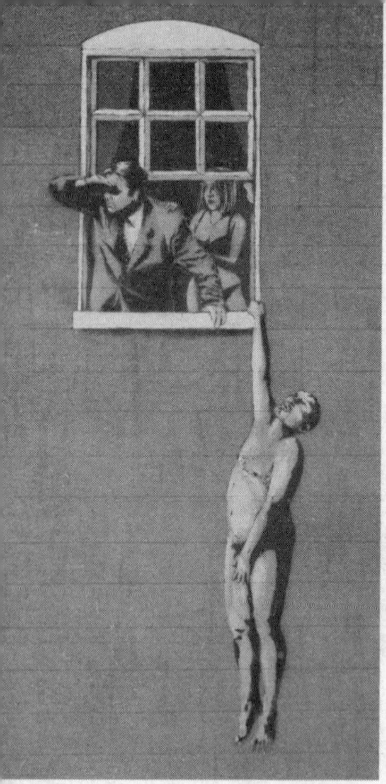

Banksy's piece on a Sexual Health Clinic for Young People in Bristol. In a referendum organised by the council 93 per cent of those who voted said it should be allowed to stay. *David Beauchamp/Rex Features*

Sunrise at Boghenge, Banksy's contribution to Glastonbury 2007. He borrowed the portaloos from Glastonbury organiser Michael Eavis and set them up in the Sacred Space field. Some of them later appeared at the entrance to his exhibition in Bristol. *David Pearson/Rex Features*

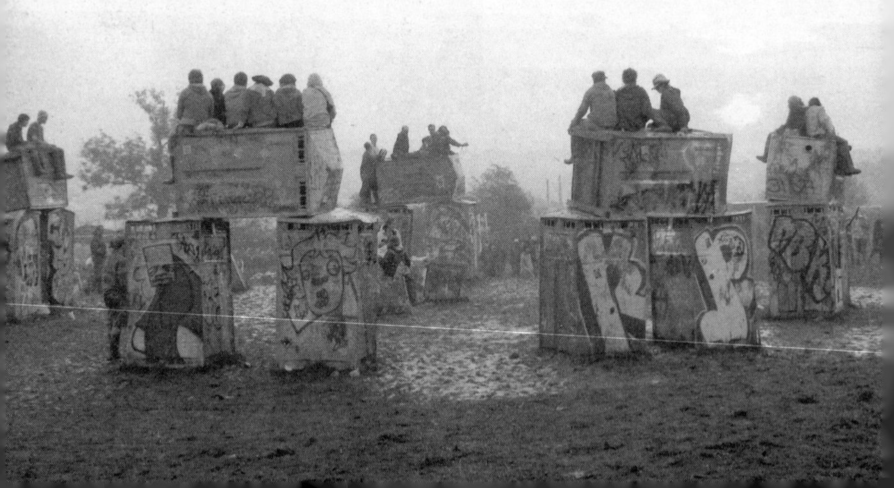

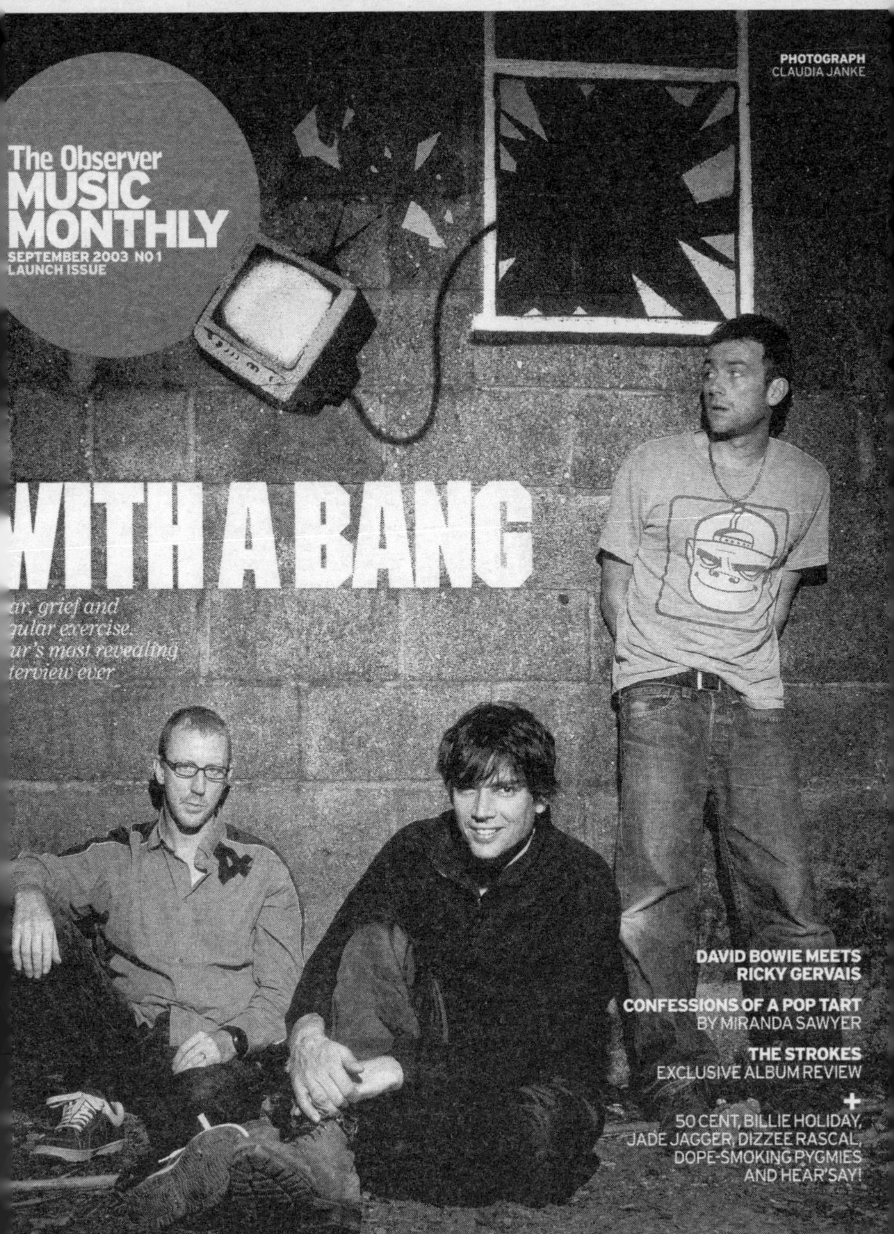


The first edition of *The Observer Music Monthly* magazine: Blur are photographed in front of the wall of a farmer's barn which Banksy had decorated with a tv being thrown out of a window in classic rock star fashion.

*© Guardian News & Media Ltd 2003; Photographer Claudia Janke*

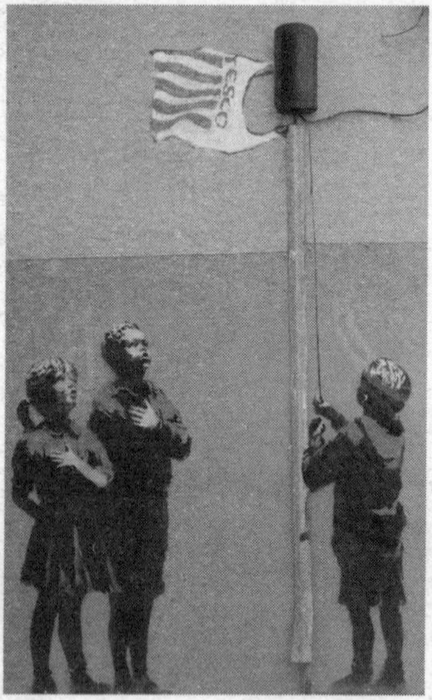

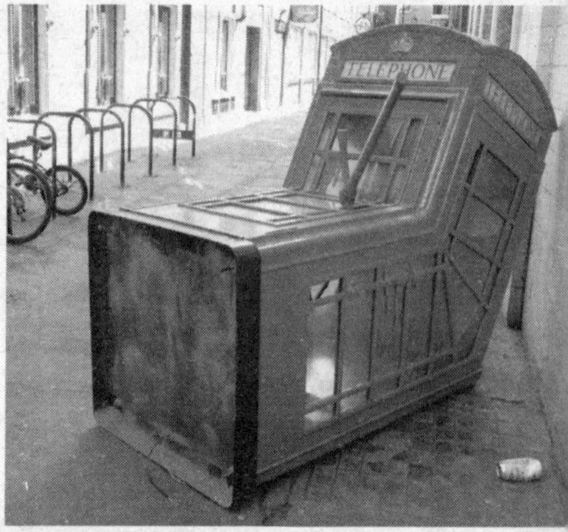


A crumpled red telephone box, complete with pick-axe, which Banksy placed in Soho. It was later sold at a charity auction in New York for $605,000. *Rex Features*

Banksy painted this homage to Tesco on the side of a chemist's shop in Essex Road, Islington in 2008. Although the children were later protected by plastic the piece has since been irretrievably defaced. *Jeff Blackler/Rex Features*

The various painted animals at Banksy's Turf War exhibition in 2003 caused animal rights protestors to object which in turn gained the exhibition more publicity. *Alex Sudea/Rex Features*

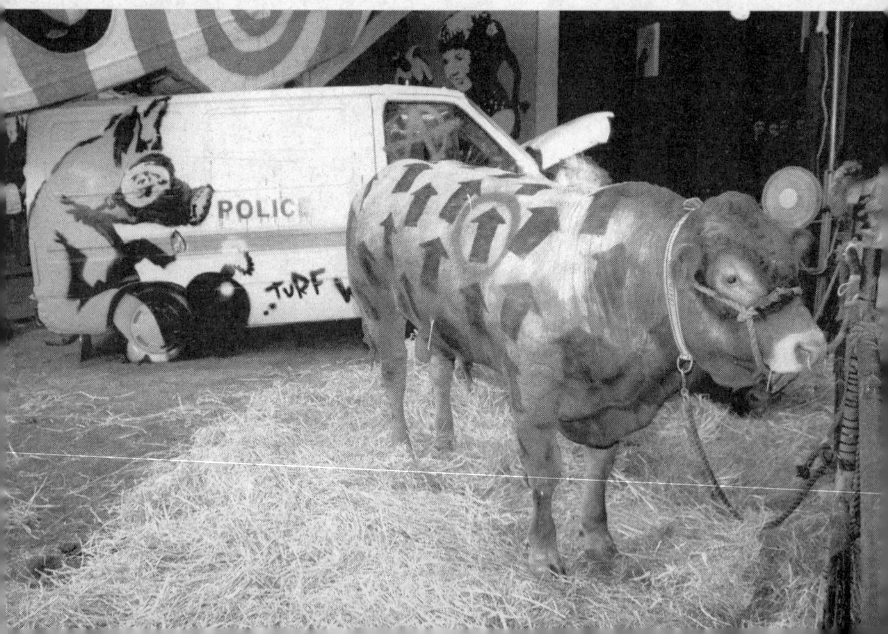

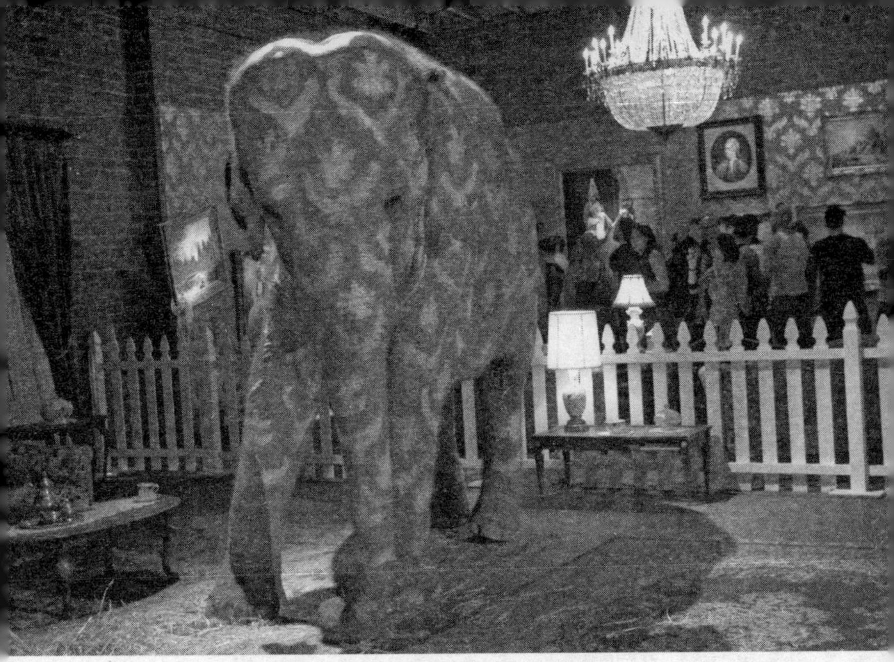

Tai, a 38 year old elephant painted (in non-toxic paint) by Banksy, became one of the stars of his 2006 Los Angeles sell-out show, Barely Legal.

*B Kvartuc/Keystone USA/Rex Features*

Banksy's Santa's Ghetto in Oxford Street, 2006; the ghetto has become an annual event around Christmas selling Banksy and other artists' work.

*Ray Tang/Rex Features*

A sign at the entrance to Leake Street, underneath Waterloo's railway tracks. Banksy rented this tunnel for a festival of street artists from around the world.

*Author's Collection*

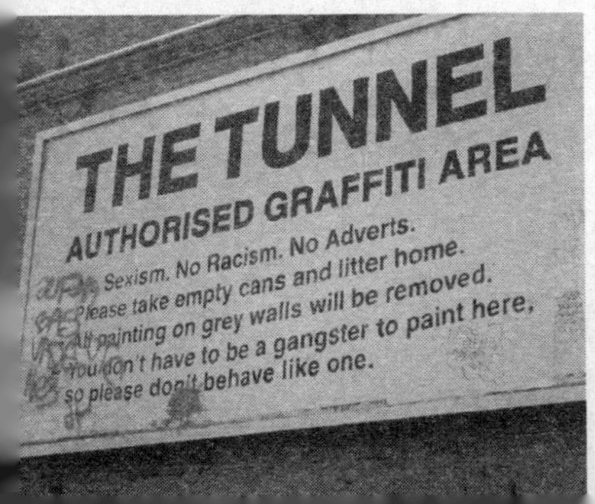


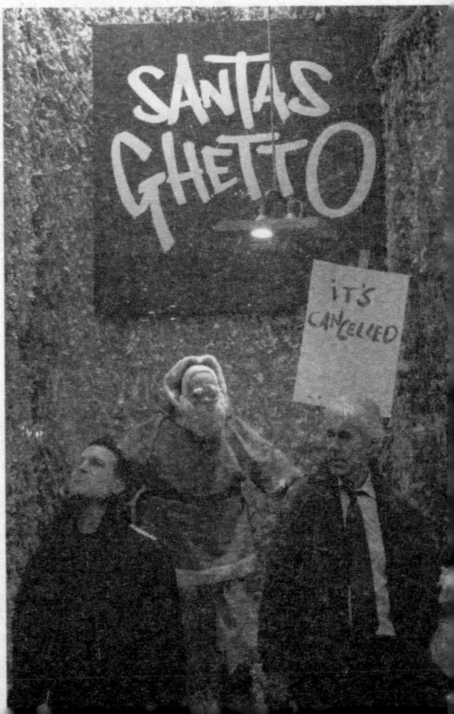

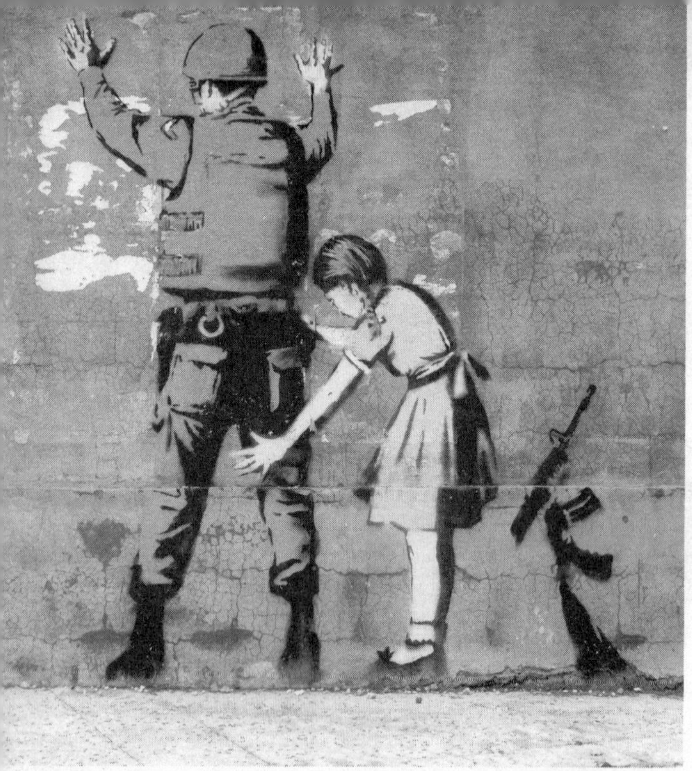

An Israeli soldier gets frisked by a young girl; painted on a wall in Bethlehem, the wall was shipped across to New York where it awaits a buyer.
*© Dan De Kleined/ Alamy*

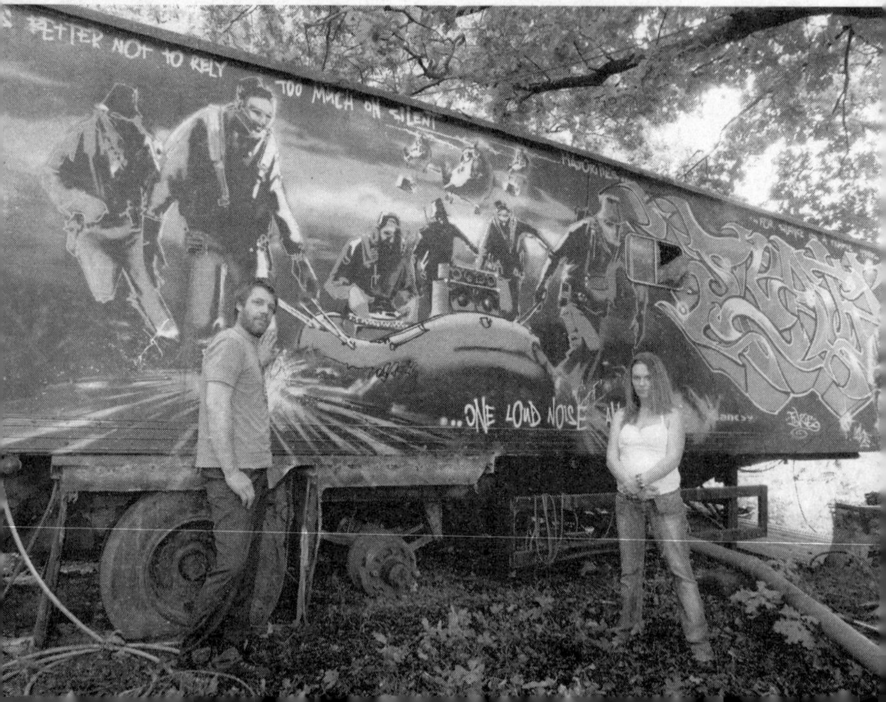


Maeve Neale and Nathan Wellard stand in front of their home, an articulated lorry that Banksy painted at Glastonbury.
*Albanpix Ltd/ Rex Features*

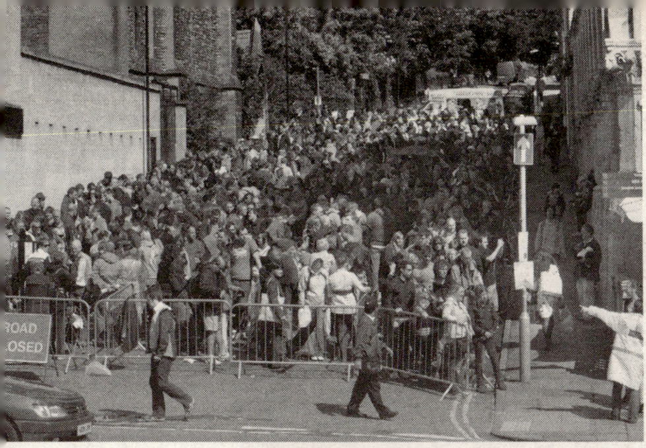


The queue for the Banksy exhibition in Bristol. It was the second most visited exhibition in Britain in 2009, just beaten by the Saatchi Gallery, and at peak times it could take four hours to get in.
*Barry Batchelor/PA Wire*

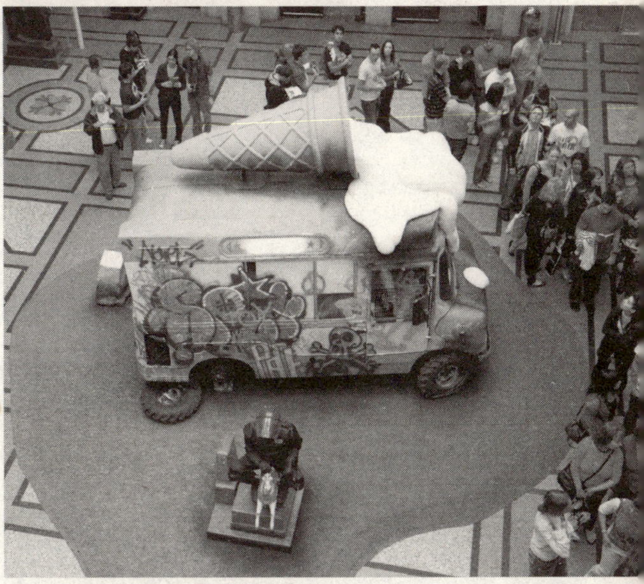

Crowds file past Banksy's ice cream van at the start of their visit to his exhibition at the Bristol City Museum.
*Jeff Blackler/Rex Features*

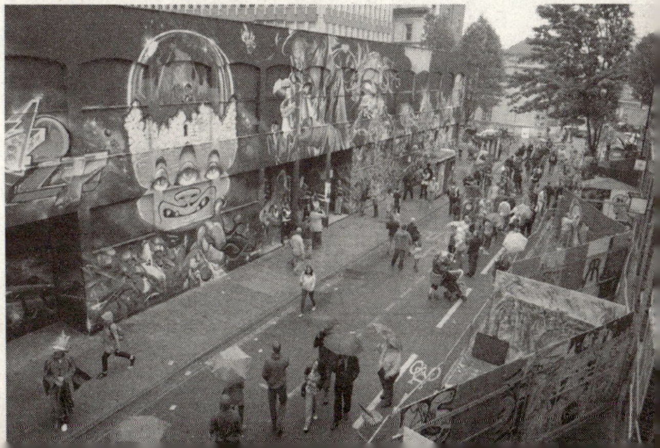

How Bristol embraced graffiti. The See No Evil street art exhibition in the city, organised by Inkie with the help of £40,000 from the city council, turned a depressing street in the city centre into one of the world's largest outdoor art exhibitions.
*PA Images*

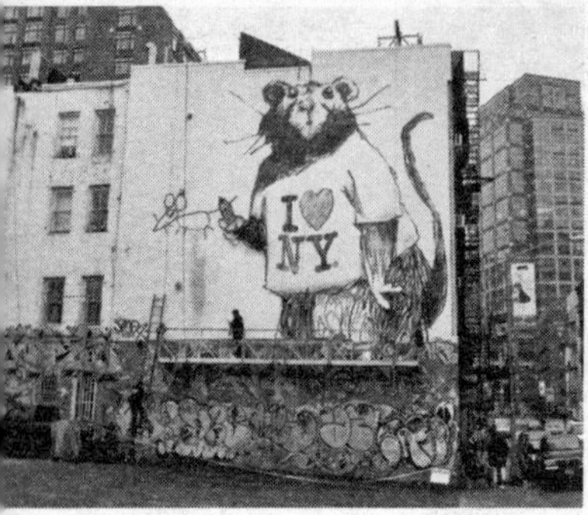


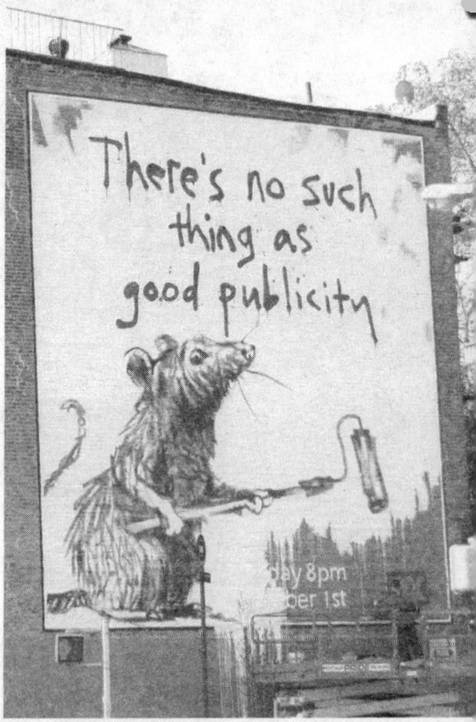


Rats in New York, two of four huge walls painted by Colossal Media following Banksy's design at the time of his Pet Shop exhibition in the city in the autumn of 2008. *Courtesy of Colossal Media*

Two animatronic chicken nuggets feed themselves at the Village Pet Store, the three-week exhibition that Banksy opened in New York in 2008. *Dima Gavrysh/Rex Features*

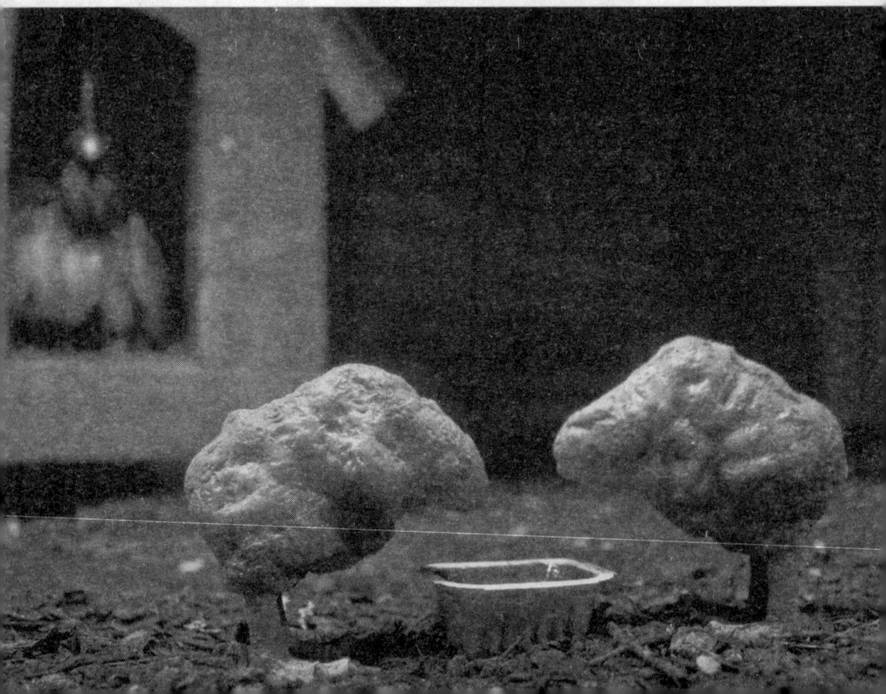

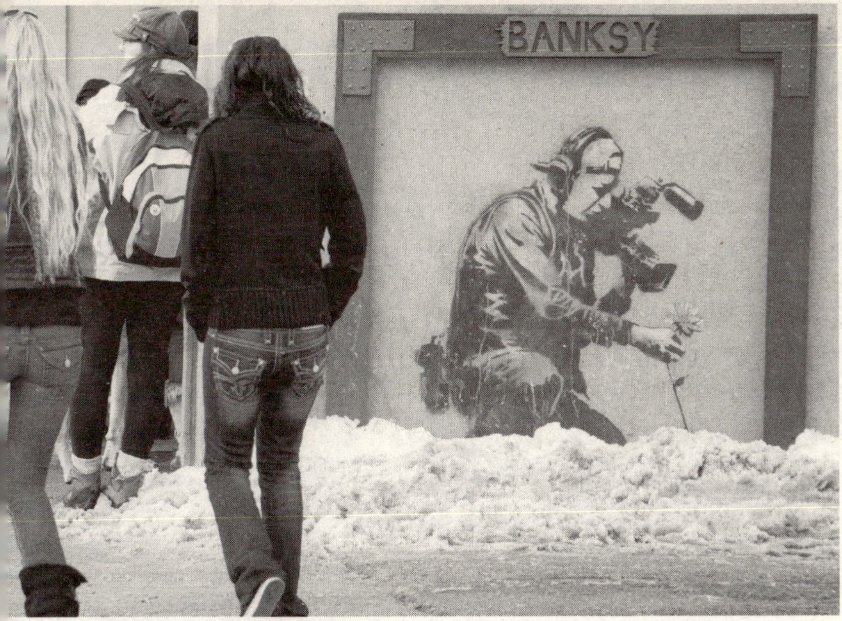


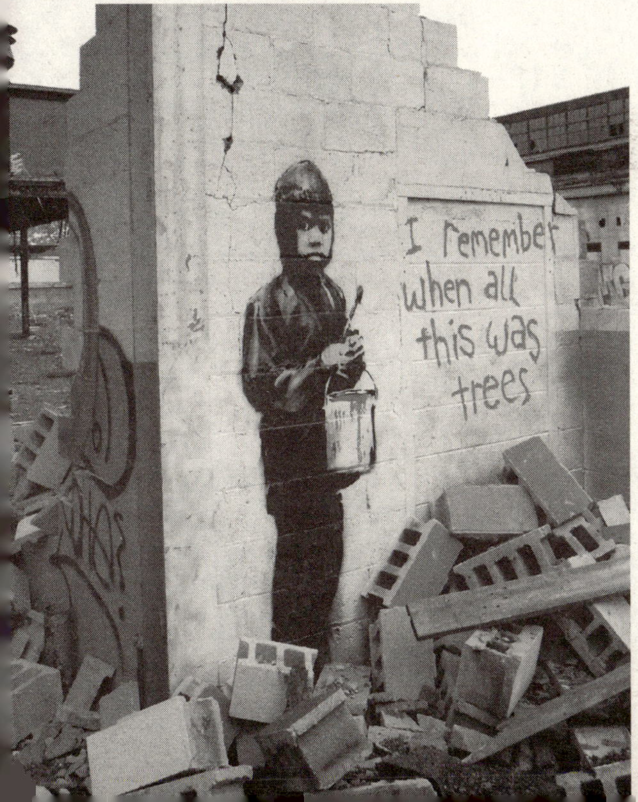


Banksy's artwork at Park City, home of the Sundance Film Festival, has been preserved behind plexiglass.
*Marcocchi Guilio/SIPA/ Rex Features*

Painted in the derelict Packard motor plant in Detroit; never authenticated but taken away to be put as a key exhibit in a new art gallery.
*© 2010 detroitfunk.com*

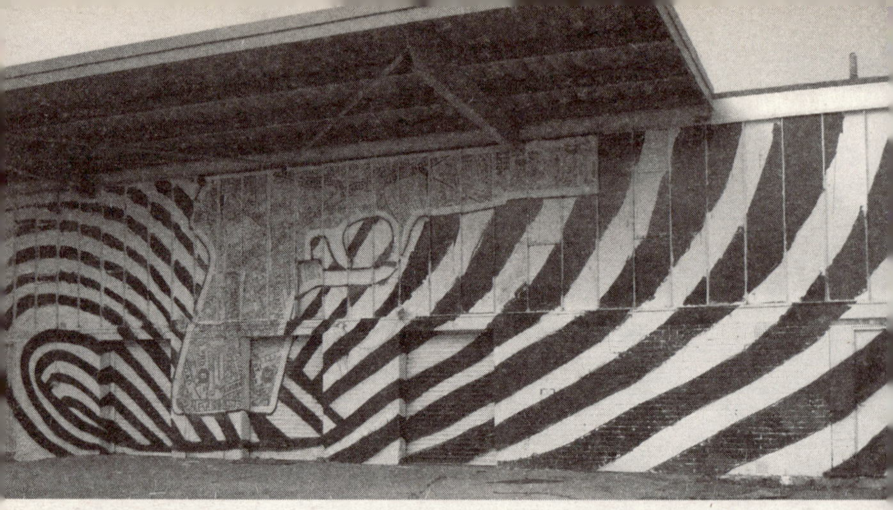

Murder Mile by Pure Evil painted in a site waiting redevelopment in north London. *Author's Collection*

Wall Street's charging bull that graffiti crochet artist Olek managed to cover up nicely in an extraordinary piece of crocheting. Her work lasted only a couple of hours before it was cut off.

*Work by Olek; Image courtesy of Jonathan LeVine Gallery*

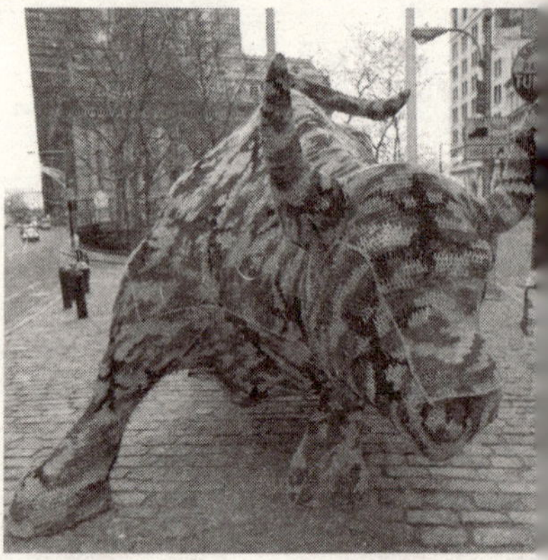

Graffiti artist Ben Eine's piece in Hackney, painted after David Cameron had surprised Eine and many others by selecting a work of his to give to President Obama on his first official visit to Washington. *Artofthestate*

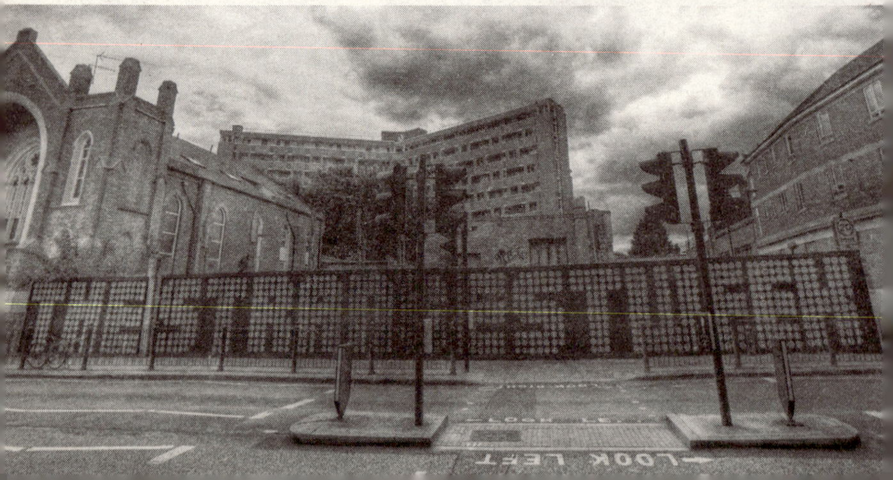

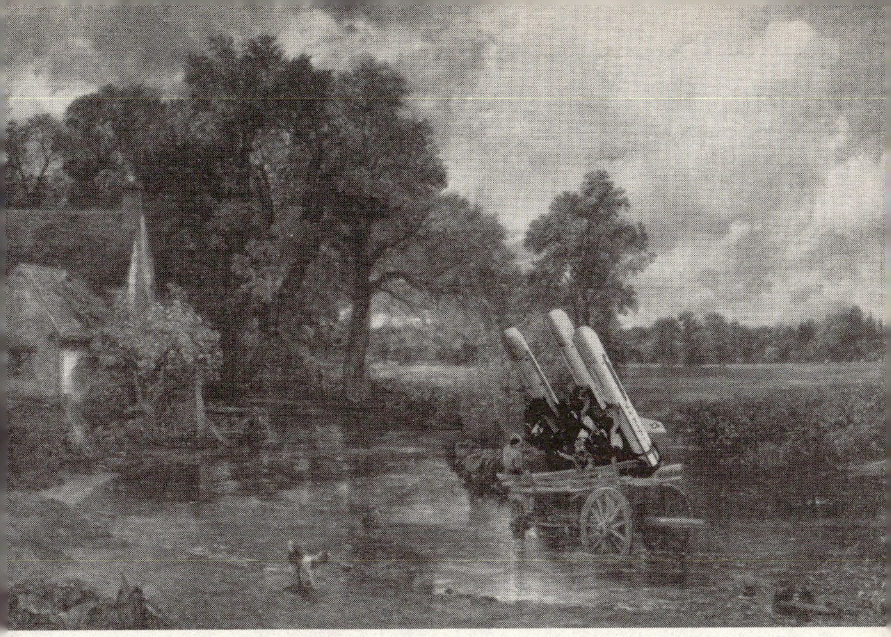

**H**aywain with Cruise Missiles (1980), Peter Kennard's detourned version of Constable's famous scene, bought by the Tate in 2007. *© Peter Kennard*

**G**raffiti for London by David Samuel. The tube map's station names have been replaced by the names of the city's top graffiti writers from 1980-2000 placed at the stop closest to where they were from. *Rarekind London*

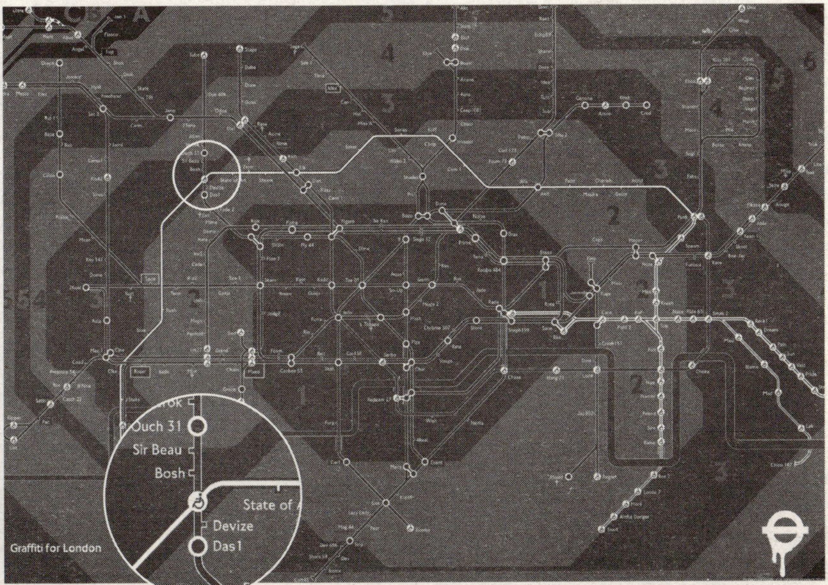

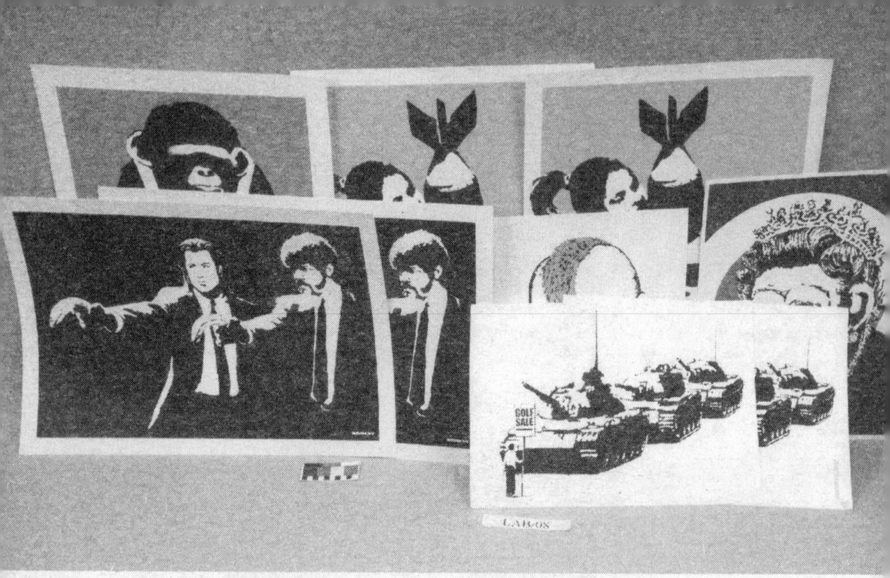


Some of the 120 fake Banksy prints discovered by the Metropolitan Police during their investigation into two men convicted of forging Banksys. *© Metropolitan Police*

A pouting girl holding an Oscar painted on a wall in Weston-super-Mare shortly after Banksy failed to win an Oscar for his film. Hailed as a new Banksy it later turned out to be a fake. *SWNS*

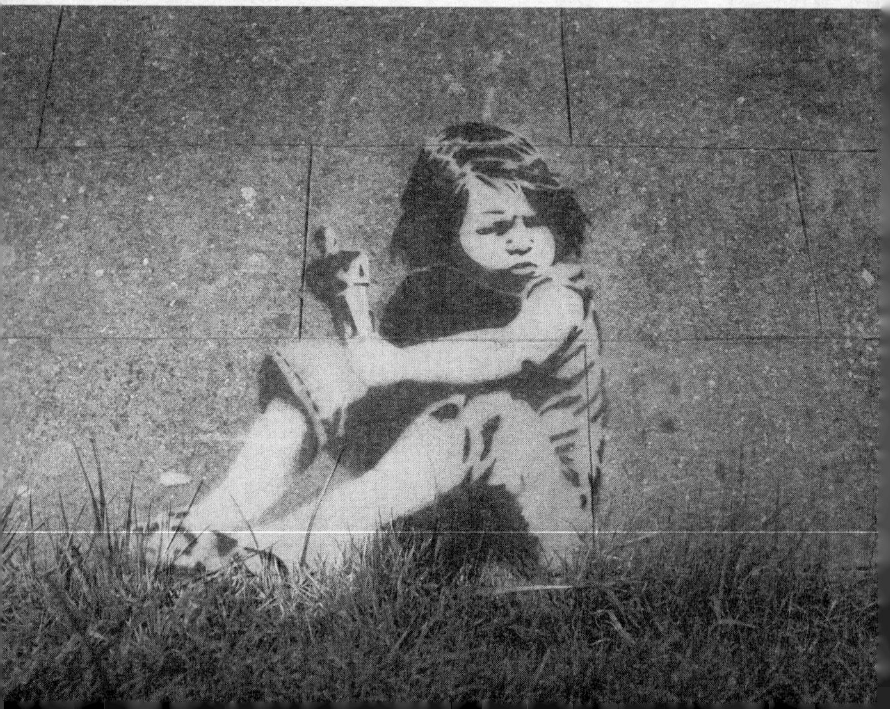

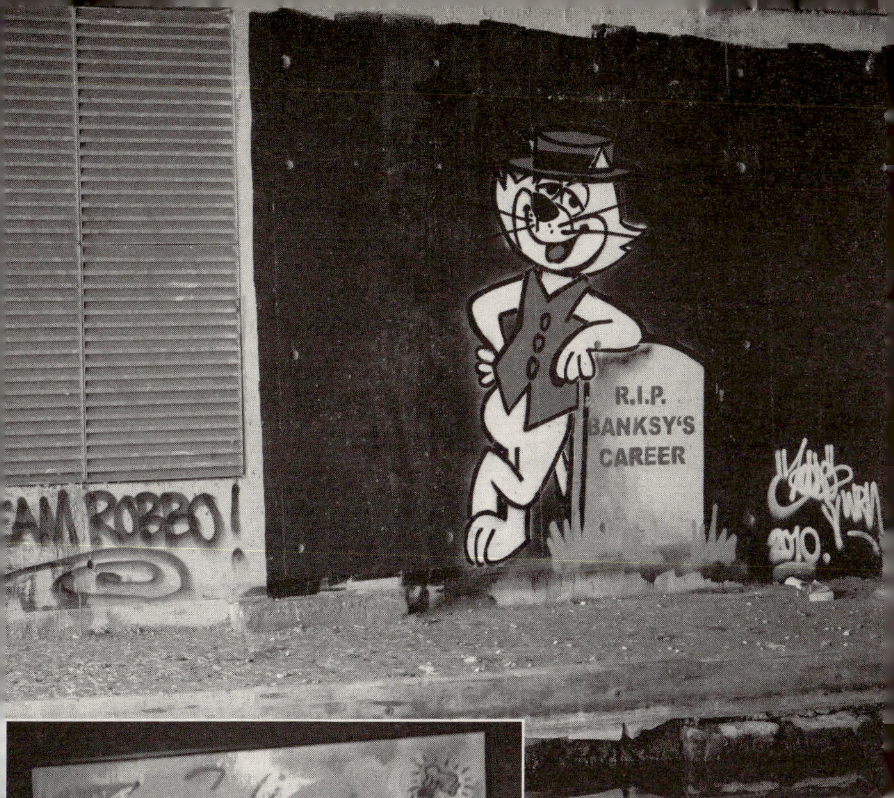


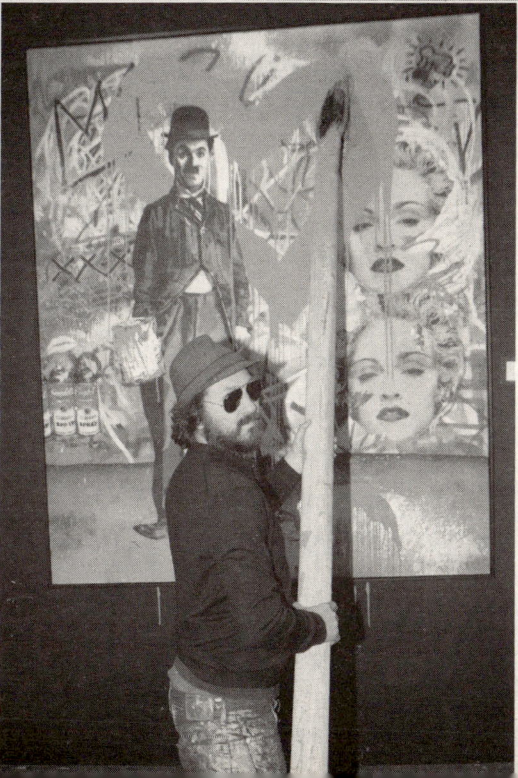

This image was painted by Team Robbo as part of the ongoing war between Robbo and Banksy over a wall beside the Regent's Canal near Camden Lock. Like others before it the image did not last long before Banksy, in turn, painted over it. *© LouisBerk.com*

Thierry Guetta or Mr Brainwash, star of Banksy's *Exit Through the Gift Shop* in front of one of his *Charlie Chaplin Pink* which sold for $122,500 at auction in New York in 2010. *AlamyCelebrity/Alamy*

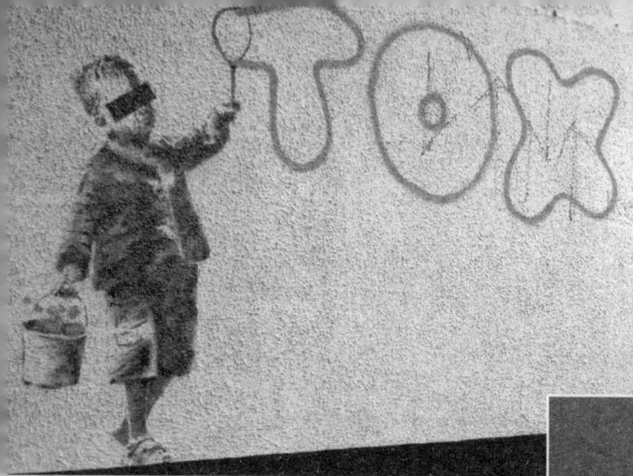


A wall in Camden with a piece believed to be Banksy in support of Tox, a graffiti artist jailed for twenty-seven months in 2011 for offences stretching back to 2000. *London News Service/ Rex Features*

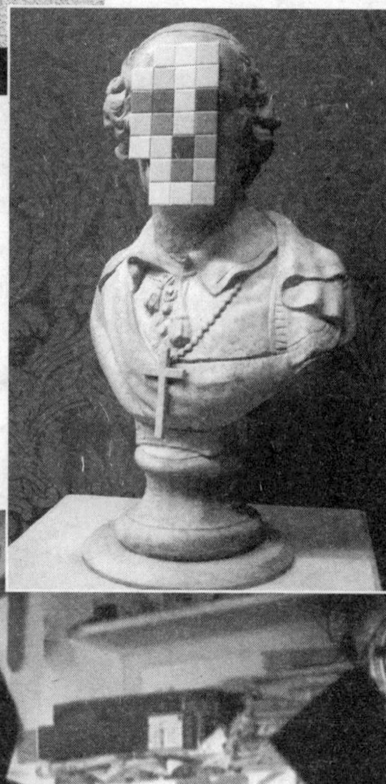

Cardinal Sin, a work given by Banksy on permanent loan to the Walker Art Gallery in Liverpool. He implied that it was a comment on the cases of children abused by Catholic priests. *Mark Sumner/Rex Features*

A well hooded Banksy, with his voice disguised, facing the camera in his film *Exit Through the Gift Shop*.
*C. Everett Collection/Rex Features*

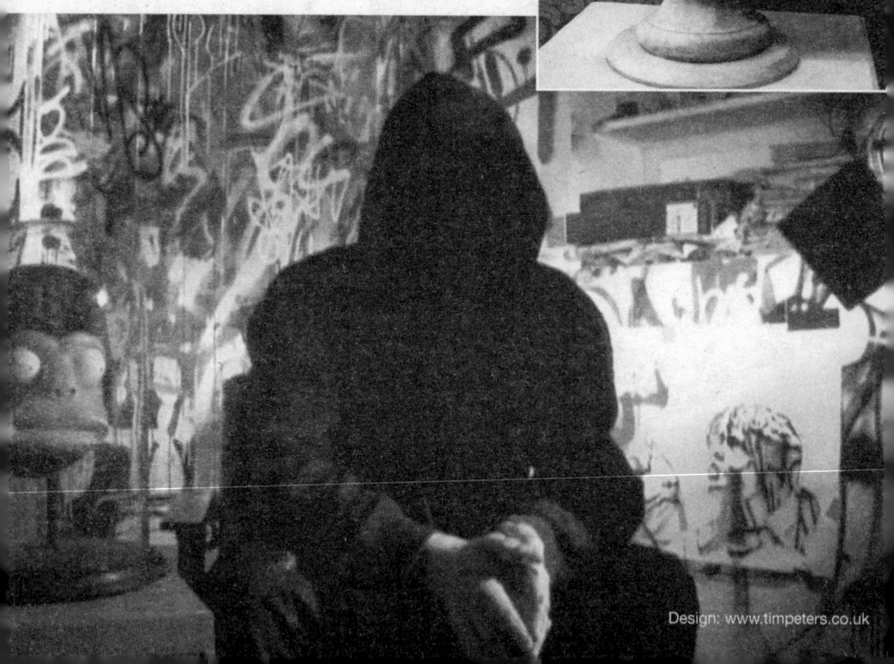

Design: www.timpeters.co.uk

Unangst remembers that when Team Banksy had been negotiating to use his warehouse they had said 'Is it OK if we bring in an elephant?' 'And I said "Sure, OK, if we get all the permits." For filming we've had horses, camels, grizzly bears, all different kinds of animals. it's not really a problem. Although they didn't really mention that they were going to paint it.'

It was quite a major point to 'forget'. For the rats, cows, pigs and sheep had all been replaced this time by just one rather big animal: 38-year-old Tai the elephant, or the 'painted pachyderm' as some journalists liked to call her. Like Banksy's previous animal props, other than the rats, she was painted – this time all over – although visitors were assured that 'non-toxic' paint had been used. She was placed in the cosy sitting room, complete with Banksys hanging on the wall, which he had constructed at the heart of the exhibition. The colours and patterns on Tai's back matched the room's wonderfully awful wallpaper. (Eventually she had to be moved to one side since she was not really suited for such cosiness.) She was supplied by a company called Have Trunk Will Travel and her handlers said she was 'regularly fed and given water, taken on bathroom breaks and driven back to her ranch every night'; but all this did little to reassure animal lovers.

The elephant was there for Banksy to make a serious point – a card handed out to visitors read: 'There's an elephant in the room. There's a problem that we never talk about. 1.7 billion people have no access to clean water. 20 billion people live below the poverty line . . .' But who cares about global poverty when there really is an actual elephant in the room? The elephant became the story – a curiosity, cruel or otherwise – and global poverty soon disappeared far into the background.

As usual the show was announced only at the last minute, unless you were a celebrity invited to the first-night preview. Banksy did his usual jokey-serious anonymous interview: 'This show has been quite a big undertaking for me; it represents nearly a month of getting up early in the morning. Some of the paintings have taken literally days to make. Essentially, it's about what a horrible place the world is, how unjust and cruel and pointless life is, and ways to avoid thinking about all that.'

There was of course no press conference but Banksy had already made his own pre-opening headlines. At the beginning of the month Team Banksy had visited forty-two record stores across Britain and replaced Paris Hilton's debut CD – 'she sounds both distracted and bored stiff', said the *Guardian* reviewer – with 500 of his own remixed Paris CDs. They came with a forty-minute rhythm track, but more important, he had brilliantly doctored the booklet that accompanied all Paris's emptiness. His trick was to keep the CDs' original barcode intact so that punters thought they were still buying the real thing. Only when they got it home would they discover that Paris was exposing a pair of enormous bare breasts; that the original song titles had been replaced and instead they were faced with a list of questions: 'Why am I famous?', 'What have I done?' and 'What am I for?'; and that there were telling thoughts from the new Paris like 'Every CD you buy puts you even further out of my league.' (No one who bought the album complained – they paid £9.99 for it and a copy of the CD complete with sleeve and case sold for £1500 at Christie's in November 2011.)

On the other side of the Atlantic a week later he visited Disneyland, with a blow-up doll stuffed into his backpack. He managed to get through the Disney security search, then sat down on a bench and calmly blew up the doll so that it turned into an orange-suited, black-hooded, manacled Guantanamo Bay detainee. He dodged the first security fence, stepped gingerly through various cacti – and stood the doll just inside, beside the railings protecting the Big Thunder Mountain Railroad ride. It was not a particularly impressive doll, but it took considerable nerve to put it there in broad daylight. And it was certainly big enough that when it was noticed after about ninety minutes, it brought the railroad to a halt while Disney disposed of the doll and checked the area. The key thing, as usual with Banksy's escapades, was that he had himself filmed as he was doing it. More headlines followed both for the detainees at Guantanamo and for his show.

Despite the last-minute panic Banksy managed to pull it off again; the show was free, and even though it was only open for three days 30,000 people managed to visit it. Unangst says, 'My first reaction was, oh my god I've got to get more toilet paper. It became a cool scene with the line outside turning it into something of a street festival.' Making the front page of the *New York Times* and the *Los Angeles Times* on the same day meant Banksy established for himself a new recognition across America, and for the West Coast fans who already knew him and followed him on the web, here was a chance to visit a gallery where they could actually see his work emerge from behind the computer screen.

(As for Unangst, he received not only his fee but also a painting traded for all the lighting he did for the exhibition. 'About a year went by and I was thinking, "These guys are going to fuck me up, I am never going to get a painting, he's too big now." But they came through, the painting suddenly arrived.')

These were all exhibitions – though perhaps the Westbourne Grove rats were, as one art critic put it, more of a happening than an exhibition – where Banksy was operating, and operating very successfully, outside the mainstream art world. But one exhibition yet to come was by far the most surprising and probably the most satisfying of all: Bristol.

# Eight
# The Outlaw Returns Home

In the autumn of 2008 officials at the Bristol City Museum and Art Gallery received a phone call from someone claiming to represent Banksy. The caller asked to be put through to the museum's director, Kate Brindley. Naturally enough it was assumed this was a bad joke and the call was not transferred. The real Banksy might have been born in Bristol, but what interest could he possibly have in the city's imposing but rather dusty museum?

But this was no joke call. The Banksy camp had made several attempts to find a personal contact who could give them an in to the museum, but without success, and eventually they had to resort to cold calling. The caller didn't make it as far as the director but did finally succeed in getting through to the museum's exhibition manager, Phil Walker. It became very clear that this was for real – not a practical joke – when the caller said Banksy would fly a representative from the museum to New York to see a small animatronic show that he had mounted there, titled The Village Pet Store and Charcoal Grill.

This show, open for three weeks, was startlingly different from anything he had done before. It was held in a tiny gallery on

Seventh Avenue, instead of 12,000 square feet in Los Angeles it occupied no more than 300 square feet, and it could hold no more than twenty people at a time. It had taken Banksy and friends a month to transform a trinket store into a 'pet' store, complete with some straw outside but with a rather confusing window display. Instead of the usual unhappy-looking hamsters and budgerigars, the shop window featured a rabbit quietly filing its nails in front of a mirror, two-legged chicken nuggets dipping themselves in sauce, and a leopard – or rather not a leopard but a leopard skin – lounging on a tree. Inside, there were swimming fish fingers in a large goldfish bowl, hot dogs squirming in their rolls, a chimp watching chimp porn on TV, a CCTV camera keeping a close eye on her young CCTV chicks in their nest, and much else. Again it came with the usual Banksy 'is he joking, is he serious?' statement; referring back to Tai the Los Angeles elephant, he said: 'I took all the money I made exploiting an animal in my last show and used it to fund a new show about the exploitation of animals. If it's art and you can see it from the street, I guess it could still be considered street art.'

Once Phil Walker had been to New York and seen the show he met up with the Banksy team, who said they wanted to bring the exhibition to Bristol and wanted to know how the museum felt about it. 'That was their first ask,' says Kate Brindley. 'It was completely their idea. We had talked in the past about working with Banksy but you could never imagine he would do it because we were a provincial museum with no money and no pulling power. It basically grew from there. Because what became quite clear quite quickly was that he knew the building very well. He had a lot of ideas about how he wanted to display the work. And we started a dialogue with him. Obviously it was not a dialogue with him but a dialogue through the mechanisms that he used, through his agents but also through a series of drawings that he produced on how he could see his ideas working within our spaces.'

Being Banksy's idea, created by Banksy, financed by Banksy, publicised by Banksy, he could write the contract he wanted. And it was a very tight contract, particularly as far as letting anyone know about the project, or indeed about Banksy. 'They were very explicit about it – if it was going to happen it had to be kept top secret,' says Brindley. 'Of course this is all very counter to how we usually work, because we spend a lot of time trying to get publicity and planning and organising involving loads of stakeholders and the team. Instantly we had to work completely differently. It was a fabulous opportunity and we needed to manage the risk because they were very categorical with us. They said, "If it gets out it's over. Nothing happens." So we had to start planning it that way.' Even among the museum staff, the number of people who were allowed in on the secret was very limited.

Even now the terms of the contract that the city had to sign are so tight that when, a year after the show was over, I approached Phil Walker to ask him more about the exhibition, he was yet another to ask me in turn if the publication 'had been authorised by the artist'. He then consulted with Banksy's PR and apologised but said he was 'contractually bound not to disclose details of the production'. However, Kate Brindley was hired away from Bristol to become director of Middlesbrough Institute of Modern Art (mima), so she was able to be interviewed – the Banksy net did not quite stretch that far. While she says, 'I don't think I would have been doing my job properly if I had said no,' she and the museum staff did much more than just say yes. Certainly it was all Banksy's idea – and no one at the museum, and probably not even Banksy, knew that it would grow and grow until it took over the whole building. But the transformation of the museum, from slightly quaint treasure trove to a place so hot and on the mark that people were ready to queue for hours to get into it, could not have happened without the very few staff who were involved being just as determined as Banksy to make it work.

The approach came in October 2008 and Banksy wanted the show to open the following June, which might seem a reasonable time gap but is a very short deadline by exhibition standards. 'We worked on very small budgets so we realised we had hardly anything to bring to the table. But they didn't worry about that, what they wanted from us was the buildings and the access to the collections and co-operation and flexibility. What they brought to the table was a huge amount of resources and contacts and an ability to make it happen within eight months, which is phenomenal for the scale of the show.'

For probably the first and last time in its history, there was no budget for the museum to stick to – an amazing luxury. In his usual jokey pre-show statements Banksy said this was the first show he had ever done where 'taxpayers' money is being used to hang my pictures up rather than scrape them off.' But actually it was his money, not the taxpayer's, that was used to hang the paintings and make the exhibition possible. Kate Brindley says: 'One of the big things about putting on exhibitions is cost control, but the pleasure of working with Banksy was he was footing the bill so I didn't have to worry in the same way. It was an odd position to be in actually, where they were saying "If there's a problem we're dealing with it." It was quite bizarre.' The deputy leader of the city council, Simon Cook, put the cost to the city at about £60,000 in extra security and the economic impact of the ten-week run at about £15 million. 'In the case of some businesses I think it literally saved them from going to the wall. Some of the retailers said that without it they would have found it difficult to continue and then promptly asked us what we were going to do next year.' Even though these figures are rough, there was certainly a Banksy bonanza. The *Bristol Evening Post* was so excited it called it 'the greatest gift he could have presented to his home city'.

To understand just how radical the exhibition was, you have to have some concept of what the museum was like before Banksy got working on it. Housed in an imposing Grade II listed building, it had been opened in 1905 as a gift to the people of Bristol 'for their instruction and enjoyment' from Sir Henry Wills, Baron Winterstoke, who had made his fortune through tobacco. 'Encyclopaedic' is a kind description, so too is 'eclectic'; 'dusty' is less kind, but they all sort of fit. A brochure you can pick up inside describes how the museum 'tells the story of our world from the beginning of time to the present day'. It is all Edwardian confidence on the outside and marble steps and brass banisters on the inside. You enter and on the left there is a gallery of British and South West wildlife, while on the right Sekhmet the lion goddess and Hapy, the god of inundation, guard the Egyptian galleries. There are dinosaurs, a world wildlife gallery full of very excited schoolchildren and an equal number of stuffed animals, there are twelve pianos and there are fossils, silver, minerals, Chinese glass and Chinese ceramics. A biplane hangs in the central hall while a gypsy caravan sits on the first floor. There is Eastern art and Bristol art, Turner and Titian, Botticelli and Bellini, Sisley and Seurat, Holbein and Harris (Rolf). There is the slightly faded swagger here of Bristol as a great trading port, stretching out its influence – collecting in its treasures – to and from all corners of the world.

And into this unruffled environment came Banksy. The *Observer* called the exhibition a 'sell-out in every sense' – meaning it was both a crowd pleaser and the moment when Banksy gave up his outlaw past and joined the established art world. In the *Sunday Times* Waldemar Januszczak, usually a supporter of Banksy, said he would rather he had not done it: 'Banksy the rebel was an artist you could trust, a free creative voice that owed nothing to anybody. Banksy the respectable museum artist is something else. What is being destroyed here is not the anonymity of Bristol City Museum, it's Banksy's raison d'être.'

Both these judgements seem incredibly harsh. The show was a huge, joyous leap of the imagination. The established context for contemporary art has become the white cube, all cool and focussed without any interruptions. It is seen as a neutral space; it is in fact incredibly loaded, and for many who are not part of the art world incredibly off-putting. But Banksy chose a completely different context and made it work brilliantly. There was no standing, staring, reading the notes on the wall and still being totally bewildered about what it might mean. No, this was part gallery show, with his pictures hanging normally – or relatively so – in one part of the museum, and part treasure hunt. A modern-day treasure hunt, a bit like the one I had enjoyed so much in London, where you had to spot the Banksy amidst the exhibits in the permanent collection, and where almost everyone came armed with digital cameras so they had a record which they could enjoy themselves and email their enjoyment to friends.

At Middlesbrough Kate Brindley now runs an institute which is all white space and high-end concepts, but she remains a great admirer of Banksy. His work, she says, is 'smart, it's intentioned. It's political, it's humorous. It's current. It's site specific, it's universal. He thinks very carefully about it but there is also a lightness and playfulness which I really enjoy about it. And there was clearly a great affection for Bristol Museum.' For, quite apart from what it did for Banksy, the exhibition brought the museum back to life, just over 100 years since it first opened.

The slim guide to the exhibition came with Banksy's usual, slightly irritating humour – the exhibition was rated PG, 'Contains scenes of a childish nature some adults may find disappointing.' The slightly over-grand 'Bristol School of Artists' he demoted to 'Artists from Bristol'; 'World Wildlife' became 'Wildlife in Glass Boxes', 'Pottery and Ceramics' became 'Boring Old Plates', and the room for under sevens became the 'Children's Shouting Area'.

But the exhibition itself was very skilfully and humorously thought out. And it showed too how Banksy could successfully push the boundaries of his work way beyond the limits of the stencil. A scaled-down version of a sculpture he had made at Glastonbury, *Boghenge* – Stonehenge constructed in Portaloos – was sitting in the entrance hall to welcome visitors. A month after the exhibition opened a rather sozzled-looking Ronald McDonald was to be found sitting precariously on a ledge outside the museum entrance, a bottle of whisky by his side. In the big hall inside there were seven sculptures, and if you hadn't got the message from Ronald McDonald and the Portaloos that this was a very different show from anything else ever seen in the museum, then there was no escaping it here.

A satisfied lion with a whip in its mouth and specks of blood on its cheeks had all too obviously eaten its trainer. Paris Hilton, or someone who resembled her, was clutching a heroic number of shopping bags. Michelangelo's David had a suicide vest strapped around him. A beaten-up Buddha, last seen painted on a wall at the Cans Festival, now came as a statue complete with a neck brace and one of his arms in a sling. A homeless Venus de Milo had her dog and a few scattered coins at her feet. An angel with rather pretty wings had a large tin of pink paint stuck over her head, its contents dribbling down to the bottom of her plinth, but happily stopping just before it reached the dedication on the pillar to Baron Winterstoke. In the centre of the hall, surrounded by these sculptures, stood a partially burnt-out ice cream van, complete with the usual irritating ice cream jingle, with graffiti on one side and on top a giant cone melting out all over the place. Next to the van was a big riot policeman, wearing a badge that bore the words 'Metropolitan Peace', all geared up and looking ridiculous as he rode a small child's mechanical rocking horse (this piece was later reported to have been sold for £140,000).

Surveying all this from the biplane on high was a new and improved version of the prisoner who escaped from Guantanamo and was last seen in Disneyland. When the life-size orange-suited doll first arrived in Bristol, he was placed on a bench in the museum. But the exhibition evolved as the weeks went on, and soon someone in the Banksy team had the bright idea of putting him in the pilot's seat of the biplane where he could see and be seen.

The New York animatronics which had started the whole idea of the exhibition had been imported wholesale and given their own space, christened Unnatural History, in the rear hall. Next to Tweetie Bird, the swimming fish sticks, the sleeping leopard skin and the rest of the cast, the museum's main exhibition space held a mocked-up version of Banksy's messy studio. The studio came complete with spray paint, stencils from some of his work and preliminary drawings of other work, used stencils of his tag, drawers of a filing cabinet labelled 'good ideas', 'bad ideas', 'other people's ideas' and 'pornography'. A pixellated – and thus frustratingly unrecognisable – self-portrait of the artist sat on an easel opposite the artist's chair with a knitted cardigan reading THUG FOR LIFE hanging off the back of the chair. (The cardigan had a pedigree: in his Los Angeles show he had painted two grannies looking a picture of happiness as they sat in their armchairs knitting contentedly. One was knitting a cardigan with PUNKS NOT DEAD on it, the other was knitting THUG FOR LIFE.) All around were the products of his real studio, a whole new array of Banksys; in total there were just over 100 exhibits in the show. But while these were the bulk of the Banksys on display, there were many more dotted around the museum. As Banksy said at the time, 'Some of the fake historical relics I've inserted among Bristol's permanent collection should be entertaining – you can't tell what's truth and what's fiction. It'll be like walking through a real-life Wikipedia.'

Simon Cook remembers he was wandering around on the last day of the exhibition 'because I wanted to get a final look at it. And up in the galleries I was watching people looking for Banksys, finding them eventually, but also looking at our permanent collection and not realising we had a Renoir and other major artists.' Yes, the museum has always had 'depth', but it needed either a certain dedication or Banksy to discover that depth.

There was everything from a dildo nestling amongst the stalagmites and a plastic salt shaker sitting among the Reserve Collection, to a muzzled lamb in amongst the World Wildlife and a hash pipe among the Pottery and Ceramics. Even the gypsy caravan had been got at: one of its wheels had been clamped and an eviction notice stuck on the front door. Banksy was clearly having great fun. Looking at these stunts on the web reminded me of my days as a prep school boy when we were taken on an outing to the local museum and got so bored that a couple of us resorted to swapping around all the exhibit captions, making a nonsense of the whole thing. Banksy received nothing but admiration, while I was hauled up before the headmaster and beaten for it a couple of days later.

More seriously, a whole string of altered paintings were hidden amongst the museum's old masters. These interventions ranged from the Virgin Mary with child and iPod, to a rat 'improving' one of Damien Hirst's spot paintings and a couple 'dogging' amidst a typical nineteenth-century English landscape scene. My personal favourite is his version of Millet's *The Gleaners*, painted in 1857 and showing three peasant women exercising their right to hunt for any bits of grain left over in the fields after the harvest. One of the women had been cut out of the canvas (it's a copy, the original is in the Musée D'Orsay) and was sitting on the corner of the frame having a fag break. This was renamed, unconvincingly, as *Agency Job*, but it brought yet another layer of humanity to this haunting picture. Like most of the other Banksys hidden among the Old Masters, it was attributed to 'Local Artist'.

Was anything that Banksy wanted to put up just a step too far for the museum? 'There were a few things,' says Kate Brindley. 'It was very little really, which was quite surprising. There was very little where we said no, that's not appropriate, and it was negotiated through as you would with any artist.'

The whole exhibition was mounted amidst great secrecy. Notices were stuck on the doors saying 'Closed for essential maintenance' and although the Banksy team had been constructing exhibits off the site for months, they had just two days to bring everything in and set it up. Anyone at the museum not yet in on the secret was told it was closed for filming. 'It was like a big sort of *Changing Rooms*,' says Kate Brindley. 'We shut and it all came in. The only reason we could do that was because they had the manpower and finances. They were incredibly professional. I am used to putting on exhibitions but it was done in such a large and accelerated fashion. It was a bit like working with a film crew.'

In television interviews at the time, she was always asked if she had met Banksy and she always gave the same answer with a big smile on her face. She knew he had been in the museum, that he had planned the show in detail. But when asked, 'So you don't know which one of the crew he is?' she replied, 'No, we still don't, and that's part of the real charm.'

The hype surrounding the exhibition was the least impressive part of it. The show was improbably titled *Banksy versus the Bristol Museum* and described as an 'audacious heist', as though Banksy had suddenly become a true vandal and gatecrashed the museum, when in fact the whole thing had been planned down to the last detail of the pre-show party and the public relations campaign that went with it. The *Bristol Evening Post* described how two of Banksy's 'PR people' had arrived at the newspaper on a 'hush hush visit' a couple of days before the show opened and 'giggled excitedly' as they described what was about to hit Bristol – hardly a 'heist'.

But even more revealing was the contract that Banksy had the council sign, which was later released – with key sections blanked out – after a freedom of information request. To be fair to Banksy, this contract revealed that he had charged only £1 for the exhibition and that he agreed to give one work to the museum (he actually gave two: the paint-pot angel and an intricate scale model of Jerusalem made in olive wood, which he bought and to which he added 284 soldiers and one terrorist). Given he was paying for virtually everything except the insurance of the exhibits, he was entitled to call the tune – which he very certainly did.

Buried amidst all the memos, the rewrites and the rewrites of the rewrites there are odd little titbits to be found in this contract. In the list of exhibits needed for the insurers, for example, it was possible to discover some but not all of the secrets of the animatronics. *Tweety Pie* was made of marine ply and Jesmonite (a solvent-free resin). The swimming fish sticks were constructed of Iroca hardwood and birch-faced ply. In another report which ended up online with the contract documents it was clear that the fish sticks were causing problems for the museum's Health and Safety Working Group. 'Concentrated chemical required to keep water clear in fish tanks has been risk assessed. Chemical now locked in plant room – large container to be taken away as only small amount will be required.' The 'trip hazards around the ice cream van' were also being monitored – it was all a far cry from an aerosol can and a wall.

But for the most part there were just pages and pages of legalese – there was the main agreement, plus a separate confidentiality agreement for the council to sign and another for individuals to sign. The museum agreed to use 'all reasonable endeavours' to ensure that the 'privacy and anonymity of the artist and those working with him is preserved . . . and acknowledges that such obligation includes an agreement not to store, distribute or in any way seek to make profit from the sale or release of CCTV footage to any third party'. If the museum was forced to make any disclosure of CCTV footage because of legal requirements 'it shall obscure the faces of all personnel including the artist'.

As for the press, Banksy was again in complete control: 'the

Museum shall obtain written approval over all publicity, media, print and website information relating to the exhibition.' He wanted to protect his identity from the press, but certainly not his presence. All media relations were to be undertaken by Banksy's PR agent, who would supply the press with any images needed. The museum merely had to provide the staff for the press call. But perhaps the arrangements for the private view of the exhibition, all laid out in great detail, demonstrated most vividly how far he had come from his days as a Bristol vandal. There were to be three sessions and reasonably enough, since Banksy could hardly apply for it himself, the museum had to be responsible for obtaining the licences for alcohol and music. In addition the museum had to submit a list of its guests twenty-one days in advance (the contract did not say what would happen if Banksy did not like any of them). Six hundred guests could be invited to each session. The first session was from 4 p.m. to 4.30 p.m. and for this session the museum had the right to select all the guests. The second session was from 4.30 p.m. to 6.30 p.m. and here Banksy could select 500 guests and the museum 100. The hours of the third session – party time – were from 7.30 p.m. to 10.30 p.m. and Banksy was entitled to select *all* the guests. No guesses as to which session everyone wanted to be invited to. Some old friends arrived at the museum to find that with their correctly coloured wristband came a note from Banksy thanking them for their silence over the years – but rule by wristband disintegrated somewhat as the night wore on.

But this control-freak contract should not be allowed to drown the fact that the show was an absolute triumph. In July 2008 the museum had 20,861 visitors; in July 2009, the year of Banksy, the total was 111,285. With just under 4000 visitors a day it was the second most visited exhibition in Britain in 2009 in *The Art*

*Newspaper*'s annual attendance survey, just beaten to the top by the Saatchi Gallery's The Revolution Continues: New Art from China. Banksy's team had warned the museum that they knew from past experience they were going to be inundated. 'We couldn't even envisage what that meant actually, if I am frank with you,' says Kate Brindley. 'I think it surprised everyone and we had to manage it.' The queues sometimes stretched for three or four hours. Simon Cook says, 'I used to feel quite embarrassed driving past.' The museum had briefly considered timed ticketing, but Banksy had been against it anyway – the idea of kicking out hardcore fans on the hour every hour would have been hard to stomach. At one point in the queue you had to have your hand stamped but some were so desperate they managed to forge this, forcing the museum to come up with a couple of rather more complicated stamps.

The *Bristol Evening Post* 'Souvenir Edition' included a map of where the visitors had travelled from – Uruguay and Taiwan being two of the more unexpected countries. But perhaps most important was the fact that a large proportion of the visitors had never been to the museum before, or had not visited it in many years – Banksy was drawing in a new crowd. However, when the visitors were categorised in the way that statisticians delight in categorising, the great majority of them were 'wealthy achievers', 'urban prosperity' or 'comfortably off', so even this, the most populist exhibition imaginable – and free at that – could not quite reach the audience that Banksy might have hoped for.

The museum did ask if they could extend the exhibition – without success; all they could do was extend the opening hours for its last two weeks. The following summer they put on Art from the New World, described as 'a big brash exhibition of the new

American art scene'. It came with the burlesque queen Dita Von Teese at the opening party and a huge fifteen-foot-high double-scoop ice cream cone in the front hall, created by Buff Monster, just to try and show that the museum would never be quite the same again. The year after that, they reverted to more familiar but very popular territory, with an exhibition of the late Beryl Cook's work. But without the magic missing ingredient, these exhibitions were never going to have quite the same pulling power.

'I thought it was a real gift that he gave us actually,' says Kate Brindley. 'He could have worked with anyone from the Guggenheim to MOMA in New York but he chose to work with the Bristol Museum. I didn't do any of the work. I allowed him through the door, that's all I did. People enjoyed it, they came out smiling, saying "I've never seen the collections before, I've never seen the museums before." They loved it.'

When Baron Winterstoke gave the museum to the people of Bristol he hoped it would provide them with both 'instruction and enjoyment'. Among the comments left by visitors was one from Vera Flemina: 'Last week I came to see the Banksy Exhibition. I am 87 years old: I can't recall when I last had such a wonderful experience. I was happy, my ancient batteries re-charged (hopeful) . . . Perhaps I will go to Glastonbury next year.' How much instruction they gained from Banksy is arguable, but there is no doubt that more than 300,000 visitors got all the enjoyment the Baron could have possibly hoped for.

# Nine
# Welcome to Team Banksy

In February 2007 the Knightsbridge dealer Acoris Andipa was skiing with his family on the Hornberg in Gstaad when he was interrupted by a furious call from someone doing PR for Banksy. 'This was my first introduction to the Banksy camp, they have a very unique way of doing things,' he says now with considerable understatement.

'There I was literally on top of the mountain and the conversation basically began by her demanding, "What the hell do you think you are doing?" I said, "Excuse me, who are you? What kind of way is this to start a conversation?"' The PR said they were representing Banksy – 'and he was very upset, and I replied that was the furthest intention from what we want.' The conversation improved slightly from there, but it is easy enough to see why the PR was so upset, for at that moment Andipa must have represented Banksy's worst nightmare. His credentials as a street artist are both genuine and important to him, but here was Andipa about to put on a Banksy exhibition in his gallery in Knightsbridge and – possibly even worse – already showing Banksys at the Palace hotel in Gstaad, so very far from 'the street' that the penthouse suite will set you back €9000 or so a night.

Although Andipa had admired Banksy's work for almost two years, previously he was never quite sure how it would sell if he tried taking it from 'underground to overground'. So he had decided to test it out. Before Christmas 2006 he put on a show entitled Hirst and his Contemporaries, and he included about eight Banksys to gauge the reaction of the Knightsbridge crowd. 'The Banksys just went,' he said, 'we sold them all on the opening night. I thought, my goodness. Wow. These were my collectors, my clients, who were here by invitation only. People who buy Picassos only from me. Who buy Damien Hirsts only from me . . .'

Vandal . . . outlaw . . . graffiti . . . Shoreditch . . . never mind, affluent Knightsbridge was gagging for him. Andipa had taken over the gallery from his mother, who used to specialise in icons. But as the market for icons disappeared he had, with some considerable family pain, moved to contemporary art. Now he was going to jump to street art. In the next couple of months Andipa moved fast, spending a lot of money rounding up enough Banksys to make a worthwhile show. Just before his own exhibition opened he took several of the pieces on his annual trip to Gstaad and the winter exhibition at the Palace. 'What surprised me was that almost every single person who came in to see the show knew about Banksy. These were high rollers and they had learned predominantly from his book *Wall and Piece*, which they'd been given as a gift or a stocking-filler.' It was during this exhibition that Andipa had received the phone call up on the mountain, which was followed up back in England by a conversation with Steve Lazarides, still Banksy's agent at the time, who thought the show was 'piracy'. Their key worry was that this whole exhibition would make it look as though Banksy had sold out to the Knightsbridge set. For the Andipa Gallery is on Walton Street, a street oozing boutique luxury, a street where Viscount Linley's wife Serena chose to open her shop selling fragrances, candles and bespoke soaps from Provence; a street where you can buy handmade Oriental rugs, porcelain, designer maternity wear, nursery furniture, monogrammed linen and the like – in short, everything that Banksy was not.

Banksy himself emailed Waldemar Januszczak: 'If I was conspiracy-minded, I'd say this was a plot to destroy my last shred of credibility. But then I do a good enough job of that myself.' Even though the exhibition was completely out of context, it was a rare chance to see a lot of Banksys in one place and over the next month about 35,000 people managed to squeeze their way into this small gallery.

'We had to bring in crowd control to manage everything on Saturdays because the queue would be all the way down Walton Street,' says Andipa. 'They were all very polite, predominantly young hoodies, very sweet and very respectful. These were the hardcore street fans who normally wouldn't dream of coming to Knightsbridge, let alone coming to an art gallery in Knightsbridge.' And however much Andipa put notices in his catalogue and on the wall of the gallery explaining he was not representing Banksy, the whole thing was too close to Harrods for a notice or two to be any comfort to the Banksy camp.

The exhibition was an outstanding success. Andipa was asking £70,000 for a canvas of *Flower Thrower with Stars*, produced in an edition of twenty-five; another canvas, *Kids on Guns*, also in an edition of twenty-five, and which depicts two children standing on a mountain of weapons clasping their balloon and their teddy, was priced at £45,000. (Another financial delight of his chosen technique is that Banksy can, if he wishes, produce more than one canvas from the same stencil.) Andipa had gambled heavily on Banksy and he was richly rewarded. Practically everything sold, and the gallery could expand into the basement to create a very smart second floor. He has put on further Banksy exhibitions in Knightsbridge and his annual Banksy show in Gstaad continues profitably. In some way he seems to enjoy the mischief he has undoubtedly been making, telling the Associated Press after one Gstaad exhibition: 'Every single person – including clients who'd come in their Lear jets – walked in and said, "Wow, Banksy – and it's only £150,000."' Andipa is one of the very few people who has operated successfully outside Banksy's control.

For, whatever the outward impression, the fact is that Team Banksy – and it is a very small team – is just as determined as any other celebrity's team to keep control of events. Take the UK launch, in March 2010, of *Exit Through the Gift Shop*. The task for any magazine editor when a film is opening is to bag the star for an interview and picture shoot and to bag him or her exclusively. No one else is allowed to have the star on their cover, no one else can brag that they have the exclusive interview. The negotiations with the PRs – 'fuck pigs' one frustrated magazine editor used to call them, but never to their face – can be endless: photo approval, interviewer approval, copy approval, all these are up for grabs even though the star seldom gets everything that they want.

For his film Banksy got it accepted that the interview – as usual – could only be by email and that his artwork would be on the cover. What was much more of a PR triumph was that there were not one but two 'exclusive' interviews. The *Sunday Times* claimed an 'exclusive interview' and an 'exclusive cover' by Britain's 'most reclusive artist'. Well, neither totally 'reclusive' nor 'exclusive', for *Time Out* went one step further, claiming a 'world exclusive' plus 'his only interview'. For a PR paid to publicise a film it was as if all her dreams had come true.

Jo Brooks, who started her own PR company and continues to run it from Brighton, is one of the key members of the team. She is described by a friend as 'brilliant, entertaining and sharp as a needle'. Her small, slightly chaotic office suits Banksy's style. Her first major job for Banksy was organising the press, or rather lack of press, for Turf War in 2003 and she has been with him ever since. He is not her only client but he is certainly her most important. Yet she has a much more difficult task than might be imagined. She has to preserve his anonymity while nourishing his fame; preserve his street credibility while his pictures earn him more and more money; give a Banksy exhibition the sense that it is somehow secret – an insider thing – while letting people know it's happening. She not only orchestrated all the PR for his exhibition in Bristol, somehow managing to convey the friendly impression that it was a heist – that he had virtually stolen the space from the Bristol City Museum – but even provided the museum with the link to the Los Angeles gallery which put on the summer exhibition the next year. And she has done all this very quietly and successfully without creating enemies for her client or for herself.

But if she is a key member of Team Banksy, she is not the most important member; that title undoubtedly goes – or rather went – to Steve Lazarides, a fellow member of the Bristol clan who was his agent, his manager, his salesman for the six most financially profitable years of Banksy's life and had a rather more informal arrangement with him for about four years longer than that. Without Banksy, Lazarides – Laz to some – would not be a key purveyor of urban art, or outsider art as he prefers to call it, in

London today; but it is also safe to say that without Lazarides Banksy would simply not have the recognition, the influence and the money that he has today.

A colleague who says he does not want to be identified remembers: 'Steve was Banksy's manager to all intents and purposes and any sort of enquiry would go through Steve. They were very close, they were really good mates, really good friends. In fact they were a bit of a double act when they were together. They were like naughty schoolboys who suddenly got lucky. Steve was an intelligent, nice, relaxed guy who really loved what he was doing. At one point I think that Banksy was even giving him his cash to put in the bank because he didn't have an account himself. He was making lots of decisions and taking the pressure off Banksy and he was very protective of him. He knew there was a risk that Banksy would get exploited and he really didn't want that to happen.'

They are not speaking to each other now. The break-up happened over several months; things started to go badly wrong at the end of 2007 and it was all over by December 2008, when Lazarides sold his shares in Banksy's Pictures on Walls back to the company. It was a big moment in both men's lives. Lazarides had lost his best client; Banksy had lost the man who made it all possible. But, like most things to do with Banksy, no one wants to talk about the break-up and when they do talk they leave far more unsaid than said. At one point Lazarides commented: 'There was no acrimony there. We'd been working together for years and it seemed the right thing to do. He has gone off to do his own thing and here I am running my gallery.'

He did however expand slightly in an interview with Susan Michals for *Vanity Fair Daily* when she asked what happened: 'We spent about 10 years together, and I wanted to branch out. You have to grow up. Otherwise you just look like a fool. We haven't really spoken to each other in a long time; to be honest, I have no idea where he is. And it gave me much more capacity to work with everyone else. It was an amazing ride and I wouldn't be here without it, but I don't necessarily miss it.'

She suggested to him it was like a relationship when people don't define you as an individual but as a couple: 'It annoys him far more than it annoys me,' he said with a laugh. 'A decade is a long time, especially when you're both as driven as we are.'

As for Banksy, almost the only thing he has said on the subject is, 'The best I can say right now is, "No comment".' But that is not quite the only thing he has said, for on his website at one point he placed a notice saying: 'Please Note: Banksy has never produced greeting cards, mugs or photo canvases of his work. He is not represented by any of the commercial galleries that sell his work second hand (including Lazarides Ltd, Andipa Gallery, Bank Robber, Dreweatts etc . . .).' Placing Lazarides in the same company as galleries that Banksy's team has always tried to fight off, Andipa and Bankrobber, was an insult, a bitchy thing to do.

It somehow doesn't fit the outlaw image, but the sad fact is that the circle around Banksy is just as full of fun but also of paranoia, unease, jealousy as any other workplace. For example, it is even suggested that Lazarides was allowed a brief appearance in *Exit Through the Gift Shop* just so they could put a caption underneath him reading: 'Banksy's former spokesman.' At the time of the split employees of both Banksy's and Lazarides' galleries were advised they were to break off contact with each other, but given the friendships that already existed at least this separation of staff did not last long.

There are all kinds of explanations floating around to explain the split. One story went that Banksy had paid a visit to the Lazarides household; he had seen the luxury, the comfort, above all the *flock wallpaper*, and had exploded. The result was a painting, first seen in February 2009, in which a young hoodie is spraying a flock pattern on a wall. The work is called, none too subtly, *Go Flock Yourself* – just to make the point. It is a good story but there is just one problem with it: it is completely untrue. For one thing, there is no flock wallpaper in Lazarides' house, and for another it is very unlikely that Banksy ever went round there to check out the wallpaper for himself.

However, another source had a different explanation: 'They certainly fell out spectacularly. It was over a magazine piece which was an interview that basically had Steve sitting on a throne in his office saying "I made Banksy". It was more complex than that but Banksy being a control freak didn't like that at all. So the king builder got dethroned. It was purely a clash of egos really.' This source has it right: the relationship had been growing very strained anyway but it was the magazine piece that blew the whole thing apart, although the article was not nearly as provocative as he remembers it to be.

In November 2007 Charlotte Eagar interviewed Lazarides for the *Evening Standard*'s *ES* magazine. Hunting for this piece I thought that it would be all about Lazarides the king-maker boasting about how he had made Banksy what he is today. But actually, when I found the right article, Banksy's reaction to it told me more about Banksy than it did about Lazarides. For while Lazarides was certainly happy to talk away about himself and his plans, there was not much in the way of strutting – nowhere did he claim to be the man who made Banksy and he certainly denied the suggestion floating around that he actually *was* Banksy. The line on the cover called him 'The man who sells graffiti to Hollywood', which is true, and inside he was called 'the man who turns graffiti into gold' and 'a marketing genius', which also happens to be true. There was no picture of him sitting on a throne, he was just leaning casually against a wall. The problem, it appears, was that it was simply a profile of an artist's manager and the artist hardly got a look in. Amazingly, from that day on it was over and the only question was how they were going to separate out their lives.

One source in Los Angeles suggests that the problem was that Lazarides 'just got too big. He had about ten or fifteen artists he was representing and he didn't have the time or even the will to devote all his energy towards Banksy. Banksy was feeling a little bit short changed and he just needed a lot of attention because he had grown up so big and fast.' But perhaps the best way the split can be explained is in biblical terms. Lazarides had taken Banksy up to the mountain top, he'd tempted him with the likes of Angelina Jolie, fame, money, success. And instead of Banksy telling him 'Get thee hence,' he had, for a time at least, lapped it all up. It was this deal with the devil that appears to have 'weirded out' Banksy and in the long run ended their relationship.

Lazarides is a very good salesman – there is something of the great American showman P.T. Barnum about him. According to the profile that ended his relationship with Banksy there was 'nothing of the sharp suit about him', but that was a few years back – nowadays he can be just as sharp-suited as any other dealer, perhaps more so. He is shaven headed but somehow his friendly smile overcomes any hint of the football yobbo and he is fast talking, entertaining, fun – you feel he could sell you anything.

Banksy is an artist who has no interest in being a celebrity and the fact that he has no interest has made him into a celebrity. It was thus a very intense marriage with considerable benefits for both of them. One of the outer circle says, 'Lazarides was representing a superstar who wanted to remain anonymous. And thus he became a superstar by proxy, he was very much seduced by fame.'

Being a showman Lazarides embroiders history a little, although probably rather less than Banksy does. His father was born in Famagusta in Cyprus, known best by Brits for its cheap package holidays – at least until 1974 when the Turkish army invaded, capturing the town from the Greeks and turning it into a ghost town. His father came to Britain and settled in Bristol where he ran a kebab shop. He married an Englishwoman – although they eventually split up – and Steve, born in 1969, was one of eight children across different marriages. Among his siblings he numbers a plumber/builder, a truck driver, an electrician, a landscape gardener, a school secretary and a pet-life insurance saleswoman. While Lazarides has driven himself way beyond his background, he is still connected – when he opened his Euro Trash show in Los Angeles, for instance, he flew his father out to join him.

By his own account Lazarides started life as a painter and decorator and occasional chicken plucker and concrete mixer, but these jobs were never going to turn into anything permanent. He tried his hand at graffiti, realised he was no good at it and at about the age of fourteen turned to photography instead. He managed to get a place on a foundation course at Filton Technical College (now Filton College) in Bristol where he happened across Inkie, the graffiti artist who was later to introduce Banksy into the city's graffiti scene. Inkie says now: 'Where I lent Banksy his "credibility" in the UK graffiti scene, Steve in turn marketed his work to make him the global phenomenon he is now.'

From there he went to Newcastle Poly to study photography while DJing in clubs at the weekend. After a couple of very short-lived jobs, first as a studio runner and then assistant to the photographer David Bailey, he finally found a permanent job painting sets for a film studio. *Wilde* and *Sliding Doors* are two of the sets he remembers and some of the people he saw on the set from afar are now his clients. From there his long-time partner Susana introduced him to a friend at *Sleazenation*, which together with its sister magazine *Jockey Slut* was aimed – unsurprisingly, with a name like that – at the youth 'subculture' slice of the market. 'They needed a picture editor, so they just gave me the job as I walked in the door,' he says. In 1997, while he was at *Sleazenation*, he went off to photograph Banksy, or rather the back of his head. Starting over a cup of coffee – as Mills and Boon might have it – the two outsiders, making their own way in the world, became friends. Banksy was soon tipping Steve off about where to find his latest stencils so he could photograph them before they were wiped out. In Banksy's first book *Banging Your Head Against A Brick Wall*, published in 2001, all the photographs – and there were a lot of them – were credited to Lazarides. At this time Banksy already had an agent from his Bristol days, Steve Earl, but it was an arrangement without a contract and it ended when Lazarides came along and showed he could do the job better.

Steve Earl's story is a sad one. He was brought up in Wakefield where his father was a bricklayer. His parents supported him while he was at college training to be a butcher. At nineteen he had gained all the qualifications he needed, but decided he was going to abandon the butcher's trade for the music industry. At that point he had what his brother Julian describes as 'a fall-out with my father. My dad said, "Well, if you're going to be a musician you're going to have to go fend for yourself."' He left home as Stephen Earl Young and ended up in Bristol as Stephen Earl, his surname abandoned. He kept in touch for a few years but the family never saw him again. Many years later his brother, with considerable help from the police, managed to track him down to a flat in Barcelona. But although he wrote to him, Steve never replied and he died alone and pretty much penniless in 2007 aged forty-three. In between Wakefield and Barcelona he had an up and down career in Bristol, London and New York as DJ, DJ's agent and Banksy's agent.

Julian talked to Steve's friends after his brother's death to try to piece together his history. 'He seemed to see a talent in people and get them to a certain stage and then someone else would come along and take them off him.' That was certainly true of Banksy, whom he represented when he first came to London but whom he fell out with in 2003. 'I don't think he had a contract or anything like that,' says his brother. 'He told a friend "That's it, I'm over with Banksy, it's all done with." But he just carried on with his life, he didn't seem to get too wound up about it.'

Martin Worster, a former music journalist, met Steve at an internet café in Barcelona where they both worked. 'He told me he had been Banksy's manager but he wasn't any more. It seemed that there had been some dispute over money. I think it was possibly over Blur but I am not sure.' As well as being entertaining and good company he was also 'an elusive guy, quite hard to pin down . . . when I first met him he reminded me a bit of an eighties pop star who had fallen on hard times.'

Both in London and Barcelona Steve was never short of a

Banksy or two. A DJ who used to visit his office in Notting Hill said it was completely full of Banksy prints and canvases. In Barcelona too he decorated his flat with an impressive array of Banksys, including one massive painting, 'an amazing piece' depicting grannies outside a burning supermarket. But he was having money troubles and he traded two Banksy stencils on board for a business debt he owed Martin – since the debt was about £500 it would have proved a bad deal for Steve in the long run, but this was in the days before Banksy had become a big name. Two years later Martin left Barcelona and lost touch until he was told of Steve's death. Steve Earl had gone out to make his own way and lived a life that had been heartbreakingly close to being a huge success, but in the end he had had to rely on a dwindling supply of Banksys to keep afloat.

Lazarides tells of his first business venture together with Banksy in various different ways, but the essentials are that Banksy needed a lift to Bristol where he was going to sell his prints for either £5 or £10 apiece, depending on which version of the story is more accurate (whatever the price, it was mouth-wateringly cheap). 'I said, "I'll buy them all and sell them on." I had friends who had a few quid who quite liked his stuff, so I wound up selling more than the person that was looking after him [Steve Earl]. And it just spiralled from there.'

So Lazarides was not quite there from day one, and he and Banksy never quite had the same symbiotic relationship as, say, Jay Jopling and Damien Hirst. But he was in the picture from early on, and Acoris Andipa says, 'It was Lazarides building it from nothing. He is the one to be credited for all the hard work he did.' Lazarides himself says, 'I think it was very much a two-way street in the sense that we helped each other in those early days. It's probable that without Banksy I may not have got to where I am today.' Note the use of the word 'probable' rather than 'certain' or 'true' – understandably he is not going to give Banksy all the credit.

He says that his route to the gallery world 'started from selling work out of the boot of my car in a pub car park'. It is so difficult to imagine now that only a few short years ago it was a real struggle to offload Banksy prints. From the car boot sale he advanced to making the rounds of London dealers. One of them remembers: 'Stephen Lazarides would come round with rolls of these prints under his arm and try to flog them off to us at, you know, £50 a pop. And we did buy them and we used to get discounts from him before anyone had even heard of Banksy prints.' From there things progressed so that Lazarides was wholesaling prints to places like Selfridges (yes, Selfridges!), the Tom Tom Gallery in London, the Green Leaf bookshop in Bristol, and Tate Modern – Banksy was not hanging on the walls but you could buy a print there. Sales soon reached a point where Lazarides no longer needed the smaller outlets. It was a fairly brutal moment. The same dealer remembers it well: 'The thing that irked us a bit was one minute we were always first to be phoned, first to be contacted about new releases, and then suddenly the gate came down. No discounts and not even no discounts, they didn't want to sell to us as dealers at all. It was a kind of mean-spirited thing more than anything else. It was just like "You've been useful to us and now bugger off."'

In 2002 Banksy released his first properly organised, editioned print run, *Rude Copper* – a stencil of a policeman giving the finger – in an edition of 250, fifty of which were signed. Originally the edition was only going to be 100 prints but at the last minute they raised it to 250 to see what happened. In those early days, says a fan who witnessed it all, everything was somewhat disorganised. 'There were 250 copies and loads of extras. Number One might be unsigned, although it would be stamped, and then someone might want the second one signed, so two or three would get signed and then there would be more unsigned. There was chaos, really, about which was part of the edition and which wasn't. And there wasn't any consistency.' These prints went for around £40; today they can be picked up at auction for about £8000, or around £13,000 for the few that have a hand-sprayed graffiti background. In the next year fourteen additional prints were released in editions that ran from 500 to 750. Ironically, given the fact that today a signed print always fetches a considerably higher price than an unsigned one, it was the signed prints, costing just that little bit extra, which were the hardest to sell – 'They used to be hanging around for ages,' says one of the team who was trying to sell them.

So, suddenly, roughly 7000 Banksy prints or more were being released on to the market and life had to get a bit more serious. Early in 2004 Pictures on Walls was formally incorporated, the first of Banksy's companies. The finance was put up by Jon Swinstead, who published *Sleazenation* and *Jockey Slut*, and POW's first base was at PYMCA, a youth culture picture agency established by Lazarides and Swinstead on the floor above the *Sleazenation* office.

By the end of 2004, Swinstead says, he had 'walked away' from POW, but he did not want to go into any further detail. Steve Parkin, who used to employ Lazarides as a DJ in his Newcastle days, replaced him and put up the second tranche of finance which kept the company afloat. The majority shareholder was – and remains – Jamie Hewlett, the creator of Tank Girl and co-creator of Gorillaz, while Lazarides had eighteen shares. Nowhere in the records is there ever a mention of Banksy – perfectly legally, without shares and without a directorship, he is relying on his friendship with Hewlett for his involvement with the company.

White cube galleries might be the holy grail for ambitious young artists, but as the demand for the prints they were releasing grew, both Lazarides and Banksy realised they had stumbled upon a new eager audience for art among people who had never set foot in a traditional gallery and had no desire to do so. Both of them enjoyed slagging off these galleries, although Lazarides is the more loud-mouthed about them and the 'chippy bastards working behind the desk'. There's nothing he hates more than a white cube gallery: 'I do black walls, I do red walls, vintage wallpaper, anything other than fucking white. I have a pathological hatred of white walls.' Banksy himself has always tended to be more rude about the art inside the galleries than the galleries themselves: 'Anti-graffiti groups like to say tagging intimidates people, but not as much as modern art. That stuff is deliberately designed to make normal people feel stupid.'

Their way of selling art sounds simple now but at the time it was revolutionary. People could see for themselves a piece of Banksy's work on the street, and if they lived too far away or it had already been washed off by the anti-vandal patrols there were always good photographs of it on the internet – it would become something of a contest to see who could get their picture up on the web first. Some of these street pieces would eventually become limited edition prints which could be bought on the web without their purchaser ever having to venture into a gallery – accidentally the piece on the street had become an advertisement for itself. These online customers buying prints give Banksy a wider and more active web base than probably any other artist, living or dead.

For those who could afford a Banksy original and wanted to see the canvas on a wall in an exhibition, then Lazarides the showman was on hand, for as Jude Law once said, 'Steve is a bit of an event himself.' Turf War in 2003, followed by Crude Oils in 2005 and then Barely Legal in Los Angeles in 2006 and Bristol (without Lazarides) in 2009, were all very different shows but they had key elements in common: they were free; they were never publicised in the usual way, the secrecy adding to the allure; there were no white walls; and they were fun – the only thing that was intimidating was the queue to get in.

And for those who wanted a gallery to come to, rather than having to brave rats and pigs and elephants and crowds at the Banksy events, Lazarides opened his own gallery in Soho in early 2006 (he now has two more: one, much bigger, in Rathbone Place, Fitzrovia and a second in Newcastle run by Steve Parkin, who left Banksy at the same time Lazarides did). True, there are no white walls, but there is no getting away from the fact that the two London galleries are pretty straightforward, however hard Lazarides attempts to add a little edginess to emphasise that he is still one step removed from the system. He talks about his gallery in Soho having previously been a former sex shop for spanking enthusiasts which came complete with a dungeon, while he says his Fitzrovia gallery, in a five-floor townhouse, used to be a former brothel. In the same way, when he gave a show in New York he was almost proud of the fact that the former kitchen warehouse where he opened the exhibition used to 'have a lot of rat shit all over the floors'. However, his gallery in Rathbone Place now comes with a studio on the top floor occupied not by an artist but by one Johnnie Sapong – according to *Esquire* 'a star in the hairdressing firmament' – who counts among his customers Bryan Ferry, Jude

Law, Orlando Bloom and Justin Timberlake and charges £420 for a consultation. Edge is everything.

And in addition to the web, the shows or Lazarides' galleries, there were always the London auction houses. While Banksy himself never sold to the big auction houses – that would be a step too far for his followers – he did sell to Lazarides (£837,000 worth of paintings recorded in the company accounts in the years 2007 and 2008). What Lazarides did with them is unclear but the belief in the art world is that some of those paintings ended up with the auction houses.

What Banksy and Lazarides had done together was to create a market for street art where none had existed before. And it paid handsomely: 'We had a spectacular year in 2007 when we took three times the amount of money we took in any other year, but the market took a battering after that,' says Lazarides. And while it will do nothing to change the mind of artists who accuse him of being a sell-out, the fact is that without Banksy there might be a street art movement but there would not be a street art market.

When Lazarides left Banksy in late 2008 he sold his eighteen shares back to Pictures on Walls for a total of £70,000. (Parkin sold his shares back for £40,000.) It was good money, but he had lost much more than that – the artist who was capable of making more money for him than any other he will ever represent. There was no doubt Banksy would survive without Lazarides, but how would Lazarides survive without Banksy? The answer is, surprisingly well up to now. 'Everything I've done so far, all the expansion, has really happened in the recession. We only really started to find some sort of momentum in 2007 just before the rug was pulled . . . I'm immensely proud of the fact that the business is still going in 2011 when all we've done is reinvest every single penny we've made into expanding the business.'

Century published his book *Outsiders*, claiming to cover both artists who work on the streets and those who have 'made their name without taking the traditional path'. Despite the book's all-encompassing if slightly ludicrous subtitle, 'Art By People', there is no Banksy in the book, and Lazarides suggested that Banksy 'is a once-in-a-generation artist, if we had put even one image of his in the book it would have become all about him.' He might well be right, but the book was published almost a year after their break-up, so there is almost certainly more to Banksy's exclusion than simple artistic judgement. In addition Lazarides has published about fifteen books himself, either on the various artists he represents or on some of his shows. *Hell's Half Acre*, for instance, was the record of an extraordinary show he put on in conjunction with the Old Vic in October 2010 in the gloomy underground tunnels next to Leake Street. This was just about as far away from white walls as you could imagine, turning Dante's *Inferno* into a darkly lit exhibition-experience with everything from an armada of forty beautiful model ships suspended from the ceiling to wriggling maggots, a globe pierced with hypodermic syringes, Bernie Madoff (the fraudster now serving a 150-year prison sentence) carved out of plaster and an incredibly irritating loud dog bark that met you at the door to hell and would not go away.

He continues to attack the American market with flamboyance, organising huge shows in New York and Los Angeles. So he is still successful without Banksy, but it is a harder and perhaps riskier job than before. The art he sells remains very different and often exciting; nevertheless it all seems quite far removed from the street. A fellow gallery owner suggests: 'The initial thing was the whole Santa's Ghetto model – find a really destroyed space and put some artwork up. Now I think it's more about finding a space that looks money and then it's easier to get people with £40,000 to spend on artwork in there. So it's kind of going along with the established ways of selling artwork.'

But if Lazarides has shown what a classy gallery owner he is even without Banksy, what of Banksy without Lazarides? There is now no public face of Team Banksy as there was in Lazarides' day. But behind the scenes Holly Cushing, who changed horses from Lazarides with a couple of other staff, is now the power in Banksyland. One insider says she is so powerful 'she *is* Banksy.' Back in 1995, when she was working in California, she was listed as a 'production office assistant' for Sean Penn's film *The Crossing Guard*. So when Lazarides was preparing for Banksy's Barely Legal in Los Angeles, he asked Cushing to round up Brangelina and other celebrities to come to the show. She did the job incredibly well. Joel Unangst, who watched her at work, says: 'Out of all the people involved in the whole thing she came out on top and it's not surprising to me at all. She's a lovely woman and very attractive, but hard as nails at the same time. She knows about power and money and celebrity and she knows how to run with that crowd – she just thrives in that world. But she takes no prisoners.' Back in England she worked for the Lazarides gallery until the break-up, helping in particular with special sales. She keeps a low profile, never giving interviews, and is no competition to Banksy in the way Lazarides was perceived to be, but she is now the nearest anyone gets to being his manager. One measure of her success is the way she has risen to the top of the film credits. No longer is she Sean Penn's 'production office assistant'; instead, for *Exit Through the Gift Shop* she is Banksy's 'Executive Producer'.

I confess I have never met Holly, but I have heard quite a bit about her. Opinions range from Acoris Andipa's – 'She seems to be a very professional, balanced individual' – to that of a gallery owner who says 'she wants to control everything'. Another source suggests 'she is the direct line to the big man.' All in all, it sounds as though she is doing the job required of her.

People might not hear much of Holly but she is a sight to see. One influential member of the contemporary art world met her for the first time in Tate Modern's café: 'I had no idea what she looked like but when she came through the entrance to the café I knew instantly it had to be her.' She favours bleach blonde hair and likes wearing bright pink or bright red, or occasionally yellow. 'You are not going to miss her,' confirms Acoris Andipa, 'but why not – after all, we are in the art game and you can be whoever you want to be. She's dynamic and I think she genuinely has the best interest of Banksy within her. You don't want to be on the wrong side of her, for sure.'

A source closer to Banksy says she is a 'hard woman, tough, mercurial, and a very good buffer protecting him. She blows hot and cold depending on what day of the week it is. But she more or less runs the business side of things and in a way she's the perfect person to represent him. As for a gallery or representation, he is in such a strong position he doesn't need one.' However, there are many things that go with promoting an edgy but now quite expensive outsider like Banksy besides simply selling a painting. Like any other primary dealer, Lazarides was there to keep the clients happy, to promote the long-term relationship and to nurse Banksy's prices up from one level to the next so he could reassure collectors that their money was safe. Banksy has changed so much in the art market, but it will take time to see if he can dispense with a Lazarides type of figure and still remain as successful.

If you ever get beyond Holly Cushing the gatekeeper, what lies the other side of the gate? Is Banksy just Banksy or does he, like Damien Hirst, Jeff Koons and Takashi Murakami, leave much of the hard work and, in his case, the illegal street work to assistants? Or would that be a step too far for a street artist? Both Hirst and Koons have employed up to 100 assistants in their time. Some of Murakami's assistants, with his encouragement, have become artists in their own right. Hirst said that he got bored after his first five spot paintings – 'I couldn't be fucking arsed doing it' – and employed assistants to do the rest. This practice has become so widely accepted that it is only the fact that he is paying his assistants comparatively little when he makes so much that raises the odd eyebrow. But for Banksy the possibility of having one assistant, let alone 100, raises yet more accusations of 'sell-out' on the web.

One of his outer circle describes how it all works: 'If you are in the team it's not like you are there nine to five every day of the week, but he can call on the team when needed – like the Bristol show, where you can see differences in the work. It has to be a team for the amount of work that is produced, but he is the conductor. He's not like Damien Hirst where people are doing everything. He is very much involved.'

His erstwhile printer Ben Eine makes much the same point. 'He's one person. Although now he's so big, he's a brand. So he has people working for him, especially when he makes big sculptures. But he still makes all his own paintings and cuts his own stencils.'

There are some pieces which he must contract out although, importantly, the creative idea remains his. Banksy might be a very good stencil artist but that does not make him a good sculptor or a good producer of animatronics. Take for example the Banksy bronze rat, as endearing a rat as you will ever see. He stands about a foot high with a pack on his back and a baseball cap worn back to front, and he is wielding a paintbrush instead of a rifle. Sculpted in bronze and first seen in the exhibition in Los Angeles, later he popped up again hiding among the exhibits at Bristol Museum.

This was a work where the inspiration came from Banksy but the key sculpting was done by one Charlie Becker, a successful New York sculptor – now resident in Los Angeles – who has done work for everyone from Faile to Nike. Back in 2007 he posted a slightly amazed message on his website: 'A little while ago I got the honor of seeing a piece that I helped bring to life (for another artist) get sold like real art gets sold. At Sothebys, alongside Warhol, Basquiat, Damien Hirst and lots more. For a grip of cash too. Man, I need to get that catalog, gives me something to aspire to.'

This was in the days when Banksy, and many others too, were bringing in funny money. The bronze rat, one of an edition of twelve, signed and dated by the artist on the underside, made £68,400 at Sotheby's. Slightly less than a year later it went on sale at Sotheby's in New York and this time the final bid was $169,000. In London in 2011 a unique version with acrylic paint on the brush made £163,250. So yes, it was a 'real grip of cash'.

Becker also had on his website a photograph of Banksy's homeless Venus, which first appeared in the Barely Legal show in Los Angeles and re-emerged in Bristol, although by this time she had acquired the sort of dog that often accompanies beggars. Since most of the other Banksy sculptures are in this style, the assumption has to be that Charlie Becker has been Banksy's favourite sculptor. As for the Pet Store animatronics that first appeared in New York in 2008 and reappeared in Bristol, they had to be made by model-makers of Hollywood standard. Hot dogs having sex, a rabbit polishing her nails – the skills to create these pieces could not be acquired overnight, even though Banksy was very much the inspiration, the creator of this wonderfully weird pet shop.

Kate Brindley, who witnessed the Banksy team at work as they put together the exhibition at Bristol, says: 'What working with Banksy means is working with a team of people who represent or are Banksy. Yes, I am sure there is an individual, but there is a whole lot of people who work with him to deliver on whatever his passion is. So whether the work is made in collaboration with them or whether it is all his idea frankly doesn't bother me greatly. It might be all his idea but I'd be surprised, because actually most things are a team effort, aren't they? Given the scale of what happened and what was produced, obviously he commissioned stuff, because it's not all him making everything. But then that's artists' practice throughout the ages. That's nothing new. Artists commission work and it's theirs, they author it – as in the Renaissance, they had schools of assistants.'

But what happens when Banksy hits the street? Are those all his pieces? The answer is that in a great majority of cases they are – but not always. There is at least one example of him paying signwriters to do his work for him – and he was open in saying what he had done. At the time of his Pet Store show in New York in 2008, four huge rats went up in the SoHo district of New York. Bloggers were excited: was it actually Banksy they had spotted on high, painting away so openly? Well no, actually it was a young ambitious company called Colossal Media, trying to reintroduce the art of hand-painted signs, who did the work.

Today Colossal Media boast in their promotional material about the rats they drew for Banksy. 'Colossal had to execute all four walls simultaneously while maintaining complete secrecy about the project.' For months they worked with Banksy's team 'on site acquisition and preparation'. Banksy provided 'digital renderings of hand drawn sketches' which they then painted on to the walls. They are proud to claim that 'Colossal's role in the project was to function as any other artist's tool – as a means to an end.'

Banksy was open about it, despite his loathing of billboards. 'I wanted to play the corporations at their own game, at the same scale and in the same locations. The advantage of billboard companies is that they'll let you write anything for money, even if what you write is questioning the ethics of letting someone write anything because they have money.'

But the next step, getting other people to do his street pieces, is more controversial and certainly less clear. Ben Eine was asked by the magazine *Very Nearly Almost*: 'You used to paint with Banksy in the city, is it true you used to paint rats as well?'

'I used to help him paint stuff on the street. At some point, yes, I would've painted a rat. But it wasn't like I was going out with his stencils doing his rats.'

The clearest statement comes from Shepard Fairey. Two possible Banksys had been spotted in Boston at the time of the release of *Exit Through the Gift Shop*, which was a cue for great excitement and efforts by the *Boston Globe* to discover whether or not they were real. The reporter could not of course get to Banksy but did talk to Fairey, who was very matter of fact: 'Banksy doesn't actually execute a lot of the street pieces anymore.' So if it was a Banksy in Boston – and Fairey was very doubtful – it was not necessarily by Banksy. It may have been by his assistants: 'To me, it doesn't matter whether he was there. He orchestrated it. If you're still into believing that Batman cleans up the city by himself, fine.'

Quite how much or how little he uses assistants, or just friends out for the joyride, will probably never be clear. But the key point is this: without Banksy as the inspiration there would be no Banksys of any kind. As he himself says, 'I paint my own pictures but I get a lot of help building stuff and installing it. I have a great little team.'

And the more I examined this team, not just the team that is ready when he needs help with a big project, but also the more permanent team protecting his reputation, his commercial rights, his prices, the more it became clear that he functions in much the same way as any commercially successful artist would – albeit outside the traditional gallery system. And it is perhaps this fact, the fact that in many ways the outsider is now an insider, rather than any real worry about his identity, that this team – which makes very few mistakes – is so determined to hide.

# Ten
# The Business of Banksy

In February 2008, seven months before the collapse of Lehman Brothers, at a time when people were still confident enough to splash big money on good causes, New York's rich and famous gathered together at Sotheby's for a night of serious spending. The event, organised by Bono, Damien Hirst, Sotheby's and the Gagosian gallery, turned out to be the biggest charity art auction ever, raising $42.5m to support AIDS programmes in Africa.

The auction had everything. As well as giving work himself, Damien Hirst hand wrote letters to each artist asking them to contribute their work. 'I didn't expect the result to be as good as it was, but everybody's dug deep and given us major works rather than drawings and that. It feels like a real exhibition,' he said. Bono was the star, wearing a black military-style jacket and sunglasses, exhorting the 700 guests to spend and spend again and, since it was Valentine's Day, giving them an a capella version of 'All You Need is Love' to set them on their way.

And he led by example, spending more than $1 million on several pieces for himself. Hirst gave seven works which made a total of just over $19 million, including *Where There's A Will, There's*

*A Way*, a pill cabinet filled with drugs for the treatment of HIV, which sold for $7,150,000.

It was a sort of *Hello!* love-in. John McEnroe, Martha Stewart, Queen Noor, Dennis Hopper, Michael Stipe, Helena Christensen, Liya Kebede, Russell Simmons, Ziyi Zhang and Christy Turlington (who spent $170,500 on a watercolour by Francisco Clemente – who some years earlier had painted her portrait) were a few of the headline names.

Banksy was one of the artists Hirst had asked for help and he gave three pieces. Lot 69, *Ruined Landscape*, one of his detourned paintings, a rural scene with 'This is not a photo opportunity' pasted across it, sold for $385,000, just above the estimate.

Lot 33A was his *Vandalised Phone Box*, a red telephone box bent to almost ninety degrees and bleeding red paint where a pickaxe had been stuck through it. The phone box had originally been placed in Soho Square but it was soon carted off by an unsympathetic Westminster Council because it did not have planning permission.

Happily Banksy was allowed to claim it back, for now it went for $605,000, double the estimated price. Three years later the buyer was revealed to be another of those millionaires that Banksy complains about: Mark Getty, grandson of J. Paul Getty. He told the *Sunday Telegraph*, 'I bought it as a joke – the phone box is being killed, see?' The joke being that there were once rumours – untrue – that his billionaire grandfather had installed a pay phone to ensure guests would not make calls at his expense and this was his – costly – way of 'killing off the phone box rumours'. The phone box now sits in front of the library on Getty's 2500-acre estate in the Chiltern Hills.

But it was Lot 34, *Keep it Spotless*, that had everyone excited. The story according to Hirst was that he had been rounding up work for the auction and Banksy told him, 'Give me a painting and I'll mess around with it.' So Hirst had given him one of his spot paintings – it has always seemed as though he has quite a few to spare – and Banksy stencilled a maid hitching up the spots as though they were part of a curtain so she could brush away the dirt underneath. It was a clever piece, and before the auction Hirst showed the work to a reporter: 'I love his work and I have to say I like my own,' he said. 'I think it looks brilliant, doesn't it? Sweeping it under the carpet.' The painting fetched $1.8 million, a price that put Banksy on a completely new level, although the joke at the time was that it was either a very expensive Banksy or a very cheap Hirst.

The sale did two things. As Bono put it, 'art and love, sex and money came together' to raise a huge amount of money for AIDS work in Africa, but the auction also established price records for seventeen artists including Marc Quinn, Howard Hodgkin and Banksy himself. There was no instant reward other than a feel-good factor for Banksy, but other artists' agents use auctions – and are sometimes actually bidding at them – as a way of establishing a public price which they can refer to when selling privately to collectors. So what this auction did for Banksy and other artists was to reassure collectors, particularly in a year when the financial world was collapsing all around them, that the prices they were paying privately were supported – and indeed in this case far surpassed – in the auction houses.

*Keep it Spotless* had all the charity hype behind it and, perhaps more important, the fact that it was a Hirst painting that Banksy had defaced. In the real world his prices were nowhere close to what was paid for *Keep it Spotless*, but they were jumping up in astounding amounts. In June 2005 a record for a Banksy original was set at £21,000; just over a year later his *Mona Lisa* sold for £57,600. In 2007, the year after Barely Legal in Los Angeles had opened up the American market, it was difficult to keep track of the increase. *Bombing Middle England* fetched £102,000 in February; *Space Girl and Bird* had an estimated price of £10,000 to £15,000 but sold at Bonhams in April for £288,000, and *The Rude Lord* reached £322,900 at Sotheby's in October. Bonhams followed this up with their first 'Urban Art' sale in February 2008, which essentially gave street artists a category all of their own – a slightly less threatening category than 'street art' itself or 'graffiti art'. But whatever it was called, it was the night that street art was seduced, without too much of a struggle, into the mainstream and Gareth Williams, Bonhams' Urban Art specialist, remembers it well. 'The first sale was phenomenal beyond belief. I had been working at an auction house for fifteen years and never seen anything like it. The global press interest was just crazy. We were late in starting the sale, so many people were there; they were queuing to register so we couldn't actually start on time. All the Banksys commanded good prices, but it wasn't just Banksy, the whole sale sold with the exception of one lot.'

So how important is Banksy in this whole urban art world? 'Very important. He kind of kick-started the market. There are lots of other artists out there who are equally deserving, but I am not necessarily convinced they would have had so much limelight and achieved such good results without him. He's a household name. Everyone's grandma knows Banksy.'

At the end of that same month Sotheby's put up for sale Banksy's *Simple Intelligence Testing* with an estimated price of £150,000. It is a work in five parts where a monkey finds the right box with the bananas hidden in it, but then outwits his intelligence testers first by eating the bananas and then by escaping through a vent in the ceiling. It fetched £636,500, which apart from that achieved by *Keep It Spotless* remains by far the highest price ever paid for a Banksy. *Simple Intelligence Testing* had been painted in 2000 and sold at the Severnshed exhibition, so it would have been the original buyer who made the money rather than Banksy.

But he would have done better out of *Rude Lord*, an eighteenth-century portrait of an aristocrat by Thomas Beach for which Banksy paid £2000 and then detourned so that the aristocrat was giving us all the finger. He finished the painting in 2006, in time for his Los Angeles show, and then Steve Lazarides sold it on to a collector who swiftly put it into auction. This very short chain of events all happened within the space of a year, so it is one painting in these early auctions where Banksy would have received, if not the auction price, then at least a decent price for his work. But for the most part, as Banksy put it, 'The auction houses were just selling paintings that I'd done years before and sold for not much money. Or paintings that I traded for a haircut or, you know, an ounce of weed and they were going for like fifty grand.'

Although no Banksy work has gone beyond the price of *Simple Intelligence Testing*, it is still a pretty golden ceiling for any artist to reach, particularly a graffiti artist. Indeed it is this street art background that is his problem. Compared to the likes of Hirst or Jeff Koons, Banksy is a pauper; comfortable, making good money, but not a multi-millionaire. He says, 'I don't have a lavish lifestyle,' and others support him. A collector agrees that 'He's pretty low maintenance' and Mike Snelle, director of the influential Shoreditch gallery Black Rat Projects, says: 'From what I'm told he's not living in a dream mansion with a pool. He lives in an ordinary house and gives a lot of the money away. People like Banksy aren't people who want to buy Porsches and Rolexes and things.'

But with graffiti there are – or there were – a different set of rules. If street art is somehow free art for the people, then what is it doing fetching such high prices in the auction houses? Andy Warhol in the past seemed positively to enjoy the fact that he could make so much money from his art, as does Damien Hirst today, but with Banksy it sits uneasily; it might well be temptingly enjoyable, but he still finds it slightly difficult to square with the softly leftish view of the world that comes through in his work.

Having complained about art galleries becoming trophy cabinets for a handful of millionaires, he has now found himself becoming one of the trophies and he doesn't like it – although the money may have proved handy. It was at the time of all the excitement about the prices he was achieving that he released a print known as *Morons*. An auctioneer is shown hard at work taking bids for a painting which is displayed on a stand next to him. The reference Banksy used in making this print is almost certainly the sale of Van Gogh's *Sunflowers* back in 1987 for what then seemed an astonishing world record price of £25 million. But the canvas the auctioneer is selling has no sunflowers, only the words 'I CAN'T BELIEVE YOU MORONS ACTUALLY BUY THIS SHIT' scrawled across it. When the print of the picture went up for sale on his website, the sales pitch was not the usual kind: 'Banksy makes a cr*p picture about how people pay a lot of money for cr*p pictures, which someone then ends up paying a lot of money for. A portion of irony eating itself, anyone?'

An edition was printed in Los Angeles at the time of his big show there and a much larger edition was subsequently issued in the UK, bringing the total number of prints to just over 1000.

Banksy took at least £120,000 from these prints; he could have taken much more, for they were soon selling in the auction houses for up to £5000, but nevertheless it was an enjoyable example of him having his cake and eating it too.

As is the case with almost any artist, the price private collectors pay for his paintings is impossible to establish accurately. However, there are two ways of getting some sort of feeling about the prices for Banksy's originals. The first is through the auction houses, where the prices are visible and can be tracked over the years. The website artnet.com, which has emerged as the art world's key recorder of auction prices on the internet, shows the way new collectors with new money bounded into the Banksy market in 2007, sustained it throughout 2008 and then paused for a very deep breath. The market in Banksys, like that in most other commodities, has yet to reach those heights again, although it would be unfair to suggest there has been too much of a bubble – his prices remain strong, just not as strong.

If you look at Banksy's prices recorded on the web, no post-2008 price comes in the top ten. *Insane Clown*, which sold in New York in November 2009 for $386,500, reaches number 11. His prices in 2010 and 2011 have averaged around £56,000. Compare this with 2008, where anyone with a Banksy on the wall suddenly realised they could be rich. The canvases coming to market were double the number available in 2010 and the average price was around £100,000 – and that excludes the three sold for record amounts in the New York charity auction. Even some of his prints were reaching figures of around £5000 and occasionally nearer to £10,000.

But if you wanted to sell, you had to hurry, because from July 2008 onwards, as the world financial markets fretted and failed, an increasing number of Banksys were marked 'Bought In' because they did not reach their reserve price. December 2008 was a particularly dismal month when twenty-eight lots were auctioned, all but one of them prints, but only two sold; the rest had to be bought in. Sellers either had to lower their prices or wait for better days. But a collector, particularly anyone buying a canvas, today can be reassured that although the market has fallen from its height, it is still a healthy one.

The other source is the accounts for Pest Control Office Ltd, Banksy's company, which has taken over his sales from Steve Lazarides. Although the details are scant, the way he has chosen to run his business life through private limited companies means, ironically, that there is probably more financial information publicly available on the anonymous Banksy than on any other artist. In June 2010 Pest Control's assets were £1.1 million, a figure that had jumped by a hefty £900,000 in the year after Lazarides left. There is no way of telling in these abbreviated accounts where exactly all this £900,000 came from, but it is a reasonable assumption to make that a very high percentage of it came from the sale of Banksy originals.

The prints are easier to track than the canvases, because they are all sold through his website and the prices have been there for all to see. Banksy's prints are a phenomenon in themselves. As we have seen, he started out like any other artist, selling prints to any gallery that would take them. You could usually pick them up for £40 unsigned or £100 signed. But then as the demand grew he discovered that he did not need galleries at all. He was selling to a computer-literate generation, and although some preferred to go to Banksy's gallery in Shoreditch and queue for hours for a newly released print, many were happy to see a print online, buy it online and then put it up on their wall without ever putting a foot inside a gallery.

If they decided they didn't like their print, or decided simply that they wanted to make money out of it, there was always eBay. They weren't stuck with it – they could make an instant profit. As one dealer says: 'Banksy wouldn't have happened if it hadn't been for eBay. The two just happened to come along at the same time. It was happenstance rather than planning. No one flipped art before then. It just hadn't happened. But with Banksy people queued for four or five hours for a print and by the time they were out of the queue it would be on eBay.'

'All of a sudden it was like the new gold rush,' says Steve Lazarides. 'You could go out, buy a Banksy print at 250 quid. The next day you could sell it for two and a half grand. What other investment is going to make ten times your money overnight?

'And then the next owner, if they were lucky, could sell it on again for five grand . . . so it was a no-brainer in those days of easy credit.

'We'd open a show and you'd have people running at you. You'd be trying to sell something to a client and you'd have someone tapping you on the shoulder . . . saying "No, no, I want to buy it." There was one instance where we caught someone flipping a work in the gallery before they'd even paid for it.'

For Banksy this posed a problem that he has never quite dealt with, one to which it is actually impossible for him to find the right answer. He wanted to keep his prints at prices not too far removed from what his original fans could pay, but as he said, 'Every time I sell things at a discount rate, most people put them on eBay and make more money than I charged them in the first place. The novelty with that soon wears off.' His prices have gone up steadily, if slowly – but so too has demand. A Banksy print can still be flipped very profitably on eBay, although the seller will not make the money they could have made in the boom years.

His print operation is unique both in its scale and in its demand. Go back through the old web postings when a rumour went out that a Banksy print was about to be launched and you will see how the hardcore Banksy fans went mental. Reading these postings now on the Urban Art Association website it seems comic, but at the time it became a matter of life and death for those involved in the chase. A millisecond after a print was released, the buyer had to be on the Banksy website and putting the print in their basket or else it was too late. Either the site crashed because everyone was on it, or the prints had all gone. Some took the afternoon off, the day off, or chose to 'work at home', while others stayed up in the hope that it would be released in the dead of night. For Banksy has always been a bit of a tease; the word would go out that a print was going to be released but no definite date or time was given as to when. Desperate buyers discussed the latest rumour on the site as they waited: 'Stuff like this makes me a nervous wreck for days and nights.' They dared not leave their computer: 'I'm a diabetic and I'm going to miss lunch because of this. If I die can I sue?' 'I need to pee. Can I wait – no. I bet it drops now.' This could go on and on for days; then suddenly, instantly it was there, and then it was gone. Despair followed: 'It's sold out, gone, goodbye.' 'f**k missed it.' 'Did anyone get one?' 'I need this. Anyone who carted it and doesn't want it I got 1000 pounds!' 'Went into a meeting and just got out and they're all sold out. Gutted.' 'I want to cry . . .' '. . . Get in the queue.' But there was also unadulterated joy: 'Got one yeahhhhhhhhhh. Three years of just losing out and now I bag my first Banksy.' And this joy was sometimes coupled with a hint of profit to come: 'Yessss. My first Banksy Yess. What's the edition size?' Recently this online agony has largely been eliminated, for there is now a lottery system online, as well as the chance to queue all night for those who don't want to trust to luck.

There is a site on the web called www.banksy-prints.com. It is a work in progress, although midway through 2010 it seemed to run out of progress, but someone with impressive dedication has tried to catalogue every Banksy print, for no visible financial reward. With the help of other websites, particularly www.UrbanArtAssociation.org. and www.thebanksyforum.com, and from talking to collectors, it is possible to give a rough outline of the Banksy print operation. In all he has created forty-eight different limited edition prints over eight years. They used to be divided unequally between signed and unsigned but more recently they are all coming signed – which makes them more difficult to fake. They have brought in at least £3.8 million and probably a fair bit more, since on the occasions when the size of the print run or the exact price is unclear I have gone in my calculations for a lower figure. In addition this sum does not account for the very limited number of artist's proofs which come with any print run. His highest figure was attained in 2006, when a run of six prints first shown in Los Angeles raised over £1 million. In 2002 he needed to sell fifteen different prints to make just under £500,000. In 2009 he could make the same money by releasing just two.

His most successful print was the portrait of Kate Moss, done in very much the same style as Andy Warhol's portrait of Marilyn Monroe, which is considered the holy grail by many collectors. It was far more expensive at source than any other Banksy print before or after, so it is not representative of Banksy prints in general; it is almost as though he was saying 'This is what I could do if I was really trying to make money.' It was first shown at the Crude Oils exhibition in Notting Hill along with all the rats. There were five canvases at £5000 each, thus £25,000, but interestingly, some fans consider the prints better than the canvases. One collector suggests, 'The image works far better aesthetically as a print: clean, graphic and luxurious. For me the texture of the canvas weakens the overall impact – looking rather cheap, like the inkjet on canvas images you can order through Snappy Snaps.'

The prints came in an edition of fifty at £1500 each – but despite the price they sold out, so that was another £75,000. Two months later, in another nod to Andy Warhol and his different colourways – *Mint Marilyn*, *Cherry Marilyn*, *Orange Marilyn* and so on – Banksy issued six further colourways. There were twenty of each colour. These prints were £2500 each – although, rather like being at a supermarket, you could have six for the price of five. So a set would cost you £12,500. This release would have brought in an additional £250,000.

At this point, with the print and the five canvases having already raised £350,000, it becomes more difficult. For there were a further twelve artist's proofs of the colourways edition and five of the original edition on canvas. It is impossible to tell what happened to these, although when Steve Lazarides opened his gallery in Soho an artist's proof of *Kate Moss* was selling for £4000. At a conservative estimate Banksy, or rather Banksy, his gallery Pictures on Walls and Lazarides, must together have made at least £400,000 from *Kate Moss*, and probably a fair amount more.

But this is nothing compared to what the buyers made. (The highest price reached at auction for *Kate* has been £96,000 in 2008, although the auction price is usually around the £40,000 to £50,000 mark.) Looking around an exhibition of prints at the Black Rat Gallery, I came across a *Kate Moss* which looked stunning hung against the gallery's bare brick walls. It was marked 'Price on

Application' and when I duly applied, Mike Snelle, the director of the gallery, told me that he was selling it on behalf of a collector who had already turned down an offer well above £100,000.

I told him how much I liked it but asked him what Kate was adding to Marilyn – she might be an icon but she is certainly not up there in the icon charts with the likes of Marilyn. There was a pause and he then replied: 'I could say Kate Moss. I guess I think it's playing with the original Warhol idea. I think the way to view it is that there is a whole generation of people now who perhaps haven't been very interested in art in the past who have come to art through street art and who will recognise the Banksy version of the Warhol over the original Warhol. I think that's a very Warhol idea.'

So will they even know that there is a Warhol version? 'I think they will, but they might know it subsequently to seeing this one. And I think there is something interesting to that idea. Something playful and clever about it.' Clever in what way? 'Clever in the idea of celebrity fame, modern culture and the idea that you can distort something to the point where you can change the meaning of it so that the original version is no longer recognised and it's a back to front thing. People are seeing that and learning about the Warhol. And there is something slightly subversive about that idea.'

At the end of 2010 I decided it was time to enter the Banksy market myself. In October a new Banksy appeared on a wall in Southwark, a barking dog painted very deliberately in the style of Keith Haring being taken for a walk on a chain by a hoodie who looked as menacing as the dog. Just over a month later Banksy opened his annual Christmas show, although this year it was called Marks & Stencils rather than the usual Santa's Ghetto.

Having heard via the web that the Southwark stencil had now been turned into a new print which would be released during this exhibition, I took myself down to the empty shop on Berwick Street in Soho which he had taken over for Marks & Stencils. Admittedly it was not a big space; nevertheless there was still a queue at the door. As I stood waiting in the freezing cold I thought it might be hype, it might be greed or, forget the cynicism, it might just actually be people interested in street art . . . but what other modern artist could set up in a shop and have a queue standing on a freezing cold winter's day waiting to get in? I stood in this queue for about half an hour. On one side of the street I could examine Banksy's shop window, inside which a newly constructed breezeblock wall advertised 'Street Art now in a gallery near you' and a teddy bear sat slightly lewdly on a plaster column (well, this was Soho). On the opposite side of the street, Seymores World offered XXX DVDs, as well as Delay Spray, Spanish Fly and Spankarama DVDs.

Eventually I was let in to two floors of Banksarama. This, like his other Ghetto shows, was anything but a white-walled space. There was *no* space on any wall; every inch was taken in a deliberate jumble of work, while the basement was given over to Dran, a vaguely subversive French street artist many of whose works were painted on cardboard. In amongst all this, but not given any special prominence, was the print of the hoodie with his dog – it now had a name, *Choose Your Weapon*. This surely was too good to be true, a Banksy print there for me after only half an hour's queuing. Of course it was a fantasy: you could look but you could not buy.

For that you had to wait for the off, announced via email by Banksy's gallery. And Banksy was teasing yet again, for almost every day there was a new email to be found from the gallery, frustratingly titillating, announcing the release of more prints from the show, but none of them by Banksy. Finally the day arrived. The price was £450. There were 175 available online – the names would be drawn by lottery, so I did not have to sit up all night hitting the refresh button. Or if you wanted to go down to queue all night at the gallery, there would be another 200 on sale.

I have to confess that the thought of an all-night queue in December in Shoreditch was too much for me. I applied online. And, reading the blog artonanisland.blogspot.com, I was very glad I did. The blogger, Evan Schiff, a Californian in his early thirties who had been living in London for three years, heard the rumour that the print was about to be released, so at 9 p.m. on Friday night he hurried down to Soho. He was about 180th in line! An hour and a half later the news was out: the prints would go on sale the next morning but they would be sold from Banksy's gallery, Pictures on Walls in Shoreditch.

'You've never seen so many people move that fast', he blogged. 'People running through the streets of central London trying to buy cabs from others who were waiting. I started a mad dash with two guys who were in back of me in line. They had a car and I did a few calculations and thought I'd get there quickest with them. I reckon it took about twenty-five minutes. We parked about three blocks before POW's showroom. In a dead sprint we ran to the queue and when the dust settled, ended up being about 150th in line. Result!

'Having come straight from work I wasn't prepared for the cold at all. No sleeping bag, no long underwear, I hadn't even worn my scarf that day. However, nervous that in the 10 minutes it would take for me to run home they'd pass out tickets and I'd miss out, I stayed the course.

'The night from 2–6am was fairly uneventful save for the odd fight (two that I counted) or figuring out who was gonna walk across the street to get tea (which started the night at about 50p a cup and ended the night at a pound a cup). However, at about 6:30 our second bout of absolute bedlam. A security guard/POW person showed up with tickets. And the queue absolutely imploded. People from the back running to the front, people at the front trying to fight them off. And perhaps worst of all, CARLOADS of people pulling up and walking right up to the ticket dude and getting their tickets. It was terrible.' He was being pushed further and further down the queue.

'Once all the touts and queue jumpers were sorted out the fat bald security guy started making his way through the line. I was nervous as hell, cracked out from being up all night, and just hoping me and the people I was with would be sorted out. As he came closer to us (I was about 10 people away at this point) he got to number 170 and said "that's it, that's the last number."

'Devastation. I can't believe I waited that bloody long for NOTHING.'

He had started on his way home when a couple of people who were behind him in the queue stopped their taxi and told him to get in. They had heard a hint that there might be a few more prints on sale back at Marks & Stencils. He arrived there to find he was number seventeen in the queue. This time they established their own rules, drawing numbers on everyone's hand.

'At 9am, the first employee showed up and we went up to him. "We're here, we will gladly go home, please just tell us if we can buy a print here." "We have 60 prints for you here." Absolute bedlam. He passes out tickets and for the next few hours we all sat around telling stories, talking art, and really enjoying each other's company.

'When my number was eventually called to go in and buy my print, I pumped my fist and walked in to the store.' He had his Banksy. He says now that it is not his favourite Banksy image but 'it was my first Banksy and one that will be on my wall for ever.'

The Banksy queue has become something of a club. One successful member of this 'club' says, 'You got to remember we meet every year and there are people there you've met at the last sale and they just come up to you saying "Oh, how you doing?"; it's lovely, it's a really nice community, but the problem you've got is that before I had collected my print of *Choose Your Weapon* somebody at the front of the queue had already put theirs on eBay for £10,000.' He says the *Choose Your Weapon* queue was the only bad queue he has experienced: 'There were fights and all sorts, it was scary.' And while in a way it seems amazing to queue all night for a piece of art, in many ways it seems rather more admirable (and profitable too, if you want it to be) than queuing all night for, say, a football ticket or a good view of the royal wedding or the New Year sales. (Banksy eventually issued a further edition of fifty-eight prints in 'Queue Jumper Edition (Warm Grey)' for those who missed out in the scrum at Shoreditch and had their names and details taken by one of his staff.) As for me, I stayed warm and comfortable, but unhappily my number never came up in the online lottery.

Banksy took close to £200,000 for this one print but did not keep any of it for himself. He donated all the money from the proceeds to the Russian art collective Voina – *war* in Russian – which performs public protest happenings that include everything from orgies to throwing cats at bored McDonald's workers on

International Workers' Day. When he decided to make the donation, two of Voina's members were in jail charged with aggravated hooliganism and facing a prison sentence of up to five years. Lucy Ash had reported on their deeds on the BBC's *From Our Own Correspondent*, detailing how they had painted an erect penis on a drawbridge across the River Neva in St Petersburg. Every time the drawbridge opened, the penis, 65m tall and 27m across, was there in all its glory opposite the building which is the local headquarters of the KGB's successors, the Federal Security Service. (The penis reached a shortlist for a state prize for contemporary art, mysteriously slipping off the list and then re-emerging as the winner, with $14,000 being awarded to the group.) Rather more seriously, the group had overturned seven police cars in protest against police corruption.

Banksy must have been one of the people listening to her report, for soon afterwards she was in Italy about to interview the mayor of an impoverished hilltop village when her mobile rang. 'It felt a bit surreal and I wondered at first if the call was a hoax,' she reported. 'After all, it is not every day you get phoned up by one of the world's most elusive artists.' It was not actually Banksy but his ubiquitous PR Jo Brooks, who told her that Banksy wanted to help.

'How much do you reckon it'll cost,' Brooks asked, 'to get them out?'

'Uncharacteristically, I was lost for words. I mumbled that I was not sure whether he could help get them out of prison, but that I was certain that the artists would be most grateful for his support.'

In very simple terms the donation worked – and there was still a lot of it to spend, which they say will in turn be used to help 'political prisoners'. Early in 2011, after almost four months in jail, they were released, having posted bail of 300,000 roubles, about

£6500 each. Although their troubles were far from over, Banksy had secured their release from prison, even if he could not get rid of the charges against them. He had also raised their profile across the web to a level they could never have dreamed of, and this perhaps had made them just a little safer.

There are many ways Banksy could make more money. He could take a few of the commercial jobs offered to him – if Blek le Rat can don a Hugo Boss suit to judge a Hugo Boss stencil competition, then why not Banksy at what would probably be a much higher price? He could license the Banksy brand. He could put up the price of his prints. He could keep more of the money he does make by cutting back on the eclectic range of good causes he supports. He could accept the sort of interior commissions now on offer – the late Gunter Sachs' castle at Lake Worth in Austria is one of the best examples of graffiti taken on to inside walls. Yet even though he does none of these things he still can't win, he will still be accused of being a sell-out. Thus he remembers the time he went to see the film *Precious*, where they played the trailer for *Exit Through the Gift Shop* before the main feature. It was not an enjoyable experience: 'Someone two rows in front shouted "OH MY GOD, BANKSY IS SUCH A SELL-OUT" and I shrank into my seat.'

Ever since starting this book I have been getting Banksy birthday cards and Banksy Christmas cards and plain Banksy cards from friends who thought I needed encouragement. Banksy makes no money out of those at all. The graffiti is 'attributed to Banksy' but the copyright of the photograph of Banksy's work is with the photographer and the card company. All the mugs, the cards, the cheaply printed canvases, the iPod skins, the laptop covers, the Banksy buttons, even the 'Banksy style' decorative wall stickers, are rip-offs. The producers of all these money-spinners are no doubt encouraged by the words of Banksy himself who told the *Sunday Times* 'if you've built a reputation on having a casual attitude towards property ownership, it seems a bit bad-mannered to kick off about copyright law.' Unless he has some secret licensing deal, which seems very unlikely indeed, he has nothing to do with any of them; he just happens to produce the art on the streets for others to profit from.

While the souvenirs could possibly be money-making ventures for him, he could make much bigger money if he was prepared to do commercial work. For, as graffiti crosses over to the mainstream – brand managers now reference his work as 'intelligent mischief' – there could be no greater prize than having Banksy as your figurehead.

As far back as 2003 he was being courted for advertising jobs. The *Guardian*'s Simon Hattenstone asked him if there was work he would turn down on principle. He replied: 'Yeah, I've turned down four Nike jobs now. Every new campaign they email me to ask me to do something about it. I haven't done any of those jobs. The list of jobs I haven't done now is so much bigger than the list of jobs I have done. It's like a reverse CV, kinda weird. Nike have offered me mad money for doing stuff.'

'Never' is a dangerous word to use, but three years later he told his friend Shepard Fairey: 'I don't do anything for anybody any more, and I will never do a commercial job again.' He explained in some detail why he had done the cover for the Blur album, not that anyone was accusing him of selling out over that. 'I've done a few things to pay the bills, and I did the Blur album. It was a good record and it was quite a lot of money. I think that's a really important distinction to make. If it's something you actually believe in, doing something commercial doesn't turn it to shit just because it's commercial. Otherwise you've got to be a socialist rejecting capitalism altogether, because the idea that you can marry a quality product with a quality visual and be a part of that even though it's capitalistic is sometimes a contradiction you can't live with. But sometimes it's perfectly symbiotic, like the Blur situation.'

Very early on in his career he said, 'I'm kind of old fashioned in that I like to eat so it's always good to earn money.' He does make good money, but he could both make more and keep more than he does. 'I have been called a sell-out but I give away thousands of paintings for free, how many more do you want. I think it was easier when I was the underdog, and I had a lot of practice at it,' he told the *New Yorker*. 'The money that my work fetches these days makes me a bit uncomfortable, but that's an easy problem to solve – you just stop whingeing and give it all away. I don't think it's possible to make art about world poverty and then trouser all the cash, that's an irony too far, even for me.' He went on, 'I love the way capitalism finds a place – even for its enemies.'

There is no Banksy Foundation giving away money publicly; it's all done on a very ad hoc basis, with no ostentation. This makes it completely impossible to give a fair picture of what he gives away. But at one end there is the £1.5 million raised at the New York charity auction. At the other end there are the smaller gifts, like the hand-finished print of *Nola* (a young girl sheltering from the rain under her umbrella, originally put up in New Orleans to commemorate the third anniversary of Hurricane Katrina) which sold for almost £7000 at the annual art auction that Inkie organises to raise funds for a complicated operation for deaf children at Great Ormond Street hospital. It all adds up.

Apart from Voina there was £165,000 for Sightsavers from the release of the print *Flag* in 2006/7. There was a further £25,000 he raised for Sightsavers in 2008 by organising a raffle at his gallery when he released his new limited edition print *Very Little Helps*. The tickets cost £1 each with a maximum of twenty per person, and people queued for up to three hours to buy them. This raffle is another good measure of his following, for these were not tickets to win the print but simply to win the right to *buy* the print. Among the auction of original work, there was the £30,000 raised for Moorfields Eye Hospital and another £30,000 for a drop-in centre for asylum seekers run by the New North London Synagogue.

Then too there was a piece sold for £46,000 for the 'Defenestration Project' in San Francisco, a hotel building abandoned since 1989 which had been turned into a piece of art with all sorts of furniture, grandfather clocks, fridges, tables, chairs, sofas creeping out of every exit at every level of the four-storey building and staying stuck there. An appeal had been launched to raise funds so that all this outside-inside furniture, and the building itself, could be given a much-needed tarting up. When I first looked at the website for the project it had one of those sort of thermometers with a $75,000 goal and a line showing $30,000 had been raised. It was the kind of device that used to sit outside churches in the hope that it would encourage people to give and which, if there was not much progress towards the target after a few years, always began to look very sad. This one too looked like it would take for ever, but suddenly Banksy came along and the thermometer must have exploded. The very nature of the project probably appealed to him too; like his street work, the entire building will disappear, probably by the spring of 2013, to be replaced by a block of affordable apartments.

There was a print that raised £8000 for Rowdy, a graffiti artist from way back who had lost his house and his studio in a fire. There was also money for the failed campaign to re-elect Ken Livingstone as Mayor of London – hardly a charity, but nevertheless Livingstone benefited by £120,000 from the auction of a canvas in a complicated but legal arrangement set up to avoid Banksy having to reveal his true name as a donor to his campaign.

And there was Santa's Ghetto in Bethlehem in 2007. Again this shows Banksy's skills not just as an artist but as an organiser, co-ordinator, target-picker, the man who can make things happen. It was Banksy who rounded everyone up. In the *New Statesman* the artist Peter Kennard later recalled: 'The phone rings; the number is withheld. It's Banksy. He wants to know whether I can go to Bethlehem over Christmas. He is putting on an exhibition, bringing together like-minded artists from all over the world to raise awareness of the situation in Palestine. Two weeks later, I find myself involved in an experience that transforms my ideas about what artists can do in the face of oppression.'

Banksy made a similar call to almost twenty different artists across the world. He and his team got there first, both to organise and to find good sites on the wall for his own work. Working to a very tight deadline, they rented a disused chicken restaurant in Manger Square, transforming it virtually overnight into an art gallery. He was followed in two bursts by the great and the good of the street art world, who would both draw worldwide attention to the wall and donate all their art for sale at Santa's Ghetto. Of Banksy's own work, a dove wearing a bulletproof vest was perhaps the most arresting image; however, my favourite, a donkey having its identity papers checked by an Israeli soldier, caused unexpected trouble since the donkey was seen by some locals as portraying Palestinians in a rather unfavourable light. His colleague Tristan Manco wrote delicately: 'Given the local problems and high sensitivities, perhaps irony is not embraced in the same way in Bethlehem as it might be in London.' But whatever anyone's sensitivities the gallery, which existed for only one month, raised over $1 million. This money went to provide thirty university places for students who otherwise would never have had the chance to get anywhere close to university, as well as other good causes in the area.

Of course this money was not all from Banksy. Every artist who arrived in Bethlehem contributed to the gallery, but again he was the man who made it all happen. There is no 'school of Banksy' but he has a remarkable if loose gang of other street artists stretched across the world who think in much the same way he does. As for the money he makes, he keeps to his word, he does not 'trouser all the cash': he gives chunks of it away, maybe not enough to satisfy his critics but enough to make a difference to the odd assortment of people and causes that he chooses to support.

# Eleven
# Faking It

I have a Banksy on my wall. If I was trying to sell it, which I am not, I suppose I would say something like: '*Girl with Balloon*, Banksy. Giclée two colour print on Matt Paper 30 by 42, unsigned.' And if anyone bought it they would be a mug, because it is barely worth the paper it is printed on. So is it a fake? Well, no. Is it an original? No, it's obviously not that either. In the world of art there are many variations possible between these extremes, and in the world of Banksy there are inevitably extra twists to the tale.

On his website Banksy has a collection of about a dozen of his pictures and he says, 'You're welcome to download whatever you wish from this site for personal use. However making your own art or merchandise and passing it off as "official" or authentic Banksy artwork is bad and very wrong.'

So I accepted his invitation and went to my local print shop, where we downloaded the print for nothing. *Girl with Balloon* is one of his most popular and poignant images and although ambiguity is part of the picture's charm, it looks to me as if the little girl watching her heart-shaped balloon float away, string still trailing, is wishing it well rather than crying after it. At first the printers muttered slightly about the print being too 'low res' (low resolution). But they had a solution: shrink it to half the size. They encouraged me by saying that the very nature of the spray-painted image worked in our favour; the image was a bit fuzzy round the edges anyway, so what difference would it make if it printed out just that little bit more fuzzy? We agreed to give it a try.

They printed it out, using an inkjet printer ('giclée' is the posh word for an inkjet print, although both the ink and the paper would usually be of a considerably higher grade than the ingredients we were using). And there it was, my very own Banksy, looking very nice too. I took it to John Lewis and splurged £25 on a wooden frame which, added to the print shop cost, meant a grand total of £40. A bargain, especially since the last price I could find at auction of an unsigned *Girl with Balloon* was £1800 for a limited edition print, or an original canvas for £46,000. I had followed Banksy's website instructions and I had not done anything that was 'bad' or 'very wrong', and the girl and her balloon sit very appropriately in my wife's therapy office, where so much of the talk is about 'letting go'.

Apart from giving me considerable pleasure – thank you, Banksy – what this print shows is just how easy it is to copy a Banksy. You can go on the web and find a whole mini-industry of Banksy copies there. In fact I could have bought my Balloon Girl from canvastown.com, which claims to be 'the largest retail Banksy graffiti specialist in the world', for £20 plus £5 delivery charge. It was unframed but it was on stretched canvas, so perhaps mine was not such a bargain. (When I telephoned canvastown.com to discuss their marketing of Banksy prints they put down the phone on me.)

But, leaving aside the question of copyright, these canvases, bought so easily on the web, are not fakes; they are simply copies. It is only when a seller attempts to deceive a buyer into believing that what is being sold is an authentic and authorised Banksy product, whether it be a print, a canvas or anything else, that a copy becomes a fake. It is tempting though, for if you want to sell your copy, claiming it is authenticated, you have the added encouragement: the artist you are faking is himself in a vague way wanted by the police. As Detective Sergeant Vernon Rapley, who headed Scotland Yard's Art & Antiques Unit for nine years, told *The Art Newspaper*, 'There is an assumption that Banksy is not going to stand up in court and say "Oi, that's my work you are copying."' This combination of relative ease and an artist who is – or was – not too bothered by copyright is altogether too much temptation for some.

But Banksy's anonymity offers another temptation too, the temptation to *be* Banksy either by trying to paint like him or by assuming his identity on the web. Not for money, but for kicks. Artists who spray Banksy-like images on walls presumably sit back and watch as the web debates whether this is a real Banksy or just a lookalike. It must be satisfying for a Banksy wannabe to witness the debate and the fact that sometimes people can't tell the difference – 'So what's Banksy got that I haven't got?' For example, in June 2010 a couple of stencils appeared on the wall of a pub garden in Primrose Hill, London. A hooded artist, who arrived in the middle of the night, was filmed at work by the pub's CCTV cameras. It looked as though he was taking too long to be a proper hit-and-run graffiti artist, but no matter, for a few excited days it was thought to be a Banksy. The pub was about to come up for auction and the owners must have hoped they would be selling off both pub and Banksy, but they were disappointed.

Before the auction took place Jo Brooks pronounced: 'It's a fake, I can't say more than that.' (The pub fetched £1.59 million anyway.)

A much more convincing stencil of a pouting girl clutching her own Oscar appeared soon after the 2011 Academy Awards ceremony on a wall in Weston-super-Mare (Banksy's film *Exit Through the Gift Shop* had been nominated for Best Documentary but failed to win, which might explain why the girl was pouting). Never mind that Weston-super-Mare is quite a distance from Los Angeles, it is only about twenty miles from Bristol, so this was hailed as Banksy's 'response' to the Oscars and very rapidly covered in Perspex to preserve it. MelroseandFairfax, the usually reliable West Coast bloggers of the LA street art scene, fell for this new Banksy and even told us what it meant. 'This new piece seems to say "I'm going to take my ball and go home" and at the same time poke fun at the very idea of the award.' However it only took a few days before the Banksy cognoscenti declared it a fake and MelroseandFairfax had to admit they had made a mistake – 'Fakesy not a Banksy.' They went on to describe the problems they face: 'Each day, we get a half dozen tips that there might be a new Banksy, and most of the time we can sift through to tell what is a Banksy and what is not. We got fooled on this one. We screwed up, and we can admit when we're wrong.'

But in addition to these Banksy wannabes there is another small but distinct group who are not interested in painting like him but in a weird and slightly spooky way want the world to accept them *as* Banksy: if the world doesn't know who he is, why can't he be me? When I first started on the Banksy trail I went on the web and very quickly – a little too quickly – came across a filmed interview with Banksy on YouTube. There he was in the flesh, eating a slice of pizza and chatting to us rather fiercely. The camera was darting all over the place but it was still very possible to identify him. He was pronouncing angrily in an accent that was more South London than Bristol, 'Don't get me wrong, I think it's great that you can make art about world poverty, hunger, violence, horror, all the fucking horrible shit that goes on in this world and then trouser loads of cash for it . . . it don't get better than that, does it?' The last time I saw the video a quarter of a million people had viewed it, probably thinking like me that they had fallen upon Banksy. But by the end of the two and a half minutes it was clear it couldn't be him: too much 'fucking this' and 'fucking that' for one thing, too many face shots for another. And perhaps most interesting was that somehow I held an image of the anonymous Banksy as being rather a nice, cuddly bloke, and this guy wasn't nice at all; he didn't fit my image of who he should be.

But at least he wasn't causing anyone any trouble. At the time of Banksy's exhibition in Bristol, however, the *Guardian* carried an interview with him at the back of the *Guide* which comes out every Saturday. It was all a bit jokey and it was conducted by email, but then it was Banksy and any paper is always more than glad to trumpet a Banksy interview. He was asked, for instance, why he hadn't charged for entry to the show at Bristol and made his fortune. 'I'm an accountant's worst nightmare. I had suggested a £20 entry with a voucher for £20 off your next purchase of any original Banksy but people didn't think it would work out.' After various responses in this vein, the last question he was asked was what he would paint on the wall of the *Guide* if he happened to break in one weekend. 'A giant comedy cock,' he replied, making the embarrassment that was to follow even worse.

Three days later the *Guardian* apologised. The interview, 'it transpires, was conducted with someone impersonating the graffiti artist', and 'we apologise to Banksy for this error and for any offence and inconvenience caused.' In a way it was another triumph for Banksy; there was more publicity for the exhibition and he both remained anonymous and had a newspaper apologising to him for an 'offence' essentially created by that very anonymity. A week later the *Guardian*'s readers' editor examined the case. Rich Pelley, the journalist, had sent his questions to an email address which his source had convinced him would put him in direct email contact with Banksy. Neither he nor the *Guide*'s editor had any doubt that the interview was genuine, particularly since it came at the time of the Bristol show when Banksy was looking for publicity. However the readers' editor suggested that this was not enough; the *Guide* should have called Banksy's 'official spokesperson' to verify the interview.

It was just such a call which saved the *Observer* from similar embarrassment. The paper's *Music Monthly* was putting together a special art and music issue. Miranda Sawyer, a writer on the paper, had been contacted by someone on Facebook who, over the course of several months, had convinced her that he was Banksy. She told Caspar Llewellyn Smith, the magazine's editor, that she would ask Banksy for a list of his top ten favourite records – a perfect fit for the issue. 'It seemed slightly odd,' he says, 'but I thought, she knows a lot of people in the art world. So it seemed plausible that Banksy would know her and I assumed that he operated under some sort of alias on Facebook.' As the deadline drew ever closer, no list had appeared but Banksy was still promising to do it, 'and because I'd met him a few times I thought if she's saying "It's for Caspar's magazine," he'll do it.'

It was as though this Banksy character was grooming Sawyer

in a deeply unpleasant way. 'He was quite friendly and had a similar sense of humour,' she says, 'and it gradually progressed and escalated . . . He was always quite flaky, quite hard to get hold of, all the stuff that you would imagine.' But slowly she got to know things about him. 'It was all kind of plausible. He kept going down to the West Country, which is obviously where Banksy is from. He was living in London on a boat on the river, which was also kind of likely. He was really, really druggy; and I thought, yeah, well maybe that's not implausible . . . We kept nearly meeting and then not meeting. And you don't want to push it because you think it's Banksy.'

'Banksy' did indeed come up with his top ten, number one being the completely plausible, very right-on 'The Revolution Will Not Be Televised' by the late Gil Scott-Heron, and it went on from there. Not only did he provide his list, but he also provided the artwork to go with it – Michael Jackson as a sort of Madonna. By the time the list arrived the deadline had almost been and gone; but the magazine needed to check the copyright on the artwork and it was at this point that Banksy's PR was asked for confirmation that this was the real thing. Llewellyn Smith says, 'She immediately came back to me saying "He's not done anything like that and he doesn't know the journalist."'

But in the anonymous world of Banksy you never quite know the rules. Was Banksy pretending it was someone else when it really was him? What was really going on? So in the meantime Miranda Sawyer was desperately trying to get hold of the man she thought was Banksy to ask him for the truth. Eventually she got a text back from him simply saying 'Hands Up.' She says now: 'I thought, you xxxxxx, I've been writing for twenty years and I nearly got completely stitched up. I had to phone the magazine and say

"Pull it now." It taught me more about the internet than it taught me about Banksy.

'What's interesting about it is the interplay of anonymity and fame. He's completely anonymous and he's really famous, so there's the flattery – somebody who you think is famous gets in touch with you. Oh, that's nice. He's Banksy and he wants to get in touch with *me*. But since he can hide behind his anonymity it could actually be anyone. It's the same with all things on the internet. I really, really felt someone was working on my goodwill. He was somebody who was quite friendly and you feel that you have let somebody in and then they are not who they say they are and you feel a bit invaded. If it had gone to print I would have just been mortified beyond belief.'

It was a very close call; in the end the *Observer* made the right checks and saved everyone huge embarrassment. Nevertheless it leaves a nasty taste in the mouth, this person who uses Banksy's anonymity to get his kicks.

The other type of fraud, impersonating not Banksy himself but his pictures, is more easily understandable. The motive is simply easy money. In the early days, it appears not to have bothered him too much. In one interview he was asked if he minded being ripped off. 'No,' he replied. 'The thing is, I was a bootlegger for three years so I don't really have a leg to stand on.' But by 2010 things had changed somewhat. On the Banksy website there appeared a 'message from Banksy's lawyer' which warned of the consequences of fraud while at the same time distancing Banksy at least one step from it all: 'As a result of complaints from members of the public several investigations are now under way by the Police and Trading Standards into incidents of fraud. These are conducted irrespective of the views of the artist and are treated extremely seriously by the authorities. Successful prosecutions may result in a custodial sentence.'

There certainly was an investigation by the Trading Standards Office involving copyright, but it came to a halt when it was made clear that at some point the investigators would need to meet Banksy. However, the scale of the ongoing forgery meant that eventually the police had to be involved.

From 2007 onwards all Banksy's prints have been signed. This makes the forger's job difficult, but still not impossible. It is the earlier prints which are the greatest problem, partly because of the lack of a signature but also because originally they were often bought for a couple of hundred pounds by buyers who simply liked Banksy and were not too interested in establishing provenance. 'I was uber cautious,' says Acoris Andipa. 'You don't have to be a rocket scientist. If someone's holding a print that they bought for £80 and it's now worth £2000 and then next week it's worth £5000 and six months later it's worth £10,000, then somebody out there is going to start copying.'

Robin Barton of the Bankrobber Gallery tells of a seller who came to him with fourteen pieces of street art. 'There were very convincing stories and convincing emails from people close to Banksy who would verify these pieces. There was a tile, there was a small work on plywood which was very nice. Three triangular road signs, a strip of plastic that looked as though it might have come off a bollard at some point. They all had rats on them, as I recall. There was even a spray can with *Banksy* written on it. It was very elaborate, he brought them in slowly over the course of a month as he tried to draw me in.

'Some of it I really liked, but there were just certain things that weren't right. I ran each piece by the people who have the largest database of Banksy artworks anywhere. They've got thousands of images. And they Photoshopped them, over-layered them and basically told me in every case: fake, fake, FAKE. It was always the scale that was wrong. He was a nice guy, he said he bought the whole collection from someone in Europe for something like £29,000. He was either the duped or he was the duper, and to this day I don't know which one he was.'

Barton managed to escape unscathed, but Keith Sekree was one of the many Banksy fans who had his fingers burnt – although in the end he got his revenge and he can laugh about it now as he tells the tale. Just turned thirty, he is a very good example of how Banksy has drawn a completely new core of people into the art world. We met on a perfect spring day close to the docks in Southampton, where he had both his office as a financial adviser and his own gallery. Since then he has ended his role as a financial adviser to concentrate full time on his gallery – the TAOI Gallery. The remarkable thing is that here is a man who had hardly ever set foot in an art gallery before he discovered Banksy, yet who now runs his own. His first interest in Banksy was sparked off not by going to an exhibition but by being pulled over for a speeding ticket. 'I was doing like 34 mph in a 30 mph area. I got really annoyed and I was literally scanning around the internet and I found this Banksy image [*Flying Copper* – a policeman all gunned up but with a smiley face], and it just related to how I was feeling about the police. So I bought it and it all flowed from there.'

He soon discovered that in those days, before the Los Angeles show, Banksy was selling for 'a hell of a lot less' in America than he was in the UK. He put in an offer on a Banksy original being sold on eBay – collection only – on a Wednesday. His offer was accepted but to make it his he had to collect it from New York by the

Saturday. He made the deadline – just – and sold it back in England for a very healthy profit two weeks later. He was on his way. 'If people like me could make money in art then anyone could.'

Next he found a print of the Banksy *Bomb Hugger* in America. This one he wanted to keep for himself, not sell. It was a print dating from 2003, a time when the majority of Banksy's prints were not signed and there was no proper authentication service. Nevertheless, as Keith says, 'This was coming from a reputable seller with as much provenance as you could hope to get.' Crucially this included the original credit card receipt from the gallery in Brighton, the start of an easily followed trail which showed that the gallery had sold it to an English buyer who then sold it on to the American. In addition the print was blind stamped. (Blind stamping is where the printer punches the paper with a stamp but no ink, leaving a permanent identifying impression on the print.) So he bought it for around £1400. 'Everything seemed to make sense about it.'

This was followed by *Turf War* – Winston Churchill with a grassy Mohican – which he was buying as a favour for one of his leading clients. He found the print by advertising on one of the Banksy forums, rather than using eBay. Again the print came with full provenance but, better than that, this time he got to see the print before he bought it and meet the seller, who was also the original purchaser. 'He said he'd bought it from the Tate – which used to sell Banksy prints – and he had the receipt to prove it. We met and had a drink in a hotel just outside Liverpool Street station. He seemed an amenable bloke, a very nondescript guy. I did make him write out an invoice for the print and put down his name, address, signature, and he had no problem doing that.' The seller wrote his real name – Grant Howard – and signed it. 'He was not at all nervous, even when we were talking about what would happen to him if I found out it was fake – he was going "Oh yeah, I totally agree."' The cost was £1250, in cash.

Very soon after this Keith was contacted by Scotland Yard's Art and Antiques Unit, who had tracked his purchase of *Bomb Hugger* on eBay. The detectives asked him to bring the print in because they believed it was one of several fakes that had come on to the market. He took *Bomb Hugger* to Scotland Yard, and it was not long before they pronounced it a fake and told him all the supporting documents were fakes too. As a safeguard, he took *Turf War* to Pictures on Walls, so they could give him the full provenance for the print, establishing beyond any doubt that it was a Banksy.

The gallery was working closely with the police and shortly afterwards came a phone call, not from the gallery but from Detective Constable Ian Lawson of the Met's Art and Antiques Unit, saying 'You're never going to believe this, but unfortunately your *Turf War* is a fake too.'

'You're never going to believe this either,' said Keith, 'but I've just had the same man on the phone offering me more Banksys.' The police, says Keith, 'were beginning to realise they had a big problem. We weren't talking about a print here and there, we were talking about hundreds of prints.' It turned out that both *Bomb Hugger* and *Turf War* had been forged by the same South London pair, Grant Howard and Lee Parker, who were producing their own copies and claiming they were part of the limited edition print run almost as fast as Banksy was producing his own prints.

Keith was asked to be the central character in a sting organised by Scotland Yard – the kind of operation you see in the movies. One of the last things he had said to Grant Howard was, 'If this isn't real, I promise you I will find out where you are and I will be very very annoyed.' It was, as Keith says, more a South Coast threat than an East End threat, but here was his chance to get even. 'They told me I couldn't push him to sell me something. He had to be offering a print. They were very careful to make sure that all of their evidence was obtained in the right way.' After two or three weeks of telephone contact he agreed with Howard on a price for another Banksy print, *Laugh Now*, again an early print the majority of which were unsigned. They arranged to meet in the same bar at the same Liverpool Street station hotel.

Was he nervous? 'Really nervous. Scotland Yard had told me that he had no history of violence but they had gone through an emergency plan if things didn't go as planned. They told me I didn't need to pay much attention because things would be OK. They didn't give me a wire or anything because they said the moment he walked in he would be arrested.

'On the day I got to the bar nice and early. I'd had a quick drink first at the bar just around the corner since I didn't particularly want the police to see me having a drink. In the hotel bar I recognised some of the people I had seen in the office at Scotland Yard sitting around casually waiting. He turned up early and he was carrying a massive art portfolio full of prints, bless him. Five or more undercover police people literally jumped on him – chairs all over the place. It was in this nice hotel and you've got other people having morning coffee and business meetings and suddenly this. They took him off to Charing Cross police station straight away and left me to pay the bar bill.'

If Banksy had drawn Keith Sekree into the art market, he had drawn the two fakers in as well. Neither of them were art market insiders: Grant Howard, forty-four, was a one-time roofer from

Croydon and his childhood friend Lee Parker, forty-five, from Eastbourne was a plumber who had hit hard times and was having trouble paying his mortgage. In the summer of 2010 they both pleaded guilty to a charge of conspiracy to defraud. They were given a twelve-month sentence suspended for two years, 240 hours of community service and banned from selling anything on the internet for five years. It turned out that Howard had already been charged with previous offences and was out on bail when he was tempted to sell Keith the print at Liverpool Street station, so he spent three months in prison before the pair were sentenced for breaching his original bail conditions.

They had used multiple eBay accounts and email addresses as well as the various Banksy forums on the web. Both had been genuine Banksy fans for years before they started faking him, so they knew what they were talking about, and according to the prosecution if they were seriously challenged by a buyer they tried blinding them with science. If that failed, on occasions they would actually refund the buyer their money. Once they even provided a genuine Banksy as a replacement to a buyer who had complained bitterly about the one they sold him being a fake.

The police found the printer, who was doing a very fine job in faking Banksys. Printing them was not a criminal offence – passing them off as Banksys was. 'Faking a Banksy is not a very difficult process but they were perfect forgeries,' says Keith Sekree. 'When I found out my *Turf War* was a forgery we took it out of the frame and weighed it and it was a quarter of a gram out compared to the genuine one. They even did a good job sourcing the paper, and sourcing the blind stamp.' A couple of their greatest hits were *Golf Sale*, which went to an American for £6500, and *Monkey Queen*, bought by a Spaniard for £4500. Again both were from 2003, when a high percentage of a Banksy edition were unsigned. In total the police discovered 120 fakes, with an estimated value of £200,000, half still with Howard and Parker and half recovered from their victims – there may well be other victims out there who still don't know their prints are fakes.

When you think about it, the very idea of faking a live artist seems absurd. A dead artist is one thing: he or she is not here any more to stand up and say 'That's not mine.' But a live artist? It has to be the fact that the perpetrators thought they could rely on Banksy the vandal never appearing in court to denounce them. For there were other fakers too. In Coventry Robert McGarry, aged twenty-seven, bought four 'Banksys' at a car boot sale for £300. He claimed to the court that he believed they were all genuine Banksy prints, but if that was the case he must have thought he had got a truly wonderful bargain. There was only one problem: he didn't have any provenance to support his belief that they were genuine. So he simply forged certificates to authenticate them. Over a period of eight months he managed to sell all four prints, using different eBay accounts: *Barcode* went for £7100 to a doctor in December 2007, *Girl With Balloon* for £1515 in January 2008 (maybe my *Girl With Balloon* would be worth that if I had slightly more impressive provenance than receipts from the copy shop and John Lewis). *Love Rat* went for £842 in June 2008. Finally *B&W Trolley Hunters* fetched £1700 in August 2008. The court reports gave a dry account of all this, but some of the pain comes out on Banksyforum, where one post reads: 'This little fucker ripped a few people off including yours truly. I was the mug who bought the Trolley Hunters.'

McGarry admitted the four charges and got away with a 32-week sentence, suspended for two years, and 120 hours of unpaid work. The prosecution accepted his story that he believed the prints were genuine and it was this that saved him from going to prison.

In 2007 the temptation to flog what in this case were 'unauthorised' Banksy prints became too much even for a few of the people working for him. *The Art Newspaper* reported that employees of Pictures on Walls were selling prints themselves and hiking the price up on eBay. Since the prints were not part of the limited edition, the most likely explanation for their existence was that they were part of the standard overrun – printer's proofs or artist's proofs or both – which come with any such edition.

Banksy's lawyers were indignant and very earnest, while in contrast Banksy himself adopted a completely different tone – almost as though he was enjoying it. His lawyers' statement read in part: 'It appears that in spite of strict fiscal controls and strict controls of the physical prints that 25 bad prints have been sold on eBay. Pictures on Walls have called on eBay to assist in tracing these sales and also in tracing the money which will inexorably lead to those that have cynically betrayed the trust of the public, the artist and the company.'

Banksy however suggested: 'They say it's better to be a fake somebody than a real nobody, but I don't think that applies to art prints. If it turns out that limited editions have not been limited in edition then I sincerely apologise. This is particularly unfortunate for the people who buy my work to flip it for a quick profit on eBay, as I wouldn't want to affect their mark-up.' It was almost as though, whatever his staff and his lawyers might say, he quite enjoyed the idea that some of the people who bought his art for a quick profit might have lost out.

In the end Pictures on Walls said they had been 'unable to find any evidence of a serial fraud being conducted by current or former members of staff as has been alleged. We are aware former staff have sold a number of prints via eBay, but we have found nothing to indicate these prints were issued fraudulently.' They promised compensation for anybody who had been supplied 'a faulty piece of art'.

(Innocent mistakes can happen. In 2004 *Heavy Weaponry* – an elephant with a missile strapped to its back – sold at Bloomsbury Auctions for £25,000. It was one of Banksy's stencils on canvas, in an edition of twenty-five, and this one was numbered 12. Twelve days later *Heavy Weaponry* sold at Bonhams for £32,000. It was the same painting from the same edition of twenty-five, but unfortunately it had the same edition number – 12. Embarrassingly, someone in the Banksy team had simply messed up.)

Nevertheless things had to change, and they did. In January 2008 a new Banksy company was established, 100 per cent owned by Pictures on Walls. Pest Control Office Limited is its full name, but it is known by everyone in the street art world as Pest Control. Now, for £65 you can get your Banksy print authenticated. And just to keep the whole thing as jokey as possible, the authentication certificate has stapled to it half a 'Di faced tenner', a £10 note faked by Banksy with Lady Diana's face on it. The tenner has a handwritten ID number on it which can be matched to the number on the other half of the note held by Pest Control. A fake to prove that you do indeed have the genuine article – what could be more Banksy than that?

And as for the pests, people like me who want information or, more usually, people who have taken Banksy pieces off the streets – whether in the form of doors, shutters, bollards, traffic cones or walls – and want them authenticated as a Banksy, we all get banished into outer darkness. Hence Pest Control. The company has had a dramatic impact on cleaning up the market, but at the same time it has infuriated those who possess what are undoubtedly genuine Banksys but which Pest Control refuses to authenticate as genuine.

# Twelve

# Psst . . . Anyone Want to Buy a Wall?

Banksy gets around, and wherever he goes he usually leaves his mark. Whereas earlier in his short career his work usually remained in place only until it was washed away by clean-up squads or tagged out of existence by other graffiti writers, now there is a third option: Banksy has become so valuable that it can be worth taking the wall down and selling it – a real piece of street art in your own home or office.

Every Banksy wall tells a different story. So I made a list of his walls and other such surfaces which have been sold, are up for sale, or have disappeared and are likely to appear on the market one day. Although this list is certainly incomplete, it gives some idea of what Banksy sees as a problem, and the wall's owners see as a good way to make a pile of money from a piece of graffiti that is – sometimes literally – on their doorstep.

There is a rat declaring, 'I'M OUT OF BED AND DRESSED – WHAT MORE DO YOU WANT?' painted on the outside of a building in Los Angeles at the time of his exhibition there – Banksy's film gives a fascinating glimpse of him cutting out the stencils for it and then putting it up. There is a water tank, also in

Los Angeles, painted when he was looking for publicity days before the 2011 Oscar ceremony; there are the two pieces from a Yorkshire farm produced when Banksy was creating the artwork for Blur's *Observer Music Monthly* cover: part of the farmer's gate (sold) and a section of the wall of a cattle barn(unsold). There are two snogging policemen somehow taken off the wall of a pub in Brighton and replaced by a copy. There is a mural of four pensioners all hooded up with a boom box and a zimmer frame, peeled off a wall in Clerkenwell, London. There are three walls from Bethlehem: the Israeli soldier demanding a donkey's identity papers, a pigtailed young girl dressed in pink frisking an Israeli soldier and a wet dog shaking itself dry.

There is a punk having trouble with a self-assembly pack marked IEAK, close enough to the IKEA store in Croydon for the connection to be very obvious; there is the steel side of a newsagent's stall in Tottenham Court Road, London, and a piece of marine ply hoarding from a building site in Liverpool. There is a Banksy boy on a wall salvaged from Islington, north London before the building was knocked down for redevelopment (it was close to a piece by the New York artists Faile – who command a price in the same region as Banksy – which at one point was being offered 'free' with the Banksy). There is a wall in the midst of disintegrating Detroit which was painted to publicise the opening of his film. There is an advertising billboard in Los Angeles, painted like the rat in the run-up to the Oscars, which Banksy altered by inserting a frisky Mickey Mouse groping the billboard's original barely clad model. On the web you can see two men come close to a fight as they battle for ownership of the billboard. Two further wall pieces in LA, also from his Oscar campaign, were swiftly cut out and should appear on the market at some point. Another website has a film of a Banksy wall being cut down in Jamaica; a lot of drink appears to have been consumed and it is a miracle that neither the wall nor its handlers were injured. So the Banksy wall industry is showing reasonable growth, and very occasionally amidst all the hype a wall actually gets sold.

Entertainingly, the *Los Angeles Times*'s architecture critic Christopher Hawthorne compared the selling of these Banksy walls to the auctioning of some of the furniture and other bits and pieces from Chandigarh, the extraordinary city 180 miles north of Delhi that Le Corbusier designed in the 1950s. For example a Corbusier-designed manhole cover has been auctioned for almost $20,000 and a concrete light fixture from the city's zoo fetched $36,000.

Hawthorne acknowledged that in Banksy's case, where the American pieces nearly all appeared at around the time *Exit Through the Gift Shop* was released or during the run-up to the Oscars, it is 'nearly impossible to tell where the art-making ends and the marketing begins'. But then he elevated the argument on to a different plane, far away from Banksy's casual beginnings: 'A broader and frankly more compelling issue is how these two stories turn inside out the relationship between patrimony and exploitation, and between local heritage and colonial privilege. It is one thing when occupying British forces forcibly remove an artwork from its setting, as they did two centuries ago with the Elgin Marbles, and ship it out of the country. It is something else entirely when the pieces at risk were created by outsiders, and locals are the ones rushing to loot as well as protect them.'

When architects like Frank Lloyd Wright and Charles and Henry Greene designed private homes, Hawthorne said, they often designed not only the building but also 'furniture, fixtures, carpets and other interior elements meant to be inseparable from their architectural containers. Pieces from such houses now fill the collections of museums around the world.'

Dismantling such 'architectural masterworks', however upsetting, at least took them from the 'private, moneyed domestic realm to the public sphere of the museum gallery'. But the journeys of Banksy and Le Corbusier illustrate 'a trip in the opposite direction, from visible to inaccessible, from public to salable'.

So there you have it. If you want to sell the Banksy equivalent of the Elgin Marbles, you are in for a tough time both from the artist and some critics. In England the man to go to if you want to buy or sell a wall is Robin Barton. He ran the Bankrobber gallery in Notting Hill until the spring of 2011, when he closed it and went off to the Hamptons outside New York to curate a whole exhibition devoted to Banksy walls. When I visited the Notting Hill gallery there was a calculated whiff of the outsider – the bankrobber – about the place, reflected by the first painting that hit you as you walked in the door: a painting of Kate Moss costing £7000 called *Love*, completed by her former boyfriend Pete Doherty, whom Bankrobber represents, shortly after their break-up. If I had had about £9000 to spare I could have bought another piece by Doherty called *Needle*. 'Pete did this when he was going out with Kate Moss and he was completely off his face. He came in here, grabbed a canvas, pulled some of his own blood – all in front of some appalled German students – and then started sketching with it. It's not high art but if you are at all turned on by that moment of time and excesses it will appeal to you.' There were, too, some pieces by Ronald Kray, which were for inspection rather than for sale: 'They are not high art in any shape or form and I wouldn't pretend they are, I collect them for fun.' Amongst all this the Hirst spot print, several Banksys on the wall, a Warhol Campbell's soup print on the floor beside Banksy's Tesco tomato soup – 'I hope to sell them as a pair to someone with money who wants to be ironic' – all seemed positively conservative.

Barton is probably Banksy's least favourite dealer, a man who operates pretty much outside his control and who takes a positive joy in irritating him. Like the other dealers in this world of urban art whom I met he exists outside the Bond Street comfort zone. He has a Union Jack ring on one finger and one of his daughter's teeth set in a silver ring on another. In his reflecting sunglasses, there is about him the air of the jokey, sharp outsider, which he needs to survive. He started out as a photographer specialising in the sort of grainy black and white pictures that the *Independent* magazine once specialised in – plenty of kudos but not much money. So he abandoned taking pictures and started selling them. He opened his Notting Hill gallery in May 2006. The idea was that it would be a photography gallery, but then he, like others who were drawn into the art world, 'just chanced upon Banksy' and realised he had stumbled on a gold mine.

The first ever Banksy exhibition in New York, at the Vanina Holasek gallery in December 2007, was billed as 'Banksy does New York'. Complete with T-shirts on sale for $50 each and white walls hung with Banksys in a deliberately topsy-turvy style, it was actually nothing to do with Banksy. True, all sixty or so exhibits were Banksys – but they were collected and curated largely by Barton, who had seen what was happening to the market in England and wanted to reach New York before anyone else did. Banksy's website said the exhibition was 'unlikely to be worth visiting' and emphasised without any apparent sense of irony that it was 'completely unauthorised'. The critics did not like it much either, and on the Banksy forums fans were outraged. The gallery was heaving every day, but the crowds had come to look not buy. Barely anything sold; however, just by putting on the show Barton had demonstrated that he could operate outside the artist's control and it gave him the publicity he needed.

So it seems only natural that if anyone is going to sell street pieces – legally obtained, he likes to emphasise – it is going to be Barton. He says, 'It's a sort of poisoned chalice, because these pieces can sit around for a very long time taking up a lot of space and causing a lot of grief. But in the end the good stuff does sell.' His argument is that if he does sell a wall – and he has sold a couple – he makes a good deal of money out of it; but more than that, he says he's doing it 'for the fun of it'. 'He pissed me off basically with his attitude. How bonkers the whole thing is. He thinks he's Robin Hood but he ain't.'

At my last count, seven walls are or have been on his books; two of these, the Liverpool marine ply hoarding and the steel section of a newsagent's stall from Tottenham Court Road, had been sold and five were still waiting for a buyer. 'The reason walls are so very hard to sell is that you are actually asking someone to give you half a million pounds for a bunch of old rubble with some stencil work on it which they probably will never be able to offload again. And there aren't many people who like spending that kind of money.'

The first work he sold was a lovely piece: a stencilled boy, clutching a dripping paintbrush in both hands, who has just painted 'WHAT?' in giant pink letters on the wall behind him. Instead of looking triumphant he looks rather sad, as though he does not know the answer to his question and no one else does either.

It sold faster than any other piece, but like most of these walls it has an involved back story. In May 2006 it was painted on the rear of a street stall on Tottenham Court Road on quarter-inch steel. Once cut out it measured 2.2 metres square. The stall was owned by one Sam Khan, who for thirty years traded in luggage and football scarves and other tourist essentials. He sold this section of his stall for £1000, which for a very short time sounded like a lot of money, but he soon discovered he had made a disastrous mistake. His story, as he told it to the *Evening Standard*, went: 'I don't know anything about art. I've been on the stall all my life trying to make an honest living come rain or snow. I've had people coming up to me saying, "How did you not know who Banksy is?" and, "Why didn't you go on the internet?" I get up at 5 a.m. and I'm on the stall for twelve hours a day. I don't follow these things.

'The guy who bought it from me came with £1000 cash and intimidated me into it. I was threatened when I asked for time to think and I had to deliver it to a storage depot in King's Cross. I've never been able to find that man again.' He said he paid £300 to have the steel panel removed and £300 for a replacement panel, leaving him with a profit of £400.

'I have no sympathy for him,' says Barton. 'He shot himself in the foot. I had nothing to do with the purchasing of the piece. All I did was display it in Bankrobber and it sold pretty much the day it went up.' He was helped by the fact that it had been featured in a paperback edition of *Wall and Piece*, the edition which had come out promising 'Now with 10 per cent more crap', so there was no doubt that it was a genuine Banksy. In addition, it was 'right in the middle of all the Banksy hysteria and it had press coverage, which always helps sell something like that because it gives it validation.'

The *Evening Standard* suggested he might be asking as much as £500,000 for this old chunk of street vendor's stall. But he says, 'I had no intention of asking that, I had no idea what to ask really.' Like most dealers he is coy about what he got for it, but the word was that it was more like £230,000 than £500,000. Whatever the final price, Barton is convinced he sold it cheap: 'The guy who bought it went off skiing and by the time he came back, in my view it would have been worth twice as much.' He is equally coy about the buyer, but sources suggest it was bought for Matthew Freud, Rupert Murdoch's son-in-law although he has never confirmed this.

His second successful sale was a piece known as *Prick*. It's a clever work in which a museum attendant sits contentedly doing his job, knees crossed, fingers interlocked, guarding a richly framed picture. But all this security, all the bureaucracy, the guard, his pass clipped to his lapel, his uniform, his cap, his stool, the protective rope railings, are for what? To guard a picture which simply has the word PRICK spray-painted across it in blue (at some later stage someone sprayed their own tag on top).

Again it was quite easy to secure, since it was on two pieces of marine ply which were being used to board up a shop in Liverpool. Banksy had hit Liverpool at the time of the Biennial Contemporary Art Festival in 2004 and this piece lasted only about six weeks before a young couple who were visiting the Biennial saw the boarded shop and paid about £500 for the hoardings. 'They came and sat in the gallery – it was just after all the press for the *What*? piece – and said "We've got a Banksy. Do you want to try to sell it for us?" They showed me what it was and I said "Yes, perfect, bring it in to the gallery and we will put it up and make a big fuss of it."' He thought the buyer of *What?* would take this one too. But Barton's suggested price of £250,000 and the sellers' valuation of

£500,000 were so far apart that they took it away to try to sell elsewhere. 'The piece went round the houses, to God knows how many galleries' before it arrived back at Bankrobber. He eventually found a buyer for it through Stephan Keszler, a dealer colleague with a gallery in the Hamptons who had recently rented a space on Madison Avenue. 'I said "If you want to up your profile give it a try."' Keszler managed to sell the piece quite quickly, but it had taken two and a half years to reach this point. Again Barton will not give the price. It is almost certainly under the £250,000 that he was suggesting, and nothing like the price the owners had originally hoped for – but not bad for an original investment of £500.

But if those are the only two wall pieces that have actually sold, what of the others that are on the market? Keszler and Barton teamed up for a huge gamble in the Hamptons in 2011 for a summer selling exhibition of seven Banksy walls, including a turtle originally painted on a condemned house in New Orleans, the two kissing policemen transferred from the side of the Prince Albert pub in Brighton and the IEAK wall from Croydon. They even brought two walls – *Stop and Search*, complete with a couple of bullet holes, and *Wet Dog*, shaking like a wet dog does – to the Hamptons from Bethlehem via England for some restoration. The project almost collapsed – literally – at the Palestinian checkpoint with Israel, where the walls had to be transferred from a Palestinian lorry to an Israeli one and amid much argument about how best to accomplish the task, *Wet Dog* fell down in a cloud of dust. The back of the wall was damaged but the shaking dog remained intact. *Wet Dog* was on sale in the Hamptons for $420,000 and *Stop and Search* had a price of $450,000.

Banksy's unique publicity tour both for the release of his film and for his Oscar campaign has provided a treasure trove for

American collectors. He had a problem with publicising the film, for as soon as it was released the distributor was pressuring him to rent billboards to help with its marketing. Given that he sees billboards as 'corporate vandalism', this put him in an awkward position; while at one moment he thought 'maybe a couple won't hurt', in the end he shunned temptation in favour of travelling across America himself, leaving his signature wherever he went. It was far more effective publicity than billboards, because there was always the frisson of a Banksy being spotted in *our* city – with the added benefit that he had not succumbed to the temptation of actually renting a billboard.

The story of just two pieces from this campaign, one in Los Angeles and the other in Detroit, illustrates the surprising ethical dilemmas that Banksy's work raised when all the poor man was trying do was first to publicise the film and then to win an Oscar.

In California a large, derelict water tank had been sitting all too visibly in the hills alongside the Pacific Coast Highway at Pacific Palisades for a number of years. But in February 2011 drivers woke up to something a little different. Someone had stencilled across it in large black letters: 'This looks a bit like an elephant.' It was Banksy and very literally he was right. He had seen what no one else had ever seen, there was a vague intriguing similarity: the tank was cylindrical, and although it stood on six steel legs rather than four animal ones, its spout had the hint of an elephant's trunk to it. Within two weeks the elephant was gone or, as one blogger headlined it, 'Banksy elephant is dead.' On banksyelephant.com (which disappeared almost as rapidly as it first appeared) you could even watch a video of the 'elephant' first being strung up to a crane in the daylight and then, as night fell, having its legs cut away by men wielding oxy-acetylene torches before finally being carted away on an American-sized truck.

What made the story even more complicated was that although the tank had not been used to store water for many years, it had housed a homeless man, one Tachowa Covington, whom YouTube videos show parading around with a crown on his head as though he owned the whole canyon. Had Banksy inadvertently turfed him out? (No, he had moved into a cave further up after a fire in his water tank home.) Was Banksy making some sort of statement about homelessness? (No, it was all about the Oscars.)

When the Banksy paintings in Los Angeles were revealed on his website (they were not going to help him much in his Oscar campaign if no one knew they were by Banksy), it was the start of a treasure hunt to find them, to photograph them and possibly even to acquire them. Christian Anthony, who owns a 'media design' company, Mint Currency, looked at the website and knew exactly where the tank was. Together with his partner in the company, who prefers to be called Tavia D, they persuaded two friends, Jorge Fernandez and Steve Gallion, to join them. These two ran a waste-disposal company and thus had all the heavy moving equipment they could need.

Banksy hunting is usually a young person's game: Tavia and Christian are in their twenties, their two friends in their thirties. 'We saw it as a very special piece,' says Tavia. When they actually went to inspect it, 'We were even more inspired, we wanted it so bad. We were both huge Banksy fans and we wanted to be a part of the whole Banksy movement.' They were determined to do everything legitimately: 'Everyone else who was trying to get the Banksys was doing it guerrilla style, going in the middle of the night or whatever, and we weren't trying to do that with a huge water tank.'

The history of the tank is complicated, but it had come to the point where although the City of Los Angeles did not own it, they were preparing to have it scrapped when Banksy suddenly arrived. The four friends bought the tank from the city: 'We paid thousands of dollars, but not many thousands of dollars for it,' says Tavia. They then went to work before anyone else could get to it. Showing Americans' usual ability to get things done, they arrived at 8.30 in the morning, and within sixteen hours they had cut down their elephant and sent it on its way to a warehouse to await a buyer.

Tavia D says, 'We thought, let's just take it off the city's hands. We wanted to save that piece of art, we were on a rescue mission.' They thought the fact that a homeless man had once lived there made it more symbolic – Banksy perhaps was trying to draw attention to homelessness, the 'elephant in the room' – although there is nothing to suggest that Banksy had any greater clue than they did that the water tank had once been someone's home. They wanted to be seen as the good guys, safeguarding an important work of art. In a statement issued at the time on banksyelephant.com, they said: 'We have personally acquired ownership to preserve and protect the work of Banksy in hopes that it will end up exhibited in a respected museum where his work will live on without harm.'

There was no doubt, however, that the museum would have to pay good money for this privilege. 'Obviously we were trying to make a profit, because we had to cover the costs we had invested to get the piece,' Tavia admitted. Some of these profits, she said, would go towards helping the homeless. But as they waited for a buyer the storage costs mounted, and she was to find that selling the elephant was much more difficult than capturing it.

Across the country a very different Banksy piece, a 7ft × 8ft cinder block wall, has caused even more controversy, giving birth to an absorbing and entirely unexpected tale involving art, money and the law. This time there is much more to the piece than seven stencilled words. A rather forlorn boy of the kind that Banksy seems to specialise in, although this time – given that its location is inner-city Detroit – he is black, stands with his paint pot and brush (no spray paint here) beside the words he has just written on the wall: 'I remember when all this was trees.'

What made this work so poignant was that it was surrounded by total urban desolation. For it sits – or rather sat – amidst the 35-acre site of the former Packard motor factory. The luxury car-maker once employed 40,000 people here, but the factory closed in 1956 and has remained abandoned ever since, a relic of Detroit's days as the automobile city that ruled the world. (The devastation is abundant enough to attract artists and photographers whose bleak images are attacked as 'ruins porn' by some in Detroit.)

In May 2010 Carl Goines, executive director and one of the co-founders of the 555 Gallery in Detroit, was tipped off by a photographer that Banksy had hit the city. The photographer, a fan, had been to *Exit Through the Gift Shop* on the Friday night when it opened in a cinema just north of Detroit; he had seen an image on the Banksy website the next day, recognised the location and went out and found the boy that night – a very short treasure hunt. Carl rounded up his father and two other artists connected with the 555 Gallery and went to inspect the site. They tried and failed to contact the people who they thought might own the site – in some parts of Detroit land and the taxes that go with it can be a burden rather than a goldmine – but crucially they did find a foreman on site, who gave them the go-ahead as long as they did not take any scrap metal. Armed with a masonry saw, an oxy-acetylene torch, a mini tractor, some plywood boards and a truck, they set to work. By the end of Monday they had cut it out, and they crated it up and off the site on Tuesday.

Goines, who is a sculptor, says he had no interest in Banksy before all this – in fact 'I was unaware of Banksy's work and his notoriety. So it's been an education for me.' For what followed was a wonderful narrative – should the 21st-century echo of the Elgin Marbles be preserved or left to die a natural death? – which took Banksy's work to a sphere he could never have dreamed of.

Goines says they realised very early on that 'selling it was an option that we couldn't do lightly.' The gallery might possibly sell the piece in years to come, but for now the only reward they would get for their efforts would be the publicity. However, the smell of money to be made always pervades anything to do with Banksy and sure enough, the owners of the site emerged from the deepest undergrowth. They wanted their wall back and they went to court for it, claiming it could be worth $100,000. They argued that the foreman who had given permission for the wall to be taken away was not their representative. 'The acts of the defendants constitute an illegal conspiracy to take wrongful possession and control of the mural and constitute a wrongful conversion of the same'; note that at the stage when Banksy's work entered the law courts, it had been elevated from a piece of graffiti to 'a mural'.

It was time for the City of Detroit to wade in. The city had had trouble establishing who exactly owned the site but now, a city official said, that it was 'clear and publicly acknowledged who the responsible party is, we will pursue all applicable areas of enforcement to hold the property owner accountable for this unsightly and dangerous situation.' It could cost up to $20 million to demolish what was left of the factory and clear the site, and now that Banksy had inadvertently established its ownership the city was threatening to do the clear-up work and send the bill to the site owner. The city was also demanding taxes on the site stretching back over five years, and this dispute still remains unresolved. So, quite apart from anything else, Banksy had brought the issue of this huge stretch of wasteland on Detroit's East Side sharply back into focus. As one comment posted on the blog dETROITfUNK suggested: 'The fucking Packard is a ridiculous and insane site, which has been allowed to sit in this condition for ages. Wide open. We live here, and we almost become blind to the insanity.'

But quite apart from ownership, should the gallery have liberated the painting? The gallery found itself in the midst of an argument so bitter that after having had the wall on display for just ten days, they decided they needed to hide it. Their fear was not so much that someone would steal it, rather that someone would destroy it in protest at the fact that it had been removed from its all-important original context. 'We had some strange threats,' says Goines, 'also some conversations with individuals saying they were going to come and load it up and just take it from us. The threats came from all sorts of people, including those who thought we should have allowed it to stay in the plant and be destroyed, as it would have been eventually.'

The argument in essence came down to this: context is all-important. There was no chance of the painting lasting in situ. Builders were salvaging scrap metal from the site, and if you look at some of the pictures of the painting before it was moved there are beams both beside and above it awaiting their fate. But that does not matter, argued those who were horrified to see it moved. If the Banksy stayed where it was, there would be pictures on the web which would provide a permanent record of the piece in the environment in which it was created.

Given that the wall was going to come down, the gallery members saw themselves as stewards preserving the piece, in much the same way that the British Museum has done for objects taken out of context but preserved over the centuries. But did the act of saving a piece of art actually destroy it? Goines has no regrets. The idea that street art has rules at all seems strange to him: 'Many times they are breaking the rules and yet they say there is a rule against removing a piece from where it is installed. It just seems contradictory to me, they are setting up rules to break rules.'

It might be out of its original site, he believed, but it was not out of context: 'I think the piece has evolved into something on its own. The whole thing has become a project in itself. It's an ongoing escapade for Banksy, it's something that he gets the ball rolling on and then it keeps on moving and becomes something more.' Banksy certainly would not support the gallery's action, but in an emailed interview conducted at the time of the Oscars he said: 'I've learnt from experience that a painting isn't finished when you put down your brush – that's when it starts. The public reaction is what supplies meaning and value. Art comes alive in the arguments you have about it.' Becky Hart, associate curator of contemporary art at the Detroit Institute of Arts, put it rather more academically, saying that the piece had acquired its own 'patina of narrative'.

Nevertheless, to read the many posts on dETROITfUNK you would think the men from the 555 Gallery were vandals. Nearly all these posts made broadly the same point and perhaps one in particular best sums them up. *@shlee* wrote:

> It makes me cringe that so many are applauding this. The mere fact you've titled this post 'Saving Banksy' is a farce. The point of 'street art' is for it to exist in its natural

environment, it is by nature temporary. Disappointing when a good piece fades away? Yes. But that's life. More meaning in that than in some art fags cutting it out and sticking it in a gallery shortly after it has appeared. The power of that piece was in its environment. Outside of that what does it say? He created this piece in the midst of demolition. The nature of the piece in that setting, is such a social commentary I just can't fathom how someone could miss the point to such a degree that they'd remove it and boast that they were 'SAVING!' it.

*ms* admits that moving Banksy does mean people who would not visit this part of town have a chance to see it:

> But one can argue it wasn't made for those types of people in the first place. Those artsy-fartsy types are the reason street art has thrived, specifically to show that art can exist outside of stuffy galleries. The entire process is always evolving, and if something were to happen to the piece, well 'them's the breaks kid.' But I'd rather venture into the Packard to see a dissed Banksy, and stand where he stood than see it butchered and hacked from the wall in some gallery. Putting it there gives it all the majesty of a lion in a cage that's far too small . . .

But context isn't everything; many of the exhibits we see in galleries have been taken from their original surroundings to give thousands the chance they would otherwise not have to see them. This was a Banksy that would remain 'social commentary' wherever it was displayed. Compare this to the Berlin Wall where, in 1990, eighty-one segments with graffiti on them were sold off at an auction in Monaco for €1.5 million. These pieces can now be seen at places as varied as the parking lot of a business plaza in California, outside the Hard Rock Café in Orlando, Florida or, almost unbelievably, behind the urinals of the men's room in a hotel in Las Vegas. Now that is vandalism for you, and that's leaving aside the fact that it took five years in the courts for the artists who were the key painters of this section of the wall to win any share of the proceeds.

As for the wall in Detroit, the law suit between the gallery and the owners of the site was finally settled in the autumn of 2011, with the gallery paying $2500 for a clear title to their wall. The plan was that by spring 2012 the wall would re-emerge from the well-protected studio where it had been locked away to go on public display in an old police station they were turning into a new gallery. 'It's been a lively debate, a great experience and absolutely worth it in the end,' said Goines.

The Detroit wall weighed in at almost one ton, but that was a lightweight compared to the one cut out near Croydon, which was made of reinforced concrete and came in at about four tons. Again this was a Banksy that really worked. It showed a punk examining the put-it-together-yourself instructions that came from a box marked 'LARGE GRAFFITI SLOGAN' and branded IEAK. He was obviously having trouble – like we all do – with these instructions, for on the wall behind him were written the words SYSTEM, POLICE, NO, MORE, SMASH and other components of a typical revolutionary placard, but he hadn't got the instructions right – the words were all jumbled up and made no sense. But unless Banksy was campaigning to get IKEA to write their instructions more clearly or asking slogan writers to show more originality, or perhaps giving a gentle rebuke to consumerism, there was no obvious message – just an enjoyable painting.

Tucked away on an industrial estate, the wall was not easy to find, and it was almost a month before two south London friends in their early thirties – Bradley Ridge, who owns a restaurant in Streatham Hill, and Nick Loizou, a builder – heard that Banksy had strayed into the deepest south of the capital. They had actually been on their way to east London on a shopping expedition for Banksy prints when they got a phone call from a friend: 'You know this Banksy, he's done one in Croydon.' They forgot the prints and a few beers later they decided that the next morning they would take a look. What they found was a wall which Bradley says 'looked a bit knackered. It was an amazing piece but it looked ruined. Nick lost a bit of interest and I got more interested and told him, "Maybe we can get it cleaned up."'

At first they were described as two scallies with no interest in art, just an eye for a quick buck, but this was unfair. While they might have a south London edge to them, Bradley had been following and collecting Banksy ever since his college days in Bristol. He even kept – and still keeps – what he calls his 'Banksy bag', stuffed full with sleeping bag, woolly boots and a few other essentials, permanently in the corner of the hall in his flat, in case he suddenly gets word that another Banksy print is up for sale. He bought his first two Banksy canvases back in 2002 and he's been buying prints ever since, including *Bombing Middle England* for just £20. But he has never yet sold a Banksy canvas or print. So yes, they both thought the wall would be profitable, but there was also the sheer thrill of doing it – of cutting out and owning, for however short a time, a Banksy wall.

It was a far more difficult undertaking than they had ever

imagined. First they had to make a few phone calls to find out if there was someone who restored walls – someone who could take off all the additional graffiti that had appeared after Banksy had painted it. Having satisfied themselves that such a man existed – thirteenth-century churches, twenty-first-century walls, they can all be restored – they then bought the wall. But the owners played by the rules: the pair had to come up with a structural engineer to do a risk assessment, a scheme of work, a schedule of work, high-vis jackets – a proper operation. And they had to provide a bricklayer to build another wall to fill the gap.

When they started work they discovered that Banksy had, by chance, chosen the only part of the wall that was made of poured concrete with steel rods through it rather than the breezeblock they expected. Unhappily this made it a massively different job than the one they thought they had embarked on and it took them nine days to complete it. Four men, including Nick, worked on the wall during the day. At night, Bradley says, 'My job was to sleep with it. I was there in the van sleeping next to it, we never left it. We had to make sure nobody came along and whitewashed it. We didn't have any taggers but we had people round who I think were trying to steal the van. I don't think they even realised what was on the wall.'

Once the wall was down and safely tucked away into its steel cage, it could be taken to a restorer to be cleaned up. Unlike the Detroit wall, which was taken down so soon after Banksy had painted it that no one had time to add their own tag, the Croydon wall was covered with a mass of additional tags that had to be dealt with. To the inexperienced eye all this additional graffiti looked as though it would make the Banksy impossible to clean up, but Ridge and Loizou had found a restorer who had tackled much harder jobs than this one. Having been stored in Lincolnshire and New Covent Garden – Bradley's father runs a greengrocery business – now it was on its way to Faversham in Kent for restoration.

There Tom Organ runs the Wall Paintings Workshop. A craftsman more accustomed to restoring twelfth-century Romanesque paintings on church walls or uncovering a fourteenth-century scene depicting the martyrdom of Thomas Becket than he is to conserving graffiti, for nine years now he has been travelling to Istanbul for a month or two at a time to work on the sixth-, ninth- and fourteenth-century mosaics in the dome of Hagia Sophia. So Banksy is not in his usual line of work, although the artist has provided the workshop with quite a few one-offs over the last few years.

He and his small team took about forty days to clean the Croydon Banksy and he says, 'It took a lot of testing and then a great deal of patience.' He explains that from the practical point of view, there is often very little between cleaning one painting and another. But the paints that are used to create graffiti (nitro-cellulose and alkyd resin binders over emulsion paint, for those who need details) have specific properties and his job was to determine which solvents could be safely used, where and when. There was one large, particularly noticeable silver tag which fortunately had enough metallic material in its structure that it could actually be taken off with a hand tool, using binocular magnifiers to do the job.

The whole operation – buying the wall, taking the wall away, constructing a cage for it, transporting it, cleaning it up and storing it – has cost in the region of £30,000. Bradley says, 'I would love to keep it but I live in a first floor flat, so that's not going to happen.' Inevitably the wall eventually appeared on the market – but, like most things to do with Banksy, it was not the usual kind of market.

*Four Rooms*, a new series on Channel 4 – described by the *Independent* reviewer as a 'kind of *Dragons' Den* for overpriced bric-a-brac' – invited viewers to bring in the treasures they would like to sell. It is not exactly Sotheby's. The idea is that the seller goes in turn to four dealers in four different rooms, hence the title, has a haggle and hears each dealer's best offer. If the seller turns down one offer in the hope of getting a better offer in the next room, then that's it: if no better offer materialises, the seller can't go back a room or two and accept the original offer. The show feels a bit like a game show, and all the drum rolls and camera cuts to the nervous sellers' twitching fingers make it much more comic than the 'real edge of your seat viewing' that Channel 4 had promised. Yet it was in this bizarre bazaar that Banksy's wall came to the market. Other items on the same programme included a pimped-up 'entertainment chair', a Victorian hangman's rope 'with full letters of provenance', a collection of Superman memorabilia and the nose off a scrapped Concorde.

The two lads said they were looking for a price in the region of £300,000. Only one dealer was prepared to go anywhere near that amount, offering what seemed an amazing £240,000. But that was not enough. The lads were not going a penny lower than £250,000. The dealer – looking rather relieved that his offer had not been accepted – would not come up. So the wall was still theirs – and by the end of December 2011 remained theirs.

If Banksy had been unfortunate enough to have tuned in to Channel 4 that night, the programme would probably have given him nightmares. Outwitting the police might be cool, but having to endure being the centrepiece of a game show along with a hangman's rope is just embarrassing.

If it was any consolation for him, the following week Tracey Emin's twin brother Paul was on the programme trying to flog a print his sister had given him entitled *Mrs Edwards We Wish You Were Dead*, a reference to a dinner lady at their old school that neither Tracey nor her brother took to. (He got £2300 for it.) Banksy probably feels the same way about the sellers every time he sees one of his walls go on the market.

# Thirteen
# How Pest Control Routed Vermin

Any reader may well ask, how on earth can a book about an artist have such a strange chapter heading? But this is Banksy and none of the usual rules apply. What follows is a story about a serious battle for control of every aspect of his art. It is a battle that Banksy – in the form of Pest Control, the organisation he established to verify his art – won decisively, driving from the field the rival organisation, Vermin, set up by dealers to authenticate Banksy's works themselves. It was a short battle and Banksy took no prisoners.

Banksy's past is always catching up with him – not in disastrous ways, but in difficult, awkward ways that force him to make decisions he would rather not have to make. Back in November 2007 a note appeared on one of the Banksy forums: 'Authentic Banksy for sale – Mystic Swing art.' The details then followed: 'It is the frontage to a fairground ride called the Mystic Swing which has attended festivals and green fairs for the past few years.' Anyone interested was given a choice of web contacts including googling 'Mystic Swing' as a phrase, 'ignoring the movie of the same name'.

This was not exactly a high-pressure sell. At the end of the message the seller warned: 'I'm not actually on the internet and use the local library for a connection so please don't expect an immediate response. Be Lucky!' It was signed 'Flatcap'.

A little later Flatcap posted more details. The ride was about thirty years old and the artwork, a collaboration between Banksy and one Dave Panit, 'the celebrated fairground artist', was completed in 2000. 'I'm just thinking that, as the work got slightly damaged this year (sometime whilst I was asleep at a festival) I'm not willing to travel this anymore. Believe me, I think it's a shame. But, I'm not rich and am looking for the cash to buy my "safe haven" as promised by thatcher (I'm not going to put a capital "t" on the start of that word) for my family.

'Anyway, I'm not having some pissed up prat playing ping-pong with his head with the artwork (my friend witnessed this one and politely told him to "go away"), nor an imbecile with a Cosworth collide with it on a roundabout (close one, that) so it's got to go.' In response to further questions he added, 'It does have a Banksy tag and I'm currently getting it authenticated to ease the cynics minds.'

Flatcap said that he was in 'no rush to sell'. Which was fortunate, for four years later the piece still sat in a shed, with nothing to fear from Cosworths but still no buyer. For Banksy, or rather Pest Control, will not authenticate it. And without their signed certificate, complete with half its Lady Di tenner, no one wants to know.

It is a big (roughly 6m × 3.5m), really enjoyable, unusual piece, with all the brighter than bright colours of the fairground, but depicting a rabbit playing the piano, a trapeze artist monkey, a performing seal tossing a TV set instead of a ball, and a couple of rabbit ballerinas en pointe wearing tutus and *gas masks*. To me it looks like Banksy at his freehand best, but is it a Banksy?

The journey to see Dave 'W.E.T.' Panit was a long one, deep into the heart of Somerset near Huish Episcopi. From a local pub I was guided down country roads which soon turned into country lanes, which eventually turned into a large field. And there sat the fairground artist and dyslexic sign writer who long ago had trouble with spelling the key words 'Wet Paint' – hence his adopted name of Panit. The long hair evident on his website had gone, and in his mid-fifties, with a beard, he looked almost like an academic, but we were definitely in the alternative world here. The field, where various neighbours seemed to pass by and where they would sometimes reside, houses his own touring van, as well as a huge ex-Teletubbies van which turns into a bar at festivals when it is needed, some mobile toilets, the caravan for his travelling freak show, and his own overstuffed studio.

He has done everything he wanted to do as a fairground artist; he painted one helter-skelter not once but twice, when fifteen or twenty years later it came back for some rehab. A couple of years back he achieved the pinnacle for any fairground artist, a 'set of gallopers' – thirty-three horses, two cockerels and a chariot. 'It took me a couple of months, it was a bloody nightmare at times but it was worth it.' We talked in his studio, which was more treasure trove than anything else, containing everything from Lord Sutch's bowler hat and a dead fairy (nothing serious, just a skeleton with fairy wings) to lots of teddy bear heads and hundreds of dolly parts, all of them waiting to be key players in his next freak show.

Flatcap had bought Mystic Swing in 2003 from Seb Bambini, a travelling showman who entertained children at festivals around

Europe. Seb had discovered the ride unused and unloved and had done an enormous amount of work getting it back into its original shape. With the help of Mike Bodyart, a UV body and make-up artist on the rave scene, he completely covered the barrel of the ride with recycled CDs to create a giant spinning mirror ball within which sixteen visitors could sit down and enjoy the illusion of being lost in space. For the front of the ride, the part that encouraged people in, he commissioned Dave with his flamboyant, over-the-top circus style to do all the lettering – or 'flashes' as they are known in the trade – and Banksy, who he knew from the music scene in Bristol, to do the illustrating.

Dave says, 'Seb approached me and asked if I would decorate the ride with Banksy and I said "No problem." I knew he was a graffiti artist but of course none of us realised what he was going to become at that time.' It was a combination that worked perfectly.

The work was done in the spring of 1999, in the back garden of a house Bambini was renting in the village of Hambridge in Somerset, and it was certainly rather more than one quick painting session. 'Banksy was funny doing this,' says Dave. 'He was getting paid to do it for a start, and as a graffiti artist you don't normally get paid, do you? And he'd been given permission to do what he liked. I was really amazed by what he could achieve with an aerosol can.'

The Bambinis provided the meals and the drinks as well as paying both artists £200 and their travel costs. There were several people, including Banksy, staying at the house and a lot of cider was being consumed. Another artist who was said to have been present says, 'Those days were a pretty hazy time. I couldn't for the life of me tell you whether I was there or not.' Banksy took time – days – to get started but when he did start, most of the work was done in one night. As recalled by Dave: 'We worked together and I thought, this is going to be interesting, how are we going to do this? All day I would be doing my bit and would he come and join in? No. He wouldn't do it during daylight hours. He waited until it got dark, put a headtorch on and got out there and did it then. That's how it was painted, one half at night and one half in the day. It was just so funny, him in the head torch. We'd all have enough bevvies by the time he started, so we'd go to bed and he'd go painting and we'd go out there and check on him once in a while to see what he was up to.'

The division of labour was quite easy. The words 'Frills', 'Spills', 'Ribtickler Entertainment', 'Mystic Swing' and the like were all Dave's, as was the edging. Banksy did the rest, and since he was the last one to paint he could overlay his work on top of Dave's, rather than the other way round. So it is an important early work, and although Dave did a skilful job on the lettering it is without any doubt at all a freehand Banksy. The only stencil is his signature, which comes just below the safety certificate the ride needed every year.

But when Flatcap approached Pest Control for authentication, he never got an answer. Flatcap, aka Jez White, a rather laid back traveller who has plans to use the proceeds from the sale to provide a winter park-up for travellers to work on their summer festival projects, does not seem especially bothered by it all. He keeps the piece dry and well locked up and hopes that one day someone will come along and make him an offer – authenticated or not.

Pest Control was set up by Banksy in January 2008. Its one shareholder is Pictures on Walls; its one director is Banksy's accountant, Simon Durban; the company secretary is Holly

Cushing, who runs it. As Simon Todd of artnet wrote at the time, 'MI5 has more information about itself on its website than Pest Control does on its own'; nevertheless it took very little time for the company to change the rules of the game. The majority of its activities have been welcomed by every dealer in town. 'We were crying out for somebody,' says Acoris Andipa. 'Holly has brought a very, very big degree of professionalism into the marketplace, in terms of what is and what isn't a Banksy.' He admits though, 'There will be grey areas and I know plenty of people who have crossed swords with them because they have hit these grey areas.'

The 'grey areas' usually come with what are known as the street pieces, whether they be Mystic Swing, walls, traffic bollards, gates or even the side of an articulated lorry. Banksy, in the form of Pest Control, will not authenticate art he has done in the street, even though a piece like Mystic Swing is undoubtedly painted by Banksy. In part this is because to authenticate a piece on the street is, as he says, 'basically a signed confession on headed notepaper'. But in addition his argument is that he has created this art to be seen and indeed enjoyed in context, and he is not going to give any help to anyone who wants to make money out of it or, indeed, simply wants to preserve it.

Banksy's venture on to a Yorkshire farm in search of a location for his illustration for Blur's *Observer Music Monthly* magazine cover shows just what a difference Pest Control has made. In 2007 the farmer's daughter sent to market part of the sheet metal gate on which Banksy had stencilled a girl happily hugging her TV set, done as a sort of trial run for the main picture, where a different TV set is being thrown out of the window. When the shed was being renovated she managed to salvage half of the gate just before it was chucked into a skip. She kept it under her bed for a year or so until a friend who worked at an auctioneer's suggested that there was money in her old gate.

In April 2007 the gate went into the same Bonhams auction as *Space Girl and Bird*, with an estimate of between £10,000 and £15,000. It was accompanied by a statement of fact about Banksy's farm visit for the *Observer* shoot and photographs of the gate still in situ, with the TV girl on it, but no other authentication. It sold for £38,400.

In July 2008 the farmer himself thought he would give it a try. He loaded on to a trailer not a gate, but the whole wall from his barn. This bore the stencil that had featured on the front of the *Observer Music Monthly*, so there was no doubt at all that it was by Banksy and the estimate, £30,000 to £50,000, reflected this. But now Pest Control existed and the farmer did not have his certificate – it seems very unlikely that he knew he needed one. Andrew Stewart, the dealer now trying to sell the wall, believes the van broke down or the trailer got a puncture on the way to London, but either way it was a long, wasted trip: the wall did not sell.

Since then, says Mr Stewart, 'We've had great fun trying to sell it. At one stage we were thinking of having a black tie do to introduce people to it on the farm.' The asking price has come down to between £20,000 and £25,000 – cheap for a Banksy wall – but there have still been no takers. 'We know it is 100 per cent right but people are quite strange about authentication letters,' says Stewart. It's hard not to feel a bit sorry for the farmer. He did Banksy and the *Observer* a big favour at very short notice, his wall is completely authentic, and if he had put it on the market six months earlier it would have sold. Banksy cannot claim he would be opening himself up to a possible prosecution if he admitted that he did the painting, since the farmer selling the wall was the man who gave him permission to spray it in the first place.

A couple of other 'salvaged' pieces also failed to sell at the same auction, one on a ceramic tile and the other on a piece of plywood; neither had the right authentication. But this was just a skirmish. The deciding battle came a little later, at the end of September 2008. The Edinburgh auctioneers Lyon & Turnbull had made a very successful foray into the London art market earlier in the year with a sale of British art from the 1960s held at the Royal Academy. Now they hoped to build on that with a second auction, this time in a deconsecrated church opposite Regent's Park. The auction was controversial enough anyway, selling off pieces from the recently closed Colony Room – the louche Soho drinking club made famous by the likes of Francis Bacon and Jeffrey Bernard – that over the years artist members had given in lieu of their bar bills. But, just as controversially, among the twenty-four Banksys for sale were five street pieces which had been authenticated, not by Pest Control but by a new organisation called Vermin. Four of the five pieces were rats. There was a photographer rat, painted on a traffic bollard and submitted to the sale by Jon Swinstead, one of the original backers of Pictures on Walls. There was a gangsta rat from Liverpool on plywood and a drill rat on MDF from Brighton. There was a refuse rat painted on a metal door that had been one of the pieces I had tried to find on my original Banksy tour – now I knew why I could not find it. The estimates for these rats were in the £20,000 to £40,000 range. Finally there was a piece called *Fungle Junk*, a huge work in three parts which had originally been painted on the side of an articulated lorry. The estimate for this was between £100,000 and £150,000.

All these pieces had been authenticated by Vermin, but would that count? Vermin was set up by four dealers. Inevitably Robin Barton of Bankrobber was key amongst them. James Allen, who more usually dealt in antiquarian books, was a second, and there were two others. They were, their anonymous spokesman said, an entirely independent body and what they could offer would be their professional opinion based on their collective knowledge of Banksy's early works.

While Banksy and many of his most committed fans thought that his works should be left to live or die on the streets, Vermin argued that they should be preserved and marketed like any other important piece of art – recognised 'for the iconic foundation stones they are'. For that to happen buyers needed to feel confident in what they were buying – one piece had been rejected from the sale because Vermin were not convinced of its authenticity.

They stressed that they were 'in no way connected to the artist', which was certainly true. So the work would be classified as authentic without Banksy ever having to own up to it. It all sounded mildly tongue in cheek, as though they were doing Banksy a favour. Unsurprisingly he did not see it that way, and nor did his fans.

'He is a cult for a lot of people,' says Barton. 'When I did that sale the forums went absolutely berserk. The vitriol was unbelievable. It was almost as if I had murdered someone. And it was all because I was going against their artist's wishes. These are forum people. They have got a computer at home and they have bought a couple of prints and therefore suddenly they are part of this bigger church. I quite like it in some ways, but it's also a bit insane really.'

Banksy's reaction was a good deal more subtle than that of his enraged fans. The day before the sale took place he issued a statement which killed both Vermin and any hope of selling any of the five pieces authenticated by Vermin. 'Graffiti art has a hard enough life as it is – with council workers wanting to remove it and kids wanting to draw moustaches on it, before you add hedge fund managers wanting to chop it out and hang it over the fireplace. For the sake of keeping all street art where it belongs I'd encourage people not to buy anything by anybody unless it was created for sale in the first place.'

If that was not clear enough, Pest Control announced on its website: 'All works authenticated by Pest Control have been done so in conjunction with the artist. Banksy does not provide this service through any other third parties and we would caution collectors against relying on such bodies.' Since its creation eight months earlier Pest Control had 'identified 89 street pieces and 137 screen prints falsely attributed to the artist . . . [he] would encourage anyone wanting to purchase one of his images to do so with extreme caution, but does point out that many copies are superior in quality to the originals.'

'If you read that story over someone's shoulder on the tube you'd think that Lyon & Turnbull were selling fakes, but when you read the small print it said nothing of the sort,' says Barton. 'There were never any fake Banksys being sold. They were just Banksys that Banksy no longer had control over. The fact that it wasn't intended for resale by Banksy is kind of irrelevant to me. If it's not stolen, if proof of ownership is there, then I am prepared to try and market the pieces.'

Whatever Barton might think, the sale was a disaster. None of the four rats sold, nor did *Fungle Junk*. These were difficult times in the auction rooms anyway, but the malaise seemed to spread like a disease from these five disputed lots to the whole auction.

Of the twenty-four works by Banksy in the sale only five managed to sell, and the overall selling rate for all the lots was under 30 per cent. Lyon & Turnbull's London ambitions were badly damaged and Vermin was destroyed – or, as a writer on one of the Banksy forums wrote with obvious glee, 'Bye, bye Vermin.' Pest Control emerged triumphant. But there was one fight Banksy failed to win.

It was not a dealer who took on Team Banksy, but the two travellers who owned *Fungle Junk*. They had been friends with him from way back in his crusty days and saw no reason why he should not help them now he had risen to such heights. They were not asking for charity, just authentication.

When they are not on the road Maeve Neale and Nathan Wellard, now both in their thirties, live in a field in Norfolk with their four children. Trying to find them is a bit like trying to find Dave Panit, although the road to their field is much more pot-holed. A decorative skull and crossbones on the gate warns you to keep out – but oddly in a rather friendly, welcoming way. When I arrived, there were children on a trampoline, dogs and horses, with lots of trailers and fairground equipment scattered about, as well as a random punch bag hanging from a tree, but there was no door and thus no door bell. A shout through the hedge, however, brought a result. Maeve came out trailing children. They had all just come back exhausted from Glastonbury where they had been supplying tents, and Nathan was already off preparing for a trip down to Cornwall for another festival the next morning.

It was a wonderful summer's day and this woodland hidey hole, deep in the middle of nowhere, the base for their hard travellers' life, seemed like some fairy-tale land entirely separate from the world the rest of us inhabit. Winter, I suspect, would be very, very different. Rickety wooden steps went up to their home, an articulated trailer, or two articulated trailers married together. A lovely wooden dog carved by a chainsaw artist met me, but the trailer spoke of a tough existence. They had created one large room for everyone to live in, along with a room for the parents, a bedroom that housed all four children, a shower and a loo on the way out. The children packed away the groceries and happily made tea for us while we sat in the sunshine and Maeve told me their story and the fight they had had with Banksy.

Their articulated trailer started life as a refrigeration unit before it became their home. They used to hitch it up and go travelling to wherever they were delivering tents. But what they saw as a home, Banksy saw as an inviting canvas; he contacted them through Seb Bambini, paid them their diesel money and in return got to paint one side of the trailer at Glastonbury in 1999. At this point, anonymity was not a major issue. 'It was performance art,' said Maeve. 'He did a show over three days in front of loads of people.' It is a huge piece covering the whole side of the lorry. There are a group of about six dodgy-looking men, vaguely military in appearance and supported by helicopters in the distance, carrying an inflatable dinghy up what is presumably a beach. The dinghy is loaded not with guns, as you would expect, but with a sound system and someone who looks like a DJ sits in the back of it on the decks. On the other half of the 'canvas', separated by a small window, Inkie went to work with some intricate graffiti lettering spelling STEALTH – although, what with all the cider and sunshine, the L vanished somewhere along the way.

Banksy finished it at the Sun and Moon Festival in Cornwall a few weeks later, doing some touching up, some outlining and adding the words which give some sort of meaning to this strange scene: 'IT'S BETTER NOT TO RELY TOO MUCH ON SILENT

MAJORITIES . . . FOR SILENCE IS A FRAGILE THING . . . ONE LOUD NOISE AND ITS GONE.' He gave the picture to the two travellers, telling them they could paint over it if they didn't like it. They never touched it and it remains on one side of the trailer, although plywood sheets now protect it from the elements and from anyone who might fancy their very remote chances of stealing a huge Banksy.

The next year Banksy did a piece on the other side of their home, although this time it was the other way round, they paid him: 'Only a couple of hundred quid, I think.' This is – or was, since it appears it no longer exists – the piece called *Fungle Junk*, which, in pictures at least, does not look nearly so interesting. Having started out with two monkeys playing keyboard and drums, surrounded on both sides by banks of speakers, it was quite heavily altered by Banksy over time, with the monkey on keyboards re-emerging as a piglet and a stencil of Sid Vicious appearing out of nowhere.

For several years this stayed on the other side of the trailer and it became something of an attraction. 'I remember waking up in Brighton,' Nathan told me later, 'getting up and going outside, only to find forty or so people taking photographs. You couldn't park it in private anywhere any more.'

Banksy stayed friends with the couple. He wasn't exactly a traveller, but for a time he was part of the whole movement. He even had his own small caravan, covered with graffiti of course, and a van covered in zebra stripes. 'He enjoyed a good party, a friendly bloke who would come to raves here and stay for a few days.'

But as the family expanded, so too did their home; the side of the trailer with *Fungle Junk* painted on it was removed and plonked fairly casually against the children's Wendy house so that a second trailer could be joined up, doubling the size of their living space – it must have been very cramped indeed beforehand. The very end section of *Fungle Junk* did not need to be taken off, so you can still stick your head inside their shower room and see that one wall has a little bit of Banksy preserved on it.

As the price of a Banksy started escalating, people from his past – like Cookie with her graffitied-up furniture removal van and Mojo with his travelling circus, as well as Maeve and Nathan with their articulated trailer – realised that they were sitting in, or on, serious money. Maeve and Nathan contacted a local art dealer and *Fungle Junk* was rescued from their field, separated into three parts and bundled up into 'museum quality' Perspex boxes so it could take off on its last journey.

The first stop was the Number Nine Gallery in Birmingham, where the owner claimed it as a real coup for the city to get their hands on a Banksy. It might have been a coup but there was no buyer. From there it travelled north to Hawick in Scotland, where Border Auctions, a family-run company that usually dealt in antiques, said they would have a go. Maurice Manning, a director, says, 'We had a lot of interest and a lot of competition.' Only two parts were put in the auction, one fetching £38,000 and the other £58,000; for a moment *Fungle Junk* looked tantalisingly close to being sold for almost £100,000. But the winning telephone bids both came with a condition: the pieces had to be authenticated. Manning says, 'Pest Control wouldn't talk to us,' and the sale never went through. Three months later they turned up at Lyon & Turnbull authenticated by Vermin and failed again.

At this point the pair had had enough. They were particularly incensed at how the impression seemed to have arisen that, says Maeve, 'we had run off with artwork that wasn't ours.' Banksy's right, she continues, 'that art done for people on street walls shouldn't be robbed and sold off, but these pieces like ours are just not in the same category . . .'

Maeve says she is an anarchist, but there is also a distinct feeling that she is a bit of a toughie. She was not about to give up on *Fungle Junk* – 'I've got four children and not much money.' Eventually she got through first to Pest Control and then to Banksy. It was, in her recollection, 'a bit of a heated conversation' over whether her intentions were 'capitalist'. 'He wasn't that unfriendly,' she said. 'He was just saying that he didn't really like the fact that people were capitalising on his paintings. Which is fair comment; it's just that he's capitalising on them too.'

'You told him that?', I asked.

'Oh yeah I don't hold back with my words.'

'And he was OK with you telling him that?'

'Yeah, he's a human being. He took it. He understood where I was coming from. Because I said I am capitalising, I totally admit it. But why not? Why shouldn't I? It's our painting to do what we like with. We didn't rip it off a wall. We didn't go and steal it from the street.'

Eventually an unusual deal was done. *Fragile Silence* received Pest Control authentication, although according to Maeve it was conditional on not talking to anyone about the deal. Were any such condition to have been imposed, however, it is difficult to see how it might be effectively enforced: 'Authenticated by Banksy, but later disowned'.

But *Fungle Junk*, which Banksy was apparently never too happy with, was different. The deal was that 'Banksy's people' would come and collect it –which they did, apart from that small section that still sits in the shower room and as far as Maeve knows it was later destroyed. This was one early Banksy that was never going to come to market. But they got more than just a certificate of authentication for *Fragile Silence*.

In February 2009 there was an auction at Selfridges, 'the first in nearly 100 years of Selfridges' history'. Some of the work was created by artists specifically to be exhibited and then auctioned off for the Prince's Trust; other pieces were included simply as part of the auction. Lot 69 was *No Ball Games*, a familiar Banksy image of two children tossing a television between them as though it was the only form of play they were allowed. What made it unique was that it was spray painted on steel. It had all the right authentication and 'it was acquired by the present owner directly from the artist.' The 'present owner' was actually Nathan and Maeve, who had been given the painting by Banksy in return for them giving him *Fungle Junk*. Even though it only reached £30,000, at the extreme low end of the estimate of £30,000 to £60,000, it was a result. They had got their way through a combination of dogged persistence and the fact that it was their home that Banksy had painted rather than some random wall.

Other friends from Banksy's past have had different experiences. Mojo's huge truck, painted on all sides by Banksy at an outdoor millennium party in Spain, was available for viewing off Oxford Street at the end of 2011. Mojo had managed to obtain Pest Control authentication and Dreweatts were offering the whole truck for sale 'signed with artist stamp on both sides of the chassis' for around £400,000 (which included a year's tax disc).

In Los Angeles, when the four partners who owned the water tank came to sell it, they very rapidly came up against Pest Control – a body which they had never heard of before. A very disappointed Tavia D tells the story: 'There were buyers who were willing to throw money at us but they needed that piece of paper. And I was like, what is a piece of paper? I was saying, "Do you consider this a piece of art? Then add it to your collection."

'This is where we started to learn more about the whole Banksy operation – like it's almost a conspiracy, because it's more of a business than it is about the art at the end of the day. If it was about the art, then why is it that a collector that truly loves art wouldn't look at this piece and say that's a piece of art no matter what anybody else says?' She is 'frustrated' with collectors who have 'lost their independence', and she is disappointed with Banksy because 'it's probably all about the business and not even about the art any more.' It has to be said, though, that their capture of the elephant was just as much about business as it was about art. Tavia explained that the cost of storing the tank in a warehouse meant that it would soon have to be scrapped and that would be 'super-sad'. Indeed in December 2011 she told me that they had eventually been forced to scrap the tank – the 'magic of the elephant remains a lost mystery'.

Inevitably Stephan Keszler's attempt to sell Banksy's wall at the summer exhibition in the Hamptons saw Pest Control in attack mode once again. They issued a statement saying: 'We have warned Mr Keszler of the serious implications of selling unauthenticated works but he seems not to care. We have no doubt that these works will come back to haunt Mr Keszler.' Although both Keszler and Barton say they never received such an 'admonishment', the effect was the same: none of the pieces sold.

Yet however much Pest Control might complain, the point is that while these walls are 'unauthenticated' they are still Banksy's work – no one has faked them. He is now in a unique position. His straightforward prints and canvases are signed by him and authenticated by Pest Control. But in addition there are the street pieces, which nowadays are usually announced on his website and in the past were sometimes found in his book. Because he does not want these pieces to be removed, Pest Control will not authenticate them. So they are Banksy works which are acknowledged in some way by him but not authenticated. Perhaps a new secondary market will eventually emerge dealing in authentic Banksys which nonetheless lack one key piece of paper.

Pest Control has strong echoes of the Authentication Board set up by the Warhol Foundation eight years after his death, and which stamps in ink DENIED on the back of any canvas it does not consider authentic, just to emphasise the point. By 2011, however, the Foundation decided it was spending too much money and time defending itself in the courts from lawsuits filed by those who considered their Warhol authentic despite being DENIED. So it shocked the art world by announcing that the Authentication Board would be closed down in the spring of 2012. In future, it appears, the market – helped by experts – will have to decide which is a genuine Warhol. Pest Control managed to establish almost the same level of control within eight months rather than eight years and so far they have not had to deal with any lawsuits. It is a measure of how successful Pest Control has been that Robin Barton says it would be 'the kiss of death' if he tried to apply for authentication. There are others who were wary of being interviewed because they feared that if, in the future, they were to apply for authentication of one of the pieces they owned they would be rejected.

So Banksy had got rid of Steve Lazarides and sorted out his team. He had established his organisation as the only one whose word dealers would accept on whether a Banksy was real or not. The price of his pictures was not spiralling upwards in the same way it had in 2007 and 2008, but it was steady. What he needed now was a new challenge.

# Fourteen
# Bonjour Monsieur Brainwash

In May 2010, Lot 437, *Charlie Chaplin Pink*, went up for sale at Phillips de Pury in New York. It featured a sort of Charlie Chaplin figure holding a can of pink paint, in front of a background of Marilyn Monroe faces with a couple of Campbell's soup cans thrown in for good measure. It was described by Vandalog in his blog as 'ugliness overload', but despite this it reached double the estimate: $122,500. In October the same sort of painting was put up for auction in London – although this time it featured Einstein, who was awkwardly holding a placard reading 'LOVE IS THE ANSWER' in front of a similar background. Not only was it signed by the artist but it was 'marked by the artist's blood on the reverse'. This went for £75,000.

Both works were by Mr Brainwash, or MBW for short, and they were being sold at a time when some collectors seriously believed that Mr Brainwash might somehow be Banksy in disguise. Since then, with the dawning of reality, these prices – apart from one auction result in France where a mixture of icons, Monroe, Mickey and Minnie Mouse and JFK fetched $82,107 – have not come anywhere near being matched. Nevertheless such prices remain an amazing triumph of marketing. For Mr Brainwash is entirely a

Banksy construct. Street art without Banksy would still exist, but Mr Brainwash without Banksy would never have arrived and never have survived.

The easiest way to grasp the identity of Mr Brainwash is to watch Banksy's Oscar-nominated film *Exit Through the Gift Shop*, now available on DVD. A brief outline goes something like this: Thierry Guetta, a Frenchman living in Los Angeles, picks up a camera and films graffiti artists – endlessly. He's a friendly guy and a persistent one too, so he makes it up through the ranks of the street artist hierarchy, filming them all until only Banksy is left. When Banksy arrives in Los Angeles to start the preliminary work on his show there, he needs a gofer. Through Shepard Fairey he finds Guetta, who soon talks Banksy into allowing himself to be filmed and indeed, for a time at least, becomes a friend.

When, later, Guetta shows Banksy his ninety-minute street art film, Banksy realises it is unwatchable – 'someone maybe with mental problems who happened to have a camera.' So he suggests that Thierry himself try his hand at street art – 'Have a little show. Invite a few people, get some bottles of wine' – and in turn Banksy will gain possession of all the tapes and use them to make a film about street art. Guetta, now known as Mr Brainwash, turns his 'little show' into a mega-exhibition entitled Life is Beautiful and every move he makes is filmed by Banksy's crew.

With testimonials of a sort from Fairey and Banksy, free prints for the first 200 people into the exhibition and a cover story in *LA Weekly*, the queue for the show stretched along three Hollywood blocks. The five-day opening was extended to two months, sales were astonishing and Guetta jumped from zero to hero. He had much more than his allotted fifteen minutes of fame and Banksy had a movie. It is a very clever, funny movie about the making and marketing of art, but it is also slightly depressing because Mr Brainwash – for a time at least – is so successful in *brainwashing* fans into believing that his hype is actually art. Prankumentary, mockumentary, docu-parody are just some of the ways critics suggest it might best be described; nevertheless it squeezes into the Documentary category for the Academy Awards, reaches the shortlist and narrowly misses an Oscar.

Banksy was undoubtedly the creative force that drove Mr Brainwash and thus the film forward; but the role he chose to play during his intermittent appearances in front of the camera was that of the naïf artist who did not quite know what he had let himself in for. Slouched in a chair, fully hooded up and with his voice distorted, it is only his hands and particularly his fat fingers that guarantee that it is Banksy we are looking at. He tells us that Thierry 'was actually a lot more interesting than I am' (unfortunately not); that 'we all needed someone who knew how to use a camera' (he picked the wrong man); that 'maybe I needed to trust somebody . . . I guess he became my friend' (sort of).

When *Exit Through the Gift Shop* first came out, critics very understandably appeared a little nervous. On the whole they liked the film but they were not entirely sure whether or not they were being conned rotten. A year after its first release the *Los Angeles Times* was still remarking: 'The uncomfortable question persists: is it real?' Was this ridiculous bumbler speaking English with an unbelievable French accent too good to be true, or was he perhaps Ali G having a laugh, or maybe even Banksy himself in disguise? Anthony Lane in the *New Yorker* was one of the few critics who did not like the film, calling it 'overstretched' and suggesting it 'feels dangerously close to the promotion of a cult – almost, dare one say it, of a brand'.

But for the most part critics enjoyed it. David Gritten in the *Daily Telegraph* called it an 'amusing curious documentary'. However, he admitted that he left the film 'not knowing quite what to think . . . Who actually made the film? What's true? What's not? Is it a Banksy stunt satirising the art world?' In the *Evening Standard* Nick Curtis neatly covered his bets: 'If art-prankster Banksy's first film is a hoax, as it just might be, it's an extremely complex and clever one.' The *New York Times* compared it to Banksy's best work: 'a trompe l'oeil: a film that looks like a documentary but feels like a monumental con'; and in *Vanity Fair* Julian Sancton wrote, 'It would actually make *less* sense if he put out a movie that wasn't in some way pulling a fast one on the audience.'

Banksy on the other hand, in the run-up to the Oscars, was having none of this. He told A.J. Schnack, whose website All These Wonderful Things specialises in documentary film, 'Ordinarily I wouldn't mind if people believe me or not, but the film's power comes from the fact it's all 100% true.' Well, up to a point . . .

It needs to be said first that despite the critics' worries, Thierry Guetta is for real, mutton-chop whiskers and all. He is not Ali G, he is not Banksy, he is a man who has miraculously landed on his feet and is enjoying every minute of it. His life before Banksy was that of a member of a comfortable French immigrant family in Los Angeles. Shortly before the Oscars the *Los Angeles Times* decided to make some background checks and Thierry, perhaps advised by the Banksy team, gave his first extended interview. His parents, Tunisian Jews, had fled to France to avoid persecution and he was born in a suburb north of Paris. He lost his mother when he was eleven and his father took the five children to Los Angeles when Thierry was fifteen.

In Los Angeles he dropped out of high school – being unable to speak English did not help – and ended up working in a vintage clothing store and then, as *Exit* suggests, owning and running the store. So he was just a shop owner who got lucky? Well again, not quite. The Guetta brothers' shop was called World of Vintage T-Shirts, 'Hollywood's top source of Vintage T's for over a decade'. His brothers Patrick and Marc had a book published by Taschen in 2010 on the same subject, its almost 400 pages depicting 650 T-shirts for the enjoyment of dedicated T-shirt fans. In his foreword to the book Patrick writes, 'My brothers, Marc (aka Tony), Thierry and I started an apparel company in 1987 called Too Cute which manufactured high-end embroidered T-shirts, licensing characters from Disney and Warner Bros to the Beatles and Betty Boop. We also developed our own characters the Junglenuts.'

The three brothers also founded TMP Enterprises – the initials of their Christian names – which is both a clothing company and a real estate company. Shepard Fairey says Thierry 'owns a lot of property around Hollywood' and according to one of his tenants, writing on the web, he was no more organised as a landlord than he was as a cameraman: 'He'd bought our house in North Hollywood and made it "look" beautiful, with polished concrete floors, vintage lighting fixtures. BUT, nothing in the house worked. The appliances were constantly breaking. The roof leaked . . .'

But whatever his abilities as a property owner, there is something rather more substantial to Thierry's background than *Exit* might suggest. Indeed, according to the successful street artist Ron English, he actually came from a wealthy French family who bought up property in Los Angeles to help them in their efforts to obtain permanent residency in the States. Part of Thierry's attraction for street artists was that he could provide 'legal' walls for them to paint on – for he, or his family, actually *owned* the buildings concerned.

However, the film's image of Thierry trekking around Los Angeles, sticking his camera up everyone's nose in the most unselfconscious way possible, rings absolutely true. Sean Bonner now writes for the website boingboing.net, but in 2005 he ran a gallery with his ex-wife Caryn called sixspace in Los Angeles and was putting on a show by the French street artist Invader (who, with awesome determination, for ten years now has been gluing on to walls around the world mosaic tiles depicting the characters from the old video game Space Invaders). Invader happened to be Thierry's cousin and his passport into the world of street art. Thierry was happy to drive his cousin wherever he needed to go, but with Thierry came his camera: 'He always had a camera and he was always sticking it into people's faces,' Sean says now. Through Invader Thierry got to know Shepard Fairey and then, through the force of his own personality, drove out a rival, persuading Shepard that he was the film-maker best able to make a documentary about him.

I had read one description of Thierry as 'klutzy' and 'bumbling', and another describing him as a force of nature. So how did Sean see him? 'I would lean more to the fumbling and klutzy. He always seemed like he was walking around and bumping into things. I would think maybe he's rude, maybe he's dumb, maybe he's whatever, but I would be talking to people and he would walk up and stick the camera in between people's faces, people who were talking to each other who couldn't see each other because he would stick a camera in front of them. So I don't think he had much comprehension of the world around him. He was like bouncing through it in a lot of ways. He was hanging around with

Shepard a lot and on some nights I would go out bombing with Shepard and he would tag along . . . Things worked much smoother when he wasn't around.'

What about the accent? 'It's for real, definitely for real.'

And what about his film-making? At one point, when a Shepard Fairey exhibition was being held in sixspace, Thierry set up a stop-motion camera that took one frame about every thirty seconds. 'It would go click and then thirty seconds later click again. He filmed everything: spreading out Shepard's work, putting it up, the opening reception, taking it down afterwards.' But no one ever saw it. 'I kept asking him for it, like "Hey, can we get that video of the stop motion thing?" And he'd say "Oh, I haven't had a chance to go through it yet." I'd say, "It's not really editing, it's simply start to finish, just give us the tape and we'll put it up." And he was like "I haven't had a chance." So after about a year of asking for that I just stopped asking. I realised I was never, ever going to see it.'

During all this time, he says, Thierry 'had no aspirations as an artist'. They bumped into each other once more before the Brainwash show. 'He told me that he was going to put on an art show and that he had gotten a really huge space in Hollywood and maybe he was going to ask me to help out with some part of it. And I said "Whatever it is, get in touch." I assumed it was an art show of other people's work. I thought he was going to open a gallery.' Little did he know how far and how fast Mr Brainwash had come. And no, he never went to the show.

Bonner is actually rather more polite than others. One source who worked with Thierry on the West Coast says, 'He was in everybody's way and in everybody's face. You just wanted to slap him really. He was so rude, the rudest most obnoxious French guy you could ever imagine. The worst . . .'

But if any more evidence is needed that Thierry is really Thierry and he really did have serious ambitions to make a documentary, then it comes from Alex Jablonski, a young film-maker who, in 2008, was just finishing the graduate film programme at UCLA. He got a phone call from a friend asking if he could help out logging and sorting what his friend said was 'tons and tons of unbelievable footage of Shepard bombing various cities, all shot by a crazy Frenchman named Thierry'. This was for a different documentary on Shepard Fairey's rise from unknown street artist to the man whose inspirational 'Hope' image became a part of Barack Obama's successful bid for the presidency. He was given all the film that Thierry had shot (at least he thought it was all the film, but when he came to watch *Exit* he discovered that Banksy had taken some of the best bits). In need of the money, he took the job, and he says, 'It was like every day you knew you were going to be locked in a room with a madman for eight hours.'

He had over 100 tapes to go through and there was no 'rhyme or reason' in how they came to him: 'The only markings might be something like "tape 71 New York, tape 72 Las Vegas".' On his website thesparrowsongs.com he explained the problem:

> Thierry shot everything. Everything. The camera never stopped rolling and the tapes were in no discernable order or grouping. The logs ended up looking something like this:
>
> TAPE 64
>
> 1 Shepard in hardware store. (6 mins).
> 2 Shepard walking down street (3 mins).
> 3 Camera left rolling on table while people eat dinner (42 mins).

TAPE 65

1 Camera still left rolling on table while people finish dinner (33 mins).
2 Camera blocked by dessert tray (6 mins).
3 Walking down street in New York (12mins).
4 Thierry talks to woman (5 mins).
5 Shepard pastes New York water tower (20 seconds).
6 Thierry getting lost near Holland Tunnel (15 mins)

. . . and so on.

He went on:

This is all to say that while I've never met Thierry in-person I've spent days and days going through his footage . . . when you spend that much time with someone's footage it feels like you're spending time with them. You see the world the way they saw it and you hear their questions, frustrations and observations. As bad as the footage was Thierry's personality came through in the tapes – he speaks in non-sequiturs, doesn't respect people's personal space and is distracted by all things equally. All of this is to say that in the time I spent with Thierry's footage I found that he is without a doubt absolutely fundamentally lacking any self-awareness . . . I know that Thierry Guetta is real because I spent weeks and weeks wishing he weren't.

So Thierry Guetta certainly exists and, give or take a little, very much in the form that Banksy portrayed him. But at this point things start getting more complicated. Yes, it's for real, Thierry is a very persistent but not very good cameraman, but is he anything more than that? *Exit* was short-listed for an Oscar in the Documentary category, but rather than a simple story about Thierry's rise to fame as Mr Brainwash, it seems much more a documentary about how Banksy constructed Mr Brainwash from the eager model that was Thierry. As Thierry told the *Los Angeles Times*, 'Banksy captured me becoming an artist, in the end, I became his biggest work of art.'

It was immediately after the point when Banksy had sat through the ninety minutes of Thierry's film and pronounced it 'unwatchable' that the whole Mr Brainwash phenomenon became very much a stage-managed documentary. When Banksy sent him back to Los Angeles to 'make some art, you know, have a little show', you might expect Thierry to be toiling away on the city's streets for years before anyone would notice him, let alone put on a show. But as soon as he was out on the streets Banksy's crew was filming him, providing the essential early scenes to go with the narrative of Thierry's metamorphosis into Mr Brainwash. Even in these very early shots Thierry needed assistants and rather than painting on walls, he was, like a considerable number of street artists, pasting up posters that had been created in a studio. From this earliest point there was no opportunity to see whether he had any practical ability to draw or spray.

What Banksy had spotted was that Thierry had enough quirkiness and endearing naïvete to be his lead actor. In his revealing email interview with A.J. Schnack, Banksy said: 'I needed the film to be fronted by a personality the audience could engage with. The producer Robert Evans said that "vulnerability" is the most important quality in a movie star and that's a hard thing to portray if all your interviewees have masks over their faces . . .

Thierry's entertainment potential wasn't difficult to spot – he actually walks into doors and falls down stairs. It was like hanging out with Groucho Marx but with funnier facial hair.'

Banksy has found the perfect character to lead a general audience into the unknown world of street art. As the producer of *Exit*, Jamie D'Cruz, says: 'To make a film about something as obscure as street art you need the guy. You need the character. Thierry was a brilliant cipher through which you can get into a world which is actually quite dull in many ways.'

There was not too much painting on the streets for Thierry to do, for the film needed a climax. It came through Mr Brainwash's massive Banksy-style exhibition in the 15,000 square foot former CBS studio building in LA where many years earlier the TV show *I Love Lucy* used to be shot. In short, Banksy asks us to believe that he suggested to Thierry that perhaps he might graduate to a genteel little gallery opening and Thierry came up with this massive event all on his own.

Banksy tells the camera that when preparations for the show begin to go a little haywire, 'I rang a few people who I thought might be able to help him out.' But he did much more than that. For instance the exhibition was produced by Daniel Salin, a 'get it done guy' who had produced Banksy's Barely Legal show in the city two years earlier. One of the artists working with Thierry says, 'Without the help of Daniel that show wouldn't have happened the way it did. He really solidified the direction as best he could under the circumstances.' Close to the deadline Banksy brought in Roger Gastman, a key fixer in the world where graffiti meets gallery, to make sure it all happened. Thierry's claims to have financed the show himself appear justified: he took out a $320,000 revolving line of credit to do so a year before it opened. But John

Sloss, a key figure in independent film circles and the film's distributor, said that he believed Thierry had 'a piece of the upside from the film' – which meant that if *Exit* ever made a profit, Thierry would have a share in it and thus a return on his investment in the show, quite apart from whether any of the pictures sold.

But if he needed massive aid from Banksy to put on the show, he also needed artists who could do the work for him, because there is no evidence in *Exit* that Thierry can paint. The only extended period where he is shown painting is in an extra that comes with the DVD of *Exit*, shot when he came to London to participate in the Cans Festival a month before his show opened in Los Angeles.

One of the artists who was painting in Leake Street with him says: 'He can be a little bit lazy. He can get other people to do the artwork for him. He did a big stencil and he didn't cut it. He just got someone else to do it for him. The general consensus was, "Who the hell is this guy coming up and just sort of doing stuff?"'

What you see on the DVD proves his point. First Thierry is shown choosing an image from a book of possibles – in the same way you might go into a carpet store and choose a carpet. He goes for a version of the Madonna/Britney Spears kiss at the MTV Awards, done in the form of a barcode. This image is then projected on to a huge expanse of paper which has been stuck to the wall of the tunnel so that someone – not Thierry, he is off talking to others – can trace the projected image. Once the lines have been traced they then have to be cut into a detailed stencil. Thierry does at least start on this painstaking work, but very soon gives up. He blames this on 'HDD', by which he probably means attention deficit disorder: 'I am a person who cannot stay so long in a space, I become crazy. Usually I have some people to cut the stencil for me. I am bored. Like I told you, I am HDD, I am going to get some help.' So others are summoned and, muttering mildly about Thierry being 'management', they do the job, but it takes them five hours. The stencil is then put up on the wall and you see Thierry up a ladder with a spray can. But the way the film is cut it is impossible to tell whether he does all the spraying. On the evidence we have seen beforehand, probably not – too boring. The end result looks good but tells you nothing about him as an artist.

Before the film was released, Shepard Fairey told an audience at a Q and A session organised by the West Coast auctioneers Bonhams & Butterfields, 'The thing about him [Thierry] is that he is motivated but he also has a lot of money and a lot of assistants. A lot of that work doesn't even have his own hand in it and you know I have mixed feelings about all of that. His show was a very manufactured thing . . .'

But if Thierry was not creating the art, who was? In many ways the film is quite open about his skills, or lack of them. When 200 of his paintings arrived at the very final minute, just in time for the show, Roger Gastman exclaimed, 'Whatever elves Thierry had making that stuff did a good job.' But it was rather more complicated than that. There is a revealing credit for David Healy, Thierry's young 'graphic designer', who is shown going through a book full of other people's art which Thierry has overwhelmed with Post-it notes. 'Thierry goes through the books, he finds the paintings that he likes and he comes up with the ideas of how to change them and we scan the image and then we Photoshop.'

The elves have been made redundant, Photoshop has taken over – although this later started creating unexpected problems for Thierry. For at the end of 2010 he was sued by Glen Friedman, a New York photographer whose iconic image of the rap group

Run-DMC was used by Thierry, changing the tone in one version and giving it a graffiti background in another, in a relatively simple piece of Photoshopping. A Federal court was asked to decide whether this was 'blatant plagiarism', as Friedman's lawyer suggested, or 'fair use', as Thierry argued. The judge eventually ruled in favour of Friedman. (In the middle of all this Thierry had to give a sworn statement to say that the piece was his work rather than anyone else's – which did at least put paid to the theory that Banksy might have done it all for him.)

As for the sculptures and installations that were very much part of the show, Thierry hired a team to do the work. Derek Walborn, a 25-year-old artist who had arrived in Los Angeles only three months earlier, got a job with Thierry when he answered an ad on Craigslist for a sculptor who could work with assorted materials. He made at least twenty-five of the exhibits in the show, so he was at the heart of the Brainwash team, and in an email kindly answering my questions he gives the clearest picture yet of what Thierry did and didn't do. 'Most of everything we did was his idea. He didn't tell us HOW to do anything (he, at least at the time, didn't really know how to do anything or know anything about tools or materials) or, for the most part, how exactly he wanted it to look and in some cases he wouldn't tell us WHAT to make it out of either. He would just kind of throw an idea at us and then we would formulate the materials and best way to make it happen. For example, he said that the air ducts in the building reminded him of a spider. He asked me if I could make it look like a giant spider was on the ceiling. I said yes. The end.

'That particular project got no more input from him aside from his excitement about how it was coming along. A common thing would be him bringing in things he had "collected" one way or another (e.g. old film reels) and saying "Make me a (something) out of this (material)." The film canister creatures, for example, were the result of him saying "Make me a person out of them". The instructions were very minimal and the freedom to create was pretty vast. He never looked at anything I did and said "No, this is not what I wanted." He seemed continually impressed and happy with us. Towards the end of the preparation some ideas were put together to fill space that Thierry was not directly involved in, but these were very few and, at this point, I can only remember one idea that was more between Daniel [Salin] and I than Thierry.

'He is not a technician. He cannot draw or paint, by his own admission and by my own observation. I have not seen him cut a stencil. Granted, I wasn't with him 24/7, but the only thing I have ever seen him do was sprinkle spray paint on some prints in order to make them each "unique." We were all very dubious about his ability to do the things he said he could do. His lack of knowledge on a lot of processes, materials, and costs of said materials would have been humorous were we not employed by him, but at the same time it allowed us a lot of breathing room when it came to the processes we used to build things.'

I had read that Walborn had put pictures of some of the work that he had done for Thierry on his own website, but I could not find them and I wondered what had happened to them. 'He didn't want images from the show anywhere that would give the impression that his work was not "his." He did not want mystery surrounding the alleged source of the art or anyone to think that "Mr. Brainwash" was some kind of collective as opposed to just one guy. At his request I took it down. Since it's not really my style anyway, I'm not too worried about it.

'Personally, I don't hold anything against Thierry. I think he is generally a nice guy. However, I struggled through the show's creation with my ability to respect him as an artist. When I think of artists I look up to I think of honesty, integrity and, of course, talent. I found it more and more difficult to find any of these attributes as time went on. If you don't physically make your own art then be clear about it. You can still enjoy the spotlight as the ideas-man, if that's in fact what you are. But as a struggling artist myself who wouldn't dream of putting my name on something that someone else created or even touched, I couldn't help but to be a little annoyed when Thierry would show people things I put together and say "see what I did?" It made me feel like I was selling my soul, to some extent. To be fair, he was pretty generous to us as far as giving us credit in some cases. I think it just depended on what kind of impression he wanted to make on who he was talking to.

'That being said, I don't have any regrets at all about my participation in the show. I made some great friends, made enough money to pay rent, and got to make sculptures all day. I got a quick ten seconds in an Oscar-nominated documentary. Not bad, right? I also think that I learned a little from Thierry. He didn't let anything stop him. In spite of my disdain for his way of presenting himself as the creator of the art, I admire that kind of thinking and I find myself applying it to my own life as a result. Maybe, in the end, that's Thierry's real true talent: the inability to allow reality to ever take the wheel.'

And what about Banksy's role in constructing Mr Brainwash? 'Banksy helped to create a monster and then set it loose. He's here to stay now. Enjoy.'

Justin Murphy was billed in the film as 'props builder', but he was rather more of an artist than that description allows. At the time when Thierry was being attacked on the web he was solid in his defence. 'I can assure all of you people, he IS an artist, just like the rest of the team that set out to produce this show. The amazing part is, none of this would have happened without this man's vision, and it's very true, that it wouldn't have been such a huge success without the team of artists that he recruited . . . MBW is a machine, and our team is the oil that keeps it going.'

Warhol might have been proud of that defence, with all its 'Factory' implications; but it is no use, as Mr Brainwash's defenders do, comparing Thierry with Warhol. Warhol had all the technical drawing skills that Mr Brainwash does not possess, but much more than that he had the original ideas: he changed the way we look at everyday objects, he changed the way art could be produced. And in doing all this he changed the nature of art.

But, quite apart from Mr Brainwash's skills or lack of them, the exhibition and its success provided the centre point for the film. Marc Schiller, who runs the influential street art website www.woostercollective.com and who helped promote the film, said that Banksy was 'making a movie that's 100 percent like a Banksy exhibition', and he was right. What Banksy had done was make a very good film about the marketing of art. It was both fun and informative, in the sense that it showed how Mr Brainwash was a triumph of marketing over talent – how easily led we all are to the next big thing. In the early days of the film's marketing both the distributor and Banksy were careful not to call it a documentary, worried that the D word itself was a box-office turnoff – 'Our distributor told me that if I call it a documentary nobody will come,' said Banksy. But as the Oscars approached, so the dreaded D word was allowed – encouraged even – to emerge again. What the film is not, however, despite Banksy's protestations that 'it's all 100 per cent true', is a documentary in the usual sense of the word.

But, Oscar or not, Banksy appears to have had the last laugh. For in much the same way as his *Morons* print mocked the people buying 'this shit' while at the same time making good money for him, *Exit* did the same thing. After the film's surprise appearance at the 2010 Sundance Film Festival there were 'a bunch of offers' from distributors, but John Sloss, the film's American sales agent, launched his own DIY distributing company to bypass the traditional distributors. It was a gambit described by one writer as 'one part innovation, one part desperation', but in this case, with the help of Banksy, the gambit worked. It also went some way to resolving Banksy's problem that with graffiti you have 'complete control over the means of distribution, with a film you have none'.

In the end just over $1 million was spent on distribution, a very sizeable sum for an independent film, but there was no movie star or famous director to do a media tour – and Banksy was both the problem and the solution. The problem according to Sloss was, 'I saw how controlling he was over the promotion of his work. So I just thought, this is a highly unlikely project for a traditional distributor because not only is Banksy very controlling, but you can't talk to him.' The solution was to transform Banksy into a vandal who was also a marketing device. Sloss saw the impact Banksy had when he hit Park City, Utah (where the Sundance Festival is held) just before the film did and realised he had the best travelling billboard he could ever have – and it was free. Banksy described how he rented a minivan so he could 'drive around and make some paintings. Me and a friend slept in it for a week at a trailer park covered in snow and full of rottweilers. I was huddled over a tiny electric heater cutting stencils on a fold-down bed surrounded by dog shit.' It was effective but it was hardly Hollywood.

As Banksy's art had brought in a new audience, so too did his film. The approach was twofold: Banksy would get to work in each major city before the film arrived and at much the same time the distributor would 'screen the hell out of it'. These invitational screenings, designed to get the word out to a wider audience, were not for any Tom, Dick or Harry, they were 'tastemaker' screenings. 'Musicians sat with film-makers, writers and graffiti vandals,' said Marc Schiller, who helped with this campaign. 'We announced the diversity at the screenings.' Once the film's 'offline presence' had been established the promoters could then go online and to Twitter. And the audience they drew in were not regular filmgoers. As Sloss said: 'They don't read the newspapers or traditional movie advertising – we were connecting with them online, from within their community.'

And it worked. Banksy told the *New York Times* that he financed the film himself, and the abbreviated 2010 accounts for his film company Paranoid Pictures show an investment of almost £1.5 million, or roughly $2.4 million. Film finance is an obscure business, to put it mildly, but the headline figures are these. The American box office was almost $3.3 million, the foreign box office was just over $2 million, making a total of $5.3 million; add to that DVD sales and television rights. By the time everyone else had taken their share Banksy might not have made a huge profit, but he certainly would not have lost money.

Banksy complained in an email to one interviewer: 'I have a great little team, but I tell you what – they all hate this fucking film. They don't care if it's effective, they feel very strongly that Mr Brainwash is undeserving of all the attention. Most street artists feel the same. This film has made me extremely unpopular in my community.' But the argument over whether Mr Brainwash deserved all the attention – and indeed whether he was 'real' – has rather overshadowed what an incredible achievement by Banksy *Exit* was. To have had the idea for a film, spotted Thierry's potential, turned him into a 'street artist' of sorts, financed the film, and pushed it through to a very successful conclusion and to a possible Oscar is almost unbelievable, but in this case it really is '100 per cent true'.

Twelve years ago Banksy produced a video for the hip-hop artist Blak Twang, filmed largely at Queens Park Rangers' football ground, and he declared afterwards that film was 'the only art form, apart from pop graffiti, that matters'. After *Exit* he had further pronouncements to make. 'If Michelangelo or Leonardo Da Vinci were alive today they'd be making Avatar, not painting a chapel. Film is incredibly democratic and accessible, it's probably the best option if you actually want to change the world, not just re-decorate it.' He has since made the *Antics Roadshow* (geddit?) for Channel 4, a quirky compilation of assorted acts of rebellion against society including a custard pie thrower, a streaker and the man who gave Winston Churchill's statue a Mohawk. His next full-length film might well be like a second novel: it will be difficult to live up to what has gone before, but he is almost bound to give it a try.

As for Mr Brainwash, John Sloss says he is 'sensitive' to 'some harsh stuff' written about his talent – and it would be hard not to be. But if his goal was fame, he has that; and if it was money he has that too. The 'ultimate validation' of Mr Brainwash's show, according to the film's narrator, 'was measured in dollars and cents – by the end of his opening week Thierry would sell nearly a million dollars' worth of art.' Leaving aside the fact that Banksy quite clearly feels this is no validation at all, it did mean money in the bank for Thierry.

And it did not stop there. Los Angeles was followed by New York and a record cover for Madonna. Being on the Brainwash email list I still receive regular notices of new prints about to be released. There was one in the spring of 2011, for instance, of John Lennon's face outlined in a sort of 'join the dots' manner and called, unsurprisingly, *Connecting Lennon.* The bulk of the edition was priced at $250 a print, although there were five gold prints costing $600 each, and the whole edition would have made $40,000 if all the various colourways sold. (On Mr Brainwash's site a couple of months later, *Connecting Lennon* was marked as sold out.) At the end of the email was the usual impressive warning that comes with Brainwash offers: 'Please note: Due to overwhelming demand on certain print releases, Paypal cannot process the orders quick enough and may oversell. Any necessary refunds will be made within the hour.' Not bad for a failed cameraman.

# Fifteen
# Art Without a Theory

'A graffiti artist has taken this year's Turner Prize,' wrote *The Times*'s art critic Rachel Campbell-Johnston as she heralded the winner of the 2009 prize. So had Banksy, the man who had once painted 'Mind the Crap' on the steps of the Tate. actually won the Turner Prize? Well, no. Unsurprisingly this was someone else entirely, someone who most street art fans had probably never heard of: Richard Wright, a painter memorably described as 'a thinking person's graffiti artist'.

Wright had covered the whole of one of the Tate's large walls with an intricate, absorbing pattern in gold leaf. It lacked the adrenalin, the speed, the lawlessness of traditional graffiti but it was certainly a painstaking and intricate work. No cutting knife and stencil for him; instead he used both a single needle and a wheel with many needles attached to punch minute holes through paper to create his pattern. Instead of a spray can he used chalk which went through these needle holes on to the wall, and on the faint outline the chalk had left once the paper had been removed he glued the gold leaf. The work, said *The Times*, 'pays homage to the cartooning techniques of the great Renaissance artists'. My instant thought on entering Wright's gallery was that it reminded me of my mother's heavy brocade curtains. It took some time to banish that thought and really start to enjoy it.

One of the visitors who left their comments on the noticeboard had a similar feeling: 'Richard Wright's work looks like the wallpaper in my nan's house.' But most visitors loved it and particularly they loved the impermanence of it, the fact that it would be painted over once the Turner Prize exhibition finished. 'His theory that nothing lasts for ever is the truth.' 'Absolutely breathtaking. Knowing his work will never last makes you appreciate it all the more.'

The art critics were equally enthusiastic, drawn in particular to the ephemeral nature of his work. 'He is a painter for our time and only for our time because he does not want his works to last.' 'What defiant integrity, what a clever comment on the transience of riches.' 'Wright suggests that we question the power of capitalist markets, perhaps. His murals cannot be owned. They will be painted over at the end of the exhibition. All that glitters is not sold in Wright's glimmering world.'

But ten months later I was at the Frieze Art Fair in Regent's Park. The smell of big money wafted through the tented encampment and my trail soon led to the stand of Larry Gagosian, contemporary art's most important dealer with eleven galleries around the world. I had read that Gagosian represented Wright, which seemed rather confusing since it appeared from the Turner Prize that there would be nothing permanent to sell.

The Gagosian stand was staffed by assistants so formidable you hardly dared look at them, let alone talk to them. Of course, when one did speak she was very nice and very helpful. She said she had two Richard Wrights available, one very intricate piece priced at

$80,000 and a smaller one at $35,000. So not all his works are as ephemeral as his fans might believe.

Here are two 'graffiti artists' who both produce work that is ephemeral, as well as studio work – in Wright's case it is work on paper rather than canvas – designed to be hung up and sold. So what does Wright have that Banksy doesn't have? Why is it that Wright has eleven pieces in the Tate collection while Banksy has none? Banksy has featured only twice in the Tate and one of those occasions was when he hung up his own picture there. (The second time was in 2007, when Mark Wallinger won the Turner Prize with a detailed re-creation of the late peace campaigner Brian Haw's Parliament Square protest, for which two paintings Banksy had given to Haw were meticulously copied – at the time of writing the originals were being held in storage in east London by the police, who removed them when Haw's space was reduced.)

Wright's work is praised for being 'wilfully elusive', as one critic put it. Banksy on the other hand is seen as almost too obvious, too *easy* to understand. There is no particular hidden meaning and none of the qualities – 'violence, chaos and paranoid mania' – that graffiti writers can sometimes offer. There are of course hidden references in Banksy's work. To take just one example, his portrait of Queen Victoria enjoying lesbian sex reflects the urban myth that she would not sign a bill outlawing homosexuality unless lesbianism was removed from it, since she did not believe women did such things. And his work does still have some of the qualities – the anti-authoritarianism, the subversiveness – of his past, although perhaps less so as the years roll on. But what you see is what you get, and in the world of contemporary art that is seldom enough.

Thirty-five years ago Tom Wolfe wrote the classic diatribe about modern art, *The Painted Word*, basing his onslaught on a paragraph written by the *New York Times*'s then chief art critic, Hilton Kramer: 'Realism does not lack its partisans, but it does rather conspicuously lack a persuasive theory. And given the nature of our intellectual commerce with works of art, to lack a persuasive theory is to lack something crucial – the means by which our experience of individual works is joined to our understanding of the values they signify.' They were words, said Wolfe, 'which gave the game away'. In short, 'Without a theory to go with it, I can't *see* a painting . . . Modern Art has become completely literary: the paintings and other works exist only to illustrate the text.'

This, one suspects, is Banksy's problem, although he certainly would not see it as a problem: there is no theory, persuasive or otherwise, behind his work. The viewer can connect instantly with what they see. Five years ago, just before Banksy – or rather his prices – took off into the stratosphere, Marc Schiller, writing on www.woostercollective.com, put a compelling case in his defence:

> We now see Banksy as the greatest thing that has happened not only to the street/urban art movement, but to contemporary art in general. Most people need entry points to become comfortable with things that are new and for millions of people Banksy is the entry point they need in not only seeing art in a new way, but in accepting art as part of their daily lives. Like Andy Warhol before him, Banksy has almost single handedly redefined what art is to a lot of people who probably never felt they appreciated art before . . .

Shepard Fairey put it rather more concisely, calling him 'the most important living artist in the world'.

'Accessible' was the adjective I heard most often when listening to people talk about Banksy, with sometimes – but certainly not always – the slight undertone that 'accessible' art is art that is all too easy. It was an attitude probably best and most harshly expressed by the *Guardian* art critic Jonathan Jones, who was on the jury that chose Wright as the Turner Prize winner. Banksy, he wrote,

> appeals to people who hate the Turner prize. It's art for people who think that artists are charlatans. This is what most people think, so Banksy is truly a popular creation: a great British commonsense antidote to all that snobby pretentious art that real people can't understand. Yet to put your painting in a public place and make this demand on attention while putting so little thought into it reveals a laziness in the roots of your being. After wallowing in this stuff for a while, I almost found myself hating Banksy's fans. But actually, it's fine to like him so long as you don't kid yourself that this is 'art' . . . in Banksy the philistines are getting their revenge.

But, being so much part of the art world, perhaps Jones underestimates how exclusionary this world can feel. In his recent book, *How Pleasure Works*, the Yale academic Paul Bloom argues that 'Traditional art is about what is in the world; more modern works are about the very process of representation. An appreciation of much of modern art therefore requires specific expertise. Any dope can marvel at a Rembrandt, but only an elite few can make any sense of a work such as Sherrie Levine's *Fountain (After Marcel Duchamp)*, and so only an elite few are going to enjoy it.'

Banksy would almost certainly be happy with the idea that 'any dope' can enjoy his work along with that of Rembrandt. Indeed in an (emailed) interview with the *New Yorker* he dared to mount an attack on the obscurity which seems to be an essential part of contemporary art. 'I don't think art is much of a spectator sport these days. I don't know how the art world gets away with it, it's not like you hear songs on the radio that are just a mess of noise and then the DJ says, "If you read the thesis that comes with this, it would make more sense."'

His 2009 exhibition in Bristol required neither a thesis nor a short explanation, just a vaguely jokey map showing (roughly) where to find his pieces among the museum's other work. In contrast, a year later the Saatchi Gallery staged an exhibition of the new generation of British artists, Newspeak: British Art Now, where it was easy to feel completely left out of the loop without the excellent notes that accompanied the exhibition. Faced with Rupert Norfolk's *Wall 2006*, consisting of 125 carved limestone rocks, it was comforting to read in the notes that the work requires 'curiosity and an investment of time to be fully appreciated'. But other works required more than that. For Pablo Bronstein's *Monument in the Style of Michael Graves on the Debris of the Bastille*, the notes told us that the painting is based on Jean-Pierre Louis Laurent Houël's *The Storming of the Bastille* given 'a facelift à la pomo architect Michael Graves' to present an 'alternate history'. But what if you don't know that? The painting does not really survive without the explanation. The late Cy Twombly produced work that was, according to *The Times*'s headline writer, 'Graffiti of the Gods'; but after visiting an exhibition of Twombly and Nicolas Poussin's work at Dulwich and reading the gallery guidance – 'the jittery tangles of pencil seemingly caught between an utterance and a stutter' – I was still mystified, left with a feeling that Twombly's work was for scholars rather than spectators.

With Banksy no one is made to feel inferior. And that's a considerable relief, relief born from the fact that we don't have to figure out the meaning of Twombly's stutters, Hirst's spots or Tracey Emin's tampons (actually Tracey Emin often explains things for us in long handwritten notes that accompany some of her pieces).

Riikka Kuittinen, who acquired several Banksy prints to add to the V&A's continually updated Print Collection, is one who uses 'accessible' as a term of approval. Having first seen his work on the streets, she was overjoyed to find he produced prints as well. 'People get it. It appeals to a wide range. You don't have to know anything about anything necessarily to get it and I think contemporary art, sometimes unfairly, has this reputation of being difficult, whereas Banksy's work isn't difficult . . . I don't think accessible means bad at all. The Van Gogh show at the Royal Academy would have got how many thousands of people visiting and still the work is good. Because something is popular doesn't mean it's bad.'

So yes, Banksy's work is much easier for the viewer than many of his contemporaries', and while the critics might not like it he has managed to attract a whole new audience into the art world. It can get embarrassing at times. The *Boston Globe* interviewed a cyclist who had ridden over to see a new Banksy put up to publicise *Exit Through the Gift Shop* in the spring of 2010. 'I have never seen something like this in Boston before,' said this fan, who was in his early twenties. 'It gives Boston a strange sense of worth.' How could Boston with all its history need Banksy to give it a sense of worth? But the Croydon builder buying a Banksy wall, many of the crowd queuing for hours to get into the Bristol Museum, the financial adviser turned gallery owner, Banksy's followers on the web, are all new converts to the incredibly broad church who have been gathered from the wilderness by Banksy and led into the art world.

In 2011 the Museum of Contemporary Art, Los Angeles (MOCA) put on the most far-reaching display of 'street art and graffiti' yet seen. It was three years behind Tate Modern's exhibition but it set out to be considerably more comprehensive. Banksy was there in impressive style, but so were about fifty other artists. The exhibition could certainly have survived without Banksy but it is impossible to believe that it would have happened in the first place but for the Banksy effect – the drawing power that both his painting and his film have given the street art world.

Matt Gleason, who runs the web-based *Coagula Art Journal*, admitted, 'I wanted to trash this show,' but in a generally favourable review he called it 'a show meant for people who don't go to museums . . . it was also MOCA putting all those academic artists on notice that "you are no longer welcome, you are no longer wanted." Your art world is over, your theory is dead. We want bodies here, we want popular artists, popularity. We want a critical mass and you are not going to get that with a lot of minimal art, you are not going to get that with a lot of abstract painting.'

One thing he noticed at the preview for the show was that people would walk up to artists and ask for their autograph – another sign, as the *Financial Times* had noted a year earlier, that 'art and artists are attracting the fans, the adulation, the attention – and the bank balances – that were once the terrain of rock stars.' It was an exhibition, Gleason said, that signalled, 'This is the new art world and it already has its own art history dating way back.'

Of course the contemporary art world is not over – as Gleason suggests it might be – but Banksy has almost single-handedly produced a new art world for a new audience, running alongside the existing world and now, slowly but surely, within it. And there is room for both.

Banksy's problem lies not in his art but in the fact that he now makes considerable money from this art market and the fans who collected him from the beginning can no longer afford him. Richard Wright can say 'I like all my work to disappear' and then sell his work on paper via Gagosian and no one seems bothered in the slightest. But it sometimes seems as though Banksy is almost considered a criminal for making money from his art. He himself recognises the problem, telling *Time Out* in New York: 'I wouldn't want to be remembered as the guy who contaminated a perfectly legitimate form of protest art with money and celebrities. I do sometimes question whether I'm part of the solution or part of the problem ... There's obviously nothing wrong with selling your art – only an idiot with a trust fund would tell you otherwise. But it's confusing to know how far you should take it.'

On the one hand he has to deal with the likes of the Splashers, a short-lived group with, one suspects, a minimal membership, which sprang up in New York towards the end of 2006 and was dedicated to splashing paint over street works by the likes of Swoon, Shepard Fairey and Banksy. The Splashers called the work of such street artists 'a trough for gallery owners and critics', arguing that once street art is introduced into the museum or the advertising world it becomes nothing more than 'bourgeois-sponsored rebellion . . . both utterly impotent politically and fantastically lucrative for everyone involved'. (The Splashers attempted to make sure that none of their work would find its way into collectors' hands by adding a short warning at the bottom of the communiqués they pasted over or next to a piece of street art. It read: 'The removal of this document may result in injury, as we have mixed the wheatpaste with tiny shards of glass.')

On the other hand there are private dealers, gallery owners, and now museums and many artists themselves, who say that while street art belongs on the streets, the studio art that has developed from it is different and can be bought and sold – as a canvas or a print – like any other artist's work. For, as Larry Gagosian says, 'Art dealers feel they have to obfuscate the mercantile part of their profession but let's not kid ourselves – it's a business. Artists have families and children and like anyone else they want to live decently – sometimes very decently.'

Their argument goes that this trading of art in the traditional way will not damage the integrity of the art still out there on the streets. When Banksy produced his Kate Moss prints or his detourned oil paintings they were never intended to be on the streets, they have not been taken out of context. It is the collectors who try to profit from the door, the water tank, the wall who are taking his art out of context.

So far he has managed to straddle the two worlds, although his subversiveness diminishes as his prices rise. But he comes from a very identifiable subculture, and he appears to have reached the awkward point where he wants to remain somehow part of that subculture while his very success makes it almost impossible for him to do so.

Take the riots in the Stokes Croft area of Bristol in the spring of 2011, which started after police raided a squat occupied by opponents of a newly opened Tesco Metro store close by. The police said the raid followed information that petrol bombs were being made at the squat. Banksy's response was to produce a £5 'commemorative souvenir poster' of a 'Tesco Value Petrol Bomb' (marked 'Highly Flammable') with its fuse alight. The proceeds, he said on his website, were to go to the People's Republic of Stokes Croft and its associates, an organisation which for several years and in various imaginative ways has been attempting to revive the neighbourhood. Despite some rain, the inevitable queue formed at the Anarchist Bookfair where the poster was being sold one Saturday, but Banksy's generosity was not universally welcomed. Although there had been criticism of the police, there were also suggestions that the anti-Tesco protest had been hijacked by outsiders and some felt Banksy was merely polishing his right-on credentials, 'supporting a load of outsiders who are destroying a local community'. Many on the web supported Banksy, some pleading for anyone in the queue to buy them a poster too; nevertheless, being denounced as a 'Champagne Socialist', as he was on one website, might have hurt a little. (The poster was soon on sale on eBay for more than £100.)

Other street artists, particularly in America, move easily between the world of the street and the commercial world without any of the qualms that Banksy has. Shepard Fairey has established an impressive business empire with three strands: OBEY Clothing, 'a brand that speaks to many different genres', his gallery Subliminal Projects, and his creative brand agency Studio Number One, whose clients include Nike, Red Bull and the Honda Civic – and that's quite apart from his work as an artist on the streets. No one comes near matching Fairey's commercial success, but other offerings from street artists include a Faile shower curtain, a $278 limited edition vibrator with a Jamie Hewlett etching on it, a lightbulb designed by New York street artist Kaws and a Pure Evil hair straightener. Indeed Pure Evil, whom I met very early on in my research, seemed rather less of an outlaw a year later when his flat was featured in the style pages of *The Times* magazine with a headline that read 'Residence Evil, the graffiti artist's home'.

Banksy is never going to let his home be photographed, but he is always having to draw fine lines in a world which has become increasingly attractive to brand managers. The work of some contemporary artists has become, as one critic put it, 'accessible honey pots to sponsors', and if Georgio Armani can sponsor an exhibition by Richard Hambleton, 'the godfather of street art', in New York, Milan and London, what price would the right brand pay to sponsor Banksy?

At the MOCA exhibition in Los Angeles Banksy managed to stay one step away from sponsorship – just. Two of the world's omnipresent brands, Nike and Levi's, were among the exhibition's key sponsors. Nike built a skate ramp for the exhibition and brought in the Nike team of skateboarders. If indeed you exited through the gift shop, you could buy Space Invader key chains for $8 each or, rather more to the point, for $250 a limited edition Levi's 'trucker jacket' with a selection of different street artists' work on the back. Banksy was not one of those artists, but Shepard Fairey's gallery 'curated' this project and one of the jackets was designed by Fairey. The museum's director, Jeffrey Deitch, admitted that there had been difficulty presenting the idea of sponsorship to many of the artists. 'We had dialogues to explain what we were doing with the artists, and made the sponsors also understand that they are not sponsoring the artists – they're simply helping the museum to make this happen,' he explained. So that was OK then.

But each step poses problems. Banksy dislikes people being charged to go to see exhibitions – his are always free – but here he was in Los Angeles, where the entry fee was $10 a head. Halfway through the exhibition he announced he was sponsoring free Mondays at MOCA, thus joining Wells Fargo Bank which was sponsoring free Thursday evenings. 'I don't think you should have to pay to look at graffiti. You should only pay if you want to get rid of it,' he said, but despite his sponsorship people would of course have to pay for most of the week. (With the help of his free Mondays the exhibition had a record 201,000 visitors during its run, just beating the previous record set by an Andy Warhol retrospective.)

He does not accept sponsors, but he was exhibiting in a gallery that needed sponsors to help make the exhibition happen. He decried galleries as 'trophy cabinets for a handful of millionaires', yet here he was in Los Angeles exhibiting in a museum which had only been saved from extinction by a $30 million 'challenge' grant not from a mere millionaire but from a billionaire, the philanthropist Eli Broad.

A few years back he was infiltrating galleries; now he is not only exhibiting at MOCA but also loaning his work to other galleries. In December 2011 he gave the Walker Art Gallery in Liverpool a work called 'Cardinal Sin' a replica of an 18th-century bust of a priest with his face sawn off and pixelated by small bathroom tiles. In case anyone failed to understand what it was about Banksy pronounced: 'at this time of year it's easy to forget the true meaning of Christianity – the lies, the corruption, the abuse.' His carefree days as the subversive vandal are surely over and he is entering a new, more complicated phase in his career.

When I first started research on this book I thought of Banksy as a sort of happy-go-lucky vandal: entertaining, a bit of a mystery and generally a force for good, popping up on walls all over the place and gone before anyone could find him. I think of him now as a much more permanent fixture; very talented and very clever, at the pinnacle of the burgeoning street art movement even though he paints some pictures that go from studio to collector without ever going near the street. He is much richer than I ever imagined and much, much more controlling. I was asked once if Banksy would like this book; the answer I am sure is no, for whatever it says about him the fact is this is a book he does not control.

His achievement is extraordinary. It is his own unique talent, nourished in the key years by the showmanship of Steve Lazarides, that has enabled him to bypass the London cognoscenti and get to where he is today. His art has attracted a whole new audience to a world badly in need of new fans. But perhaps he now has to accept that while he is a very good artist and a very good film-maker, he is no longer part of the subculture he sprang from. He is not a revolutionary and never will be, although images like the girl floating with her balloons over the Israeli wall, the OAPs using bombs as bowls, the CCTV cameras watching over the idyllic countryside, need no thesis alongside them and speak directly and succinctly to the viewer. There are times when his pronouncements sound pompous and irritating – clichés wrapped up as deep thoughts. But the images are different – they make us admire him, make us laugh and make us think, not so much about what the painting means but about the subjects he has taken on. As for his film, while people argue about *Exit Through the Gift Shop* they tend to forget that it is a wonderful commentary on the way that art can be produced and marketed in the twenty-first century.

And that should be enough. Perhaps the time has come when he will have to change his own rules. He can remain sort of anonymous for as long as he likes, but he cannot remain the subversive street rebel for ever, juggling £5 Molotov cocktail posters with £50,000 pieces in the auction rooms. The more Banksy and his team – which is tighter than ever – try to control his image, to authorise his unauthorised life, to pretend he is the same rebel he was a decade ago, the more difficult it becomes and the more they cloud his enormous achievements. Eventually his joke *I can't believe you morons actually buy this shit* might begin to wear thin.

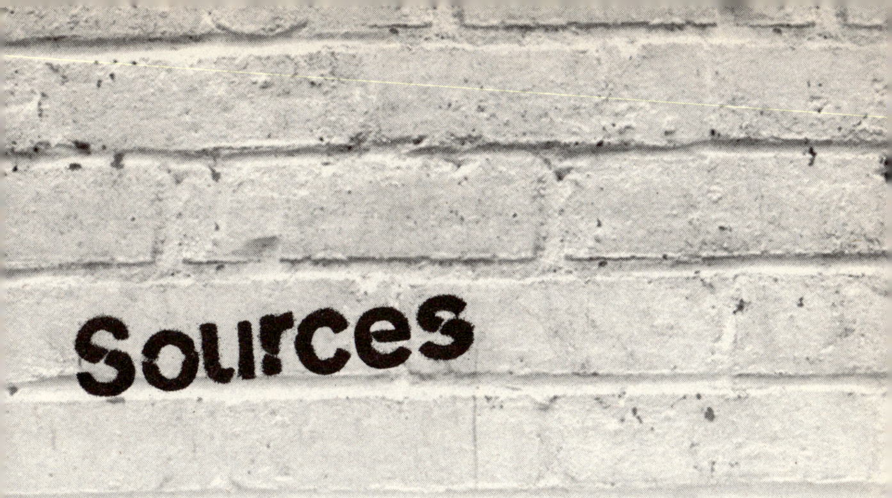

# Sources

There are two Banksy websites. www.banksy.co.uk is the one where you will find the biggest selection of his art. When the cry goes up 'there's a new Banksy' then, if it is genuine, it will usually appear on this site a couple of days later although, confusingly, this does not give it authentication. Occasionally a picture of a new piece will appear here before anyone has spotted it.

If you want to buy a Banksy print (good luck) or prints from a list of almost sixty artists who they also sell, then go to www.picturesonwalls.com, Banksy's online gallery. You can also visit the gallery at 46–48 Commercial Street, London E1 6LT.

Three sites that I used follow Banksy in fine detail, providing a huge amount of useful information if you have time to go through all the posts. The site I probably made most use of is www.UrbanArtAssociation.org. This is the original Banksy Forum site set up in 2006. I also used www.thebanksyforum.com, as well as the Banksy group on flickr: www.flickr. com/groups/banksy. The site www.banksy-prints.com gave a very helpful list of Banksy prints and the prices they were issued at, but this record unfortunately seems to have come to a halt in the middle of 2010. However the site's founder says it will be fully operational again in 2012.

The one blog I get sent and read every day is Vandalog, which you can find at http://blog.vandalog.com. Founded in 2008 by R.J. Rushmore, who divides his time between London and Philadelphia where he is at university, it is a very good record of what is happening in the street art world and where; there are many things I would have missed but for Vandalog pointing them out. I even bought a couple of T-shirts off this site at Christmas.

On the East Coast the key site is www.woostercollective.com. The founders of the site, Marc and Sara Schiller, have close links to Banksy – his New York museum incursions, for instance, were first announced on this site. Wooster carries street art pictures from around the world but is less newsy than Vandalog. Another New York-based site, http://thestreetspot.com/, concentrates more exclusively on the city. On the West Coast probably the site I used the most was http://melroseandfairfax.blog spot. com – again very useful, although I certainly was not on it every day.

Other sites that I have used regularly include:

http://arrestedmotion.com/
http://www.neublack.com/
http://nuart09.blogspot.com
http://boingboing.net/
http://www.ukstreetart.co.uk/
http://streetartlondon.co.uk/
http://unurth.com/

Good pictures of all of his exhibitions, photographed extensively by fans, can be found via Google. One of the best sites for Banksy photographs is http://www.flickr.com/photos/romanywg/. Other flickr sites that Vandalog rates include: http://www.flickr.com/photos/nolionsinengland/ (London), http://www.flickr.com/photos/lunapark/ (New York) and http://www.flickr.com/photos/lord-jim/ (Los Angeles).

**Banksy interviews**

These are the interviews with Banksy that I used or consulted; it was only while compiling this list that I realised quite how often Banksy goes public, like any other artist, when he thinks he needs to. Some articles are full interviews with him (almost all by email), others include within them some emailed quotes from him. Most are easily found on the web and I will only give exact web references where they take a bit of hunting down. There may be one or two instances where a fake Banksy has crept in but I am sure that the great majority of these interviews are genuine.

'Banksy (Yes Banksy) on Thierry, EXIT Skepticism & Documentary Filmmaking as Punk, All These Wonderful Things'. A.J. Schnack, http://edendale.typepad.com, 21 December 2010

'Exclusive: Banksy in his own words'. Nick Francis, *Sun*, 4 September 2010. (This is an accurate transcript of the Banksy interview included as one of the extras in *Exit Through the Gift Shop*, so it is not exactly exclusive, but it is useful.)

Banksy's first Australian interview. Kylie Northover, *The Age*, 29 May 2010

'Banksy Talks Art, Power and *Exit Through the Gift Shop*'. Nancy Miller, *Wired* magazine, April 2010

'Street (il)legal: Q&A with Banksy'. David Fear, *Time Out*, New York, 12 April 2010

'Banksy Revealed?' Shelley Leopold, *LA Weekly*, 8 April 2010

'World Exclusive: Banksy'. Ossian Ward, *Time Out*, 4 March 2010

'Banksy Woz 'Ere'. Eleanor Mills, *Sunday Times* Magazine, 28 February 2010

'Banksy goes home to shake-up Bristol'. Waldemar Januszczak, *Sunday Times*, 14 June 2009

'Breaking the Banksy'. Lee Coan, *Mail on Sunday* Live magazine, June 2008

'Banksy was Here. The invisible man of graffiti art'. Lauren Collins, *The New Yorker*, 14 May 2007

'Banksy: The Naked Truth'. Interview with Shepard Fairey, *Swindle* magazine, no. 8, Autumn 2006

'Banksy hits the big time'. Luke Leitch, *The Times*, September 2006

'Beware it's Banksy'. Roger Gastman, *LA Weekly*, September 2006

'Give me Monet, that's what I want'. Morgan Falconer, *The Times*, 11 October 2005

'Art Attack'. Jeff Howe, *Wired* magazine, August 2005

'Need talent to exhibit in museums? Not this prankster'. Randy Kennedy, *New York Times*, March 2005

'British prankster smuggles art into top NY museums'. Reuters, March 2005

'Something to spray'. Simon Hattenstone, *Guardian*, 17 July 2003

'Banksy, graffiti artist', Emma Warren, *Observer*, 26 May 2002

The collection of interviews below can be found through the Urban Art Association,

the Banksy Forum or the banksy flickr group and some are on all three sites.
'Banksy'. *Design is Kinky* magazine, November 2002
'Creative Vandalism'. Jim Carey, *Squall* magazine, 30 May 2002
'Banksy and Shok1 chatting'. *Big Daddy Magazine*, issue 7, 2001
There is also a 'transcript of an interview with Banksy by Squall back in 2001'. This may well be from the short film *Banksy, Boom or Bust*, Squall Productions for Channel 4, August 2001.
'Painting and Decorating'. Si Mitchell, *Level* magazine, June/July 2000
'The Enemy Within'. Boyd Hill, *Hip-Hop Connection*, no. 136, April 2000

**Radio and television**
Santa's Ghetto in Bethlehem. Paul Wood, BBC Radio 4 *PM*, Christmas 2007
Interview at the time of the publication of *Wall and Piece*. Zina Saro-Wiwa, *The Culture Show*, November 2005
Interview at the time of his incursions into New York's museums. Michele Norris, National Public Radio, March 2005
Interview before his Severnshed exhibition. Fergus Colville, BBC Radio Bristol, February 2000

**Steve Lazarides**
'Urban Renewal'. Andrew Child, *Financial Times*, 28 January 2011
'Steve Lazarides: Tunnel visions'. Alice Jones, *Independent*, 12 October 2010
'Banksy's Ex-Gallerist talks about their breakup, Depictions of Hell'. Susan Michals, *Vanity Fair Daily*, 11 October 2010
'On the run with London's bad-boy gallerist'. Michael Slenske, www.artinfo.com, 1 October 2010
'Steve Lazarides: Graffiti's Uber-dealer'. Luke Leitch, *The Times*, 11 July 2009
'Keeping it real'. Alice O'Keefe, *New Statesman*, October 2008
'The Banksy Manager'. Charlotte Eager, *ES* magazine, November 2007
'A shop window for outsiders'. Alastair Sooke, *Daily Telegraph*, August 2007

**Exit Through the Gift Shop**
'Ron English Revelations'. Jim Vorel, http://www.herald-review.com/blogs/decaturade/article_2217fed0-cf18-11e0-9659-001cc4c002e0.html, 25 August 2011
'Getting at the truth of *Exit Through the Gift Shop*'. Jason Felch, *Los Angeles Times*, 22 February 2011. This was the lengthiest and most detailed interview with Mr Brainwash that I read.
There was a 40-minute interview with the film's producer, Jamie D'Cruz, and editor, Chris King, which I found on www.viddler.com but which is now not easily accessible.
'Hyping the "Gift Shop"'. Eric Kohn, www.indiewire.com, 15 November 2010
'Banksy docu marketers let auds help out'. Caroline Ryder, www.variety.com, 19 June 2010
'Thierry Guetta is real'. Alex Jablonski, http://sparrowsongs.wordpress.com, 22 April 2010
Shepard Fairey interviewed by WNYC radio about Mr Brainwash and Banksy. http://www.youtube.com/watch?v=KiVxOzMFX gw&feature=related, uploaded 21 April 2010
'Banksy movie boasts strong opening numbers in non-traditional release'. Peter Knegt, www.indiewire.com, 19 April 2010. Also on the same website by the same writer: 'Exit strategy: Bringing Banksy to the Masses', 7 April 2010
'Moment of truth: Banksy is selling, but are you buying?' S.T. Vanairsdale, www.movieline.com, 15 April 2010

'Is Banksy's Mr Brainwash an Art-World Borat?' Logan Hill, *New York* magazine, 14 April 2010
'Riddle? Yes. Enigma? Sure. Documentary?' Melena Ryzik, *New York Times*, 13 April 2010
'Here's why the Banksy movie is a Banksy prank'. Alissa Walker, www.fastcompany.com, April 2010
'*Exit Through the Gift Shop*: The enigma known as Banksy'. Steven Zeitchik, *Los Angeles Times*, 30 March 2010
'The latest Banksy Hoax? A real artist'. Tom Shone, *The Times*, 27 February 2010
'Brainwashed'. Andrew Russeth, www.artinfo.com, 16 February 2010
'Shepard Fairey speaks at Bonhams and Butterfields Panel', 5 November 2008. On YouTube. There are different segments of this discussion; Fairey speaking about Mr Brainwash comes halfway through a video which is 10 min, 10 sec. long.
'Mr Brainwash Bombs LA'. Shelley Leopold, *LA Weekly*, 11 June 2008
'Featured Artist – Mr Brainwash'. www.neublack.com, June 2008. Short interview with Mr Brainwash, pictures of the show followed by a long interesting discussion on his art.

The news of Glen Friedman's case against Mr Brainwash was first broken on www.hollywoodreporter.com. Sean Bonner at www.boingboing.net supported Friedman, while RJ – 'Mr. Brainwash is getting his ass sued' – came to the defence of Mr Brainwash at http://blog.vandalog.com. The whole question of appropriation or 'referencing' of images was covered at www.theartnewspaper.com in March 2011. Also: 'Obey plagiarist Shepard Fairey'. Mark Vallen, http://www.art-for-a-change.com, December 2007.
Derek Walborn at www.derekwalborn.com is the sculptor employed by Mr Brainwash who answered my questions about what he did and did not produce for Mr Brainwash.

**Incursions**
'A Wooster Exclusive: Banksy Hits New York's Most Famous Museums'. www.wooster.collective.com, 23 March 2005
'Graffiti artist cuts out middle man to get his work hanging in the Tate'. Steven Morris, www.guardian.co.uk, 18 October 2003
'Street artist Banksy dons disguise to install his picture on gallery wall'. Arifa Akbar, www.independent.co.uk, 18 October 2003

**Bristol show**
'Banksy charged Bristol Museum £1, contract papers reveal'. www.culture24.org.uk, 14 August 2009
'Banksy vs Bristol Museum', review. http://martinworster.wordpress.com, 2 July 2009
'Banksy takes over the Bristol City Museum'. Waldemar Januszczak, *Sunday Times*, 21 June 2009
'Banksy: The graffitist goes straight'. Tim Adams, *Observer*, 14 June 2009
'Banksy comes home for Bristol show'. www.thisisbristol.co.uk, 12 June 2009
Banksy Souvenir Supplement, *Evening Post*, 2 September 2009
Bristol City Council graffiti policy can be found at: http://www.bristol.gov.uk

**Robbo**
*Graffiti Wars*, Channel 4, 14 August 2011 (see also 'Banksy accuses Channel 4 film of distortion over "war of the

walls"'. Dalya Alberge, www.guardian.co.uk, 3 September 2011)
'The gloves are off: Graffiti legend King Robbo has resurfaced to settle a score with Banksy'. Matilda Battersby, www.independent.co.uk, 21 April 2011
'Banksy graffiti feud given a fresh coat'. Alexandra Topping, www.guardian.co.uk, 23 April 2010
'A game of tag breaks out between London's graffiti elite'. Gabriele Steinhauser, http://online.wsj, 3 March 2010
'Banksy's rival King Robbo sprays the final word in street art feud'. Fiona Hamilton, www.timesonline.co.uk, 30 December 2009

**Reviews/critics**

'The death of Banksy'. http://blog.vandalog.com/2011/01/the-death-of-banksy/. An interesting discussion on whether, given Banksy's anonymity, his art could continue without him.
'The strengths and limitations of Banksy's "guerrilla" art'. Paul Mitchell, www.wsws.org, 10 September 2009
'Should Banksy be nominated for the Turner prize?' Jonathan Jones, www.guardian.co.uk, 15 April 2009
'Banksy's ideas have the value of a joke'. Matthew Collings, *The Times*, 28 January 2008
'Banksy's Progress'. Waldemar Januszczak, *Sunday Times*, http://times online.co.uk, 11 March 2007
'Best of British'. Jonathan Jones, www.guardian.co.uk, 5 July 2007
'Why all the fuss over Banksy?' Jonathan Jones, www.guardian.co.uk, March 2007
'When graffiti crosses that fine line'. Charles Schultz, http://white hotmagazine.com, March 2007
'The Banksy Effect'. Marc Schiller, www.woostercollective.com, 13 February 2007
Followed by 'Marc Schiller on Commerce', www.papermag.com, 10 October 2008
'Supposing . . . subversive genius Banksy is actually rubbish'. Charlie Brooker, www.guardian.co.uk, 22 September 2006
'Art: Who's afraid of the big bad guy? Is art vandal Banksy mellowing with age?' Waldemar Januszczak, http://times online.co.uk, 23 October 2005

**MOCA**

'Radical graffiti chic'. Heather MacDonald, http://www.city-journal.org/2011/21_2_vandalism.html, Spring 2011
'A risk-taker's debut'. Guy Trebay, www.nytimes.com, 22 April 2011
'Art in the Streets', review. Mat Gleason, http://coagula.com, 15 April 2011
'Street art at Moca'. Shelley Leopold, http://www.laweekly.com, 7 April 2011
'Tag He's It'. Steffie Nelson, www.nytimes.com, 11 March 2011

**Walls**

'555 Gallery gets OK to display Banksy mural'. Mark Stryker, http://www.freep.com/article/20110911/ENT05/109110402/, 10 September 2011
'Galleries defend controversial Banksy show'. Rachel Corbett, http://www.artnet.com/magazineus/news/corbett/keszler-gallery-on-banksy-controversy-9-1-11.asp, 31 August 2011
'Banksy fans decry removal of street art works from Palestine'. http://www.artnet.com/ magazineus/news/artnetnews/banksy-

palestinian-works.asp, 30 August 2011
A film about Banksy walls being transported from Bethlehem to New York via London was put up by the Keszler Gallery on YouTube in August 2011. See: Banksy Keszler.mov.
The website carrying an impassioned debate about whether the Detroit Banksy should have been 'saved' is http://www.detroitfunk.com
'Did Banksy's latest work bring misery to a homeless man?' Guy Adams, http://www.independent.co.uk/news/world/americas/, 19 March 2011
'Remove art from its architectural context, and what's left?' Christopher Hawthorne, *Los Angeles Times* architecture critic, http://articles.latimes.com, 12 March 2011
'Graffiti artist Banksy leaves mark on Detroit and ignites firestorm'. Mark Stryker, http://www.freep.com, 15 May 2010
'Banksy's Wall'. Channel 4 News, February 2010. A nine-minute film about the wall in Croydon. This can be found on various different sites. I used http://www.artisan-pictures.co.uk/and then clicked on films
'Entire Banksy mural removed by Croydon-Beddington wall's owner'. Leanne Fender, http://www.suttonguardian.co.uk, 11 November 2009
'Banksy's art found on farm's barn wall'. Charles Heslett, http://www.yorkshireeveningpost.co.uk, 3 October 2008
'Vermin on the loose'. Simon Todd, www.artnet.com, September 2008
'All the way to the Banksy. A piece of art made by Banksy for the *Observer Music Monthly* could fetch a tidy sum this week'. Caspar Llewellyn Smith, Observer, 22 June 2008
'Victim of the Great Banksy Robbery'. Rashid Razaq and Esther Walker, http://www.thisislondon.co.uk, 8 March 2007

**Art general**

'The problem with authenticating Warhol'. Charlotte Burns, www.theartnewspaper.com, 7 November 2011
'Off the Wall. Graffiti has made the transition from vandalism to fashionable art, but how did the street become domesticated'. Victoria Maw, *Financial Times*, 15 July 2011
'I'm proud to be a Twombly cultist'. John Waters, *The Times*, 9 July 2011
'Graffiti of the Gods. Amid the squiggles Cy Twombly, who died this week, created profound art'. Rachel Campbell-Johnston, *The Times*, 6 July 2011
'Beyond Graffiti. A new generation is making street art that is conceptual, abstract, and even sculptural in nature'. Carolina A. Miranda, www.artnews.com, January 2011
'The Thing is Dave, Giving is an art. But not that sort of art'. Catherine Bennett, *Observer*, 25 July 2010
'It was a stunning work of art – so why is the Wall hanging in a Las Vegas loo?' Germaine Greer, *Guardian*, 15 February 2010
'Top of the Pops. Did Andy Warhol change everything?' *The New Yorker*, 11 January 2010
'My Week: Richard Wright. The better the picture, the more I long to destroy it'. *Sunday Times*, 13 December 2009
'All that glitters is not sold in this glimmering world'. Rachel Campbell-Johnston, *The Times*, 8 December 2009
'The medium is the market'. Hal Foster, *London Review of Books*, 9 October 2008

'How the Tate got streetwise'. Alice Fisher, *Observer*, 11 May 2008

**Art and fashion**

'Richard Hambleton pop-up show @ The Dairy, London'. Patrick Nguyen, *Arrested Motion*, 6 December 2010

'Terms of Engagement'. Lucia van der Post, *Financial Times*, 27 February 2010

**Voina**

'How Banksy bailed out Russian graffiti artists Voina'. Lucy Ash, www.bbc.co.uk, 5 March 2011

'Banksy supports Voina, controversial Russian art group'. Lucy Ash, www.bbc.co.uk, 13 December 2010

'Banksy pledges cash to Russian art "hooligans"'. Tom Parfitt, *Guardian*, 13 December 2010

A website in support of Voina: http://en.free-voina.org/

**Israel**

'Art attack'. Peter Kennard, http://wwwnewstatesman.com, 17 July 2008

'Santa's Ghetto Bethlehem'. www.tristanmanco.com, 1 January 2008

**Prices**

For prices I used http://artnet.com and sometimes http://www.arcadja.com. Late in the day I also learned of another site: http://expressobeans.com/, a 'not-for-profit community resource' tracking prices.

'When the bottom fell out of the market'. Charlotte Higgins, www.guardian.co.uk, 15 October 2009

'Quick Fix. Laughing all the way to the Banksy'. www.economist.com, 10 November 2008

**Fake Banksys and dodgy Banksys**

'When can we stop wondering what Banksy looks like?' Adam Clark Estes, www.salon.com, 4 March 2011

'Suspended sentence for two men who sold fake Banksy prints'. http://cms.met.police.uk, 1 July 2010

'Croydon Banksy forger avoids jail term for selling fake prints'. Mike Didymus, www.croydonguardian.co.uk, 1 July 2010

'Revealed: the ebay Banksy print fraud'. William Oliver and Cristina Ruiz, www.theartnewspaper.com, 25 September 2007

**Knitting and crocheting**

'Wool Britannia'. Maddy Costa, *Guardian*, 11 October 2010

Interview with street crochet artist Olek, showing just how dedicated she is to her work. http://www.streetartnews.net/2010_12_01_archive.html, 31 December 2010. Olek's website is: http://agataolek.com/home.html

**Galleries**

David Samuel, my guide around Leake Street, has his own online gallery: www.rarekindlondon.com, which has now developed into an illustration agency.

My thanks to Matthew Rich, the dedicated printer at Jealous Gallery in Crouch End who very patiently spent an afternoon showing me how screen printing worked: www.jealousgallery.com

Other galleries that were helpful in one way or another:
www.lazinc.com
www.andipa.com
www.blackratprojects.com
www.pureevil.eu
http://www.weaponofchoicegallery.co.uk/

www.nellyduff.com
www.bankrobberlondon.com
www.taoigallery.com
http://www.visitmima.com/

**Miscellany**

The Shepard Fairey equivalent of the Banksy forum is http://www.thegiant.org/. Another magazine that covers street art and graffiti among other things is http://www.juxtapoz.com/.

Evan Schiff, who waited all night for his Banksy print, is at http://artonanisland.blogspot.com

'Fashion's most wanted – Mrs Jones interview'. Christina Lindsay, http://fashionsmostwanted.blogspot.com/2010/09/fashionss-most-wanted-mrs-jones.html, 3 September 2010

'Want to be famous? Then better stay anonymous'. Philip Hensher, *Daily Telegraph*, 20 August 2010

The interview where Blek le Rat was slightly more critical of Banksy than usual was on a San Francisco arts website: http://www.fecalface.com/SF/index.php?id=1056&option=com_content&task=view

Interview with Inkie. Roly Henry, www.kmag.co.uk, 7 July 2010

'On the Foundry: Not all art is meant to last for ever'. Nosheen Iqbal, www.guardian.co.uk, 12 February 2010

'Banksy and a tunnel vision'. Louise Jury, thisislondon.co.uk, 2 May 2008

For a short video of Banksy's printer in America getting a little frustrated about Banksy's concept of keeping a deadline, see: http://printingbanksy.com/

For a slide show of art at the Carlton Arms hotel go to: http://travel.guardian.co.uk/flash/page/0,,2258955,00.html

An interview with John Ogren, general manager of the Carlton Arms Hotel, can be found at www.nypress.com

'Tag we're it'. Geoff Edgers, *Boston Globe*, 15 May 2010, for the reaction of Boston to Banksy and Shepard Fairey's remarks about Banksy using assistants

A site attempting to have a laugh at Banksy's expense: http://notbanksy.co.uk

'Spray it loud', Dom Phillips, *Venue* magazine, May 1990, for the early days at Barton Hill

The website of the sculptor who has worked for Banksy: http://www.charliebecker.net/site/category/news/

Late in the day I was recommended this site for the harder edge of graffiti: http://hurtyoubad.com/

The website of the firm employed by Banksy to paint four huge billboards in New York: http://colossalmedia.com/case-studies/banksy

Figures for the impact of the Banksy exhibition on Bristol were provided by Destination Bristol at http://visitbristol.co.uk/site/destination-bristol

For a film of See No Evil in Bristol, go to http://www.you tube.com/watch?v=O2Mqeqg4guc

# Bibliography


**Books**

Banksy. *Banging Your Head Against a Brick Wall.* Banksy, 2001.

Banksy. *Existencilism.* Weapons of Mass Destruction, 2002.

Banksy. *Cut It Out.* Banksy, 2004.

Banksy, *Wall and Piece.* Century, 2005.

Blackshaw, Ric and Farrelly, Liz. *Scrawl: Dirty Graphics and Strange Characters.* Booth-Clibborn Editions, 1999.

Bloom, Paul. *How Pleasure Works.* The Bodley Head, 2010.

Braun, Felix. *Children of the Can: 25 years of Bristol Graffiti.* Tangent Books, 2008.

Bull, Martin. *Banksy Locations and Tours.* Shellshock Publishing: 3rd edition, 2008.

Bull, Martin. *Banksy Locations (And a Tour),* Vol. 2. Shellshock Publishing, 2010.

Cooper, Martha and Chalfant, Henry. *Subway Art,* 25th Anniversary Edition. Thames & Hudson, 2009.

Cresswell, Tim. *In Place, Out of Place: Geography, Ideology and Transgression.* University of Minnesota Press, 1994.

Debord, Guy. *Society of the Spectacle.* Editions Buchet-Chastel, 1967; English edition, Black & Red, 1970, reprinted 2010.

Forsyth, Freddie, ed.; Robson-Scott, Will, photographer. *Crack & Shine.* FFF London, 2009.

Huber, Joerg, *Paris Graffiti.* Thames & Hudson, 1986.

Lazarides, Steve. *Outsiders: Art by People.* Century, 2008.

Lazarides, Steve. *Hell's Half Acre.* Lazarides, 2010.

Mailer, Norman; Naar, Jon, photographer. *The Faith of Graffiti.* It Books (HarperCollins), 1974; new edition, 2009.

Manco, Tristan. *Stencil Graffiti.* Thames & Hudson, 2002, reprinted 2006.

Manco, Tristan. *Street Sketchbook.* Thames & Hudson, 2007, reprinted 2009.

Marcus, Greil. *Lipstick Traces: a Secret History of the Twentieth Century.* 1989; Faber and Faber, 2001.

Nguyen, Patrick and Mackenzie, Stuart. *Beyond the Street: The 100 Leading Figures in Urban Art.* Gestalten, 2010.

Parry, William. *Against the Wall: the Art of Resistance in Palestine.* Pluto Press, 2010.

Scherman, Tony and Dalton, David. *POP: the Genius of Andy Warhol.* HarperCollins, 2009.

Snyder, Gregory J. *Graffiti Lives*. New York University Press, 2009.
Swoon. *Swoon (Graffiti artist)*. Abrams, 2010.
Thompson, Don. *The $12 Million Stuffed Shark*. Aurum Press, 2008.
Walde, Claudia. *Street Fonts*. Thames & Hudson, 2011.
Walsh, Michael. *Graffito*. North Atlantic Press, 1996.
Wolfe, Tom. *The Painted Word*. Picador, 2008.
Wright, Steve. *Banksy's Bristol Home Sweet Home: the Unofficial Guide*. Tangent Books, 2009.

**Periodicals and essays**

Henry, Rolland. 'Eine'. *Very Nearly Almost* magazine, issue 13, 2010.
Braun, Felix. 'Jody: Dark Space'. *Weapon of Choice* magazine, issue 5, Spring 2010.
Cockroft, James. 'Street Art and the Splasher: Assimilation and Resistance in Advanced Capitalism'. MA thesis, Stony Brook University, Stony Brook, New York, 2008. <http://www.jamescockroft.com/graffiti/street_art.html
Hartley, Liane. 'Written in Stone: Territoriality, Identity and Vandalism in Cardiff's Urban Graffiti'. BA thesis, Oxford University, 1999.

**Film**

Banksy. *Exit Through the Gift Shop*. DVD, Paranoid Pictures, September 2010.

# Index